MOZART'S OPERAS
A COMPANION

MARY HUNTER

MOZART'S OPERAS

A COMPANION

YALE UNIVERSITY PRESS
NEW HAVEN AND LONDON

For information about this and other Yale University Press publications please contact:

U.S. Office: sales.press@yale.edu   yalebooks.com
Europe Office: sales@yaleup.co.uk   www.yalebooks.co.uk

Set in Minion by J&L Composition Ltd, Filey, North Yorkshire
Printed in Great Britain by TJ International, Padstow, Cornwall

Library of Congress Control Number 2008934939

ISBN 978–0–300–11833–9

A catalogue record for this book is available from the British Library
10 9 8 7 6 5 4 3 2 1

To Jim
with all my heart

CONTENTS

ILLUSTRATIONS

ACKNOWLEDGEMENTS

First of all, thanks go to the libraries that generously supplied the illustrations: in Bologna, Arnaldo Forni Editore; in Dresden, the Staatliche Kunstsammlungen; in New York, the Metropolitan Opera Archive; in Stockholm, the Sveriges Teatermuseum; in Vienna, the Österreichisches Nationalbibliothek, the Österreichisches Theatermuseum, the Wienbibliothek in Rathaus, and the Wien Museum; in Washington DC, the Library of Congress.

Secondly, my profound thanks to the exceptional undergraduate students in the seminar on Mozart's operas I taught at Bowdoin College in the Fall of 2006 as I was writing the bulk of this book: Adam Cohen-Leadholm, Jessie Ferguson, Jay Huber, Tim Kantor, Jin Kyung Kim, Seoung-Yeon Kim, Kate Lebeaux, Rogan McCally, Kathryn Skaggs, Eric Sofen, and Lydia Yeh. Their enthusiasm for the operas, their wonderfully inventive ideas about how they might be produced, and their occasional quizzical expressions on encountering some of my more tangled prose were invaluable. This book is really for them. Another undergraduate, Nick Kasprak, was a remarkable, assiduous, and very able assistant, whose work made mine a lot easier. My colleague Anne Thompson provided support and commentary. Nancy Gerth did the index with expertise and dispatch.

My thanks also to Yale University Press in London: Malcolm Gerratt, who solicited the book and has been unfailingly supportive and patient, and Stephen Kent, who has dealt skillfully and imaginatively with the process of production. Vanessa Mitchell has been a thoughtful copyeditor.

Finally, thanks to my family. My sons Sandy and Jacob are the indispensably supportive and challenging background to everything I do. My opera-loving and widely-read mother Shelagh Hunter read the whole manuscript in record time and made invaluable suggestions. My husband Jim Parakilas is the dedicatee of this book: I only hope that it lives up to his love of these works and to his expectations of writing for a not-only-musicological audience.

CHAPTER I

INTRODUCTION

Mozart wrote operas throughout his life. It was clear from his earliest days that he had the temperament to write music for the theater, as even at the age of nine he could on a moment's notice improvise amorous and rage arias to doggerel texts.[1] His adolescent and adult correspondence is full of references both to his delight in operatic composition and to his sense that this was the best genre in which to make a reputation for himself. His first operatic work was written when he was eleven, in 1767; this is the school drama *Apollo et Hyacinthus*, written for the *Gymnasium* (high school) in Salzburg. He wrote operas until only a couple of months before his death in December 1791: *La clemenza di Tito* was performed in Prague on 6 September of that year, and *The Magic Flute* was premiered at the end of the same month. Seventeen completed operas remain from Mozart's 35 years on earth; in addition there are three operas left incomplete for various reasons, and about 70 freestanding operatic arias, designed either for concert performance or for insertion in his own or (more often) other composers' operas. He wrote in all the operatic genres available to him: Italian-language opera seria (essentially grand opera), including its associated court genres of the pastoral and the *azione teatrale*; opera buffa (Italian-language comic opera); and German-language Singspiel; he also composed some more or less experimental music to accompany speech, as in his unfinished *Zaide*. His choice of genre was always determined by the venue and occasion for which he was writing, and his operas are striking, though by no means unique in his time, in the extent to which he wrote to fit the voices of his singers "like a well-made suit of clothes."[2]

Although Mozart wrote seventeen operas in all, the seven mature full-length works that he wrote between 1780 and 1791 – *Idomeneo* (1781), *Die Entführung aus dem Serail* (1782), *The Marriage of Figaro* (1786), *Don Giovanni* (1787), *Così fan tutte* (1790), *The Magic Flute* (1791), *and La clemenza di Tito* (1791) – are the works most often considered to be indispensable pillars of the Western canon, and of these seven, two of the three operas he wrote with the librettist Lorenzo Da Ponte (*The Marriage of Figaro* and *Don Giovanni*), plus *The Magic Flute*, are the first operas in history to have been in the repertory essentially continuously since their inception.

This is, then, to understate the case, a well-known, much-loved and unimpeachably canonic body of work. Most major opera houses include a Mozart opera in their repertory at least every other year, and during the anniversary years of Mozart's birth and death even the less familiar works appear in multiple performances. All the operas are available in sound recordings and almost all in videorecorded form, many of them in multiple performances. This is a relatively recent circumstance, and the newly easy availability (via purchase or rental) of DVDs of these operas is one of the bases for the structure and content of the present book.

To be able to see these operas as well as hear them, and often in multiple productions, is an enormous privilege. However, most of the available videorecordings have remarkably little documentation about either the content or the context of the opera they present. The first half of this book, then, is designed to serve essentially as a supplement to an increasing plethora of scantily documented videos and DVDs, with the idea that plainly-organized and consistent information about each opera might be helpful in confronting the brave new world of almost infinite choice. I have grouped the notes on individual operas by genre (opera seria first, then Singspiel, then opera buffa), with an essay about the genre preceding the discussions of the individual operas, which are arranged chronologically within the genre divisions. (Please see page 245 for a simple chronology of the works.) Each treatment of an individual opera begins with a list of characters and a plot synopsis for each work: if the plot is complicated there is a summary of the main story followed by a scene-by-scene description; if the plot is transparent there is no summary. The descriptions of the scenes begin with the stage sets as given in the original libretti. This synoptic material is followed by a basic "biography" of the work: its parents (composer and librettist), its birthplace, and a sketch of how it came to be, to the extent that that can be known. A commentary addressing any issue germane to the work concludes the treatment of each opera.

The commentaries on the mature operas are, unsurprisingly, longer than those for the early works. They follow the basic pattern just described, but each is divided into three sections: "origins," "reputation," and a short discussion of a different topic for each work. The topics have been chosen in part because they relate to the kinds of choices directors and performers have to make in staging these operas, and in part because they represent or comment upon one main thread of discourse about the work in question. The material on each work's reputations over time is intrinsically interesting, but it also reminds us that the meanings and value of these operas have changed considerably in the course of two hundred-plus years – it is important to remember that "The Mozart Operas" are more a moving target than a monolithic monument.

To say that these operas are a moving target is not simply metaphorical. Even their content has, in many cases, changed over the years. Nineteenth-century productions, for example, were (to modern sensibilities) incredibly cavalier about what they included and excluded under Mozart's name. Numbers from different operas were substituted at will, the stories were rewritten, characters were added and subtracted, titles were changed, and so on. (Some of these "updatings" of the operas are mentioned in the individual essays about the operas.) But even now, when scholarly editions of the operas are available, and when the ethos is that only Mozart's music for a given opera should be included in a production of that opera, productions differ in what they include. This is largely because Mozart himself altered his operas either in the process of production or for subsequent productions, and there is no single inarguably perfect text for most of these works. Don Ottavio's two arias in *Don Giovanni*, for example, were written for different productions, each of which only included one, but modern productions often include both. The favourite "Champagne" quartet in the second-act finale of *Così fan tutte* seems to have been omitted in the first performance, but it is almost unthinkable to perform the opera without it today. The essays on the individual operas mention the most frequent issues of this sort.

Like the first part of the book, the second part also connects to the profusion of on-screen performances of these works, but in a different way. This part consists of three essays addressing questions relevant to performance and production, and whose overall point is, again, to suggest the variety of meanings these works have borne over the history of their time on stage and in the public consciousness. Directors of modern productions of these works inevitably wrestle – both more and less consciously – with a variety of simultaneous histories: the recent history of other productions (or lack thereof), the history of the different versions Mozart left as equally valid, and the history of the world depicted in the opera. Modern audiences also deal with history in asking how a given production might realize Mozart's "intentions," even though in the strict sense those are almost completely unknowable. History is also involved in the question of how a production differs from other interpretations of the same opera; and again in the apparently simple question of whether we enjoy seeing a given work translated to a twenty-first century terrorist stronghold, or "reconstructed" in a barely-refurbished eighteenth-century theater with flickering candle-like light bulbs and a bewigged orchestra. I have tried to weave these questions about the different histories of and in production through the three last chapters.

This book does not attempt a general overview of the history of Mozart production.[3] In Chapters 7 and 8 I have, rather, given a glimpse of the worlds in which Mozart's operas originated and raised questions about how modern productions use, discard, ignore and change that historical information. The first of these chapters describes the remarkably foreign and fascinating culture of later eighteenth-century theater-making and -going, and suggests that even the most rigorous historical reconstructions of these works are, for reasons both inevitable and willed, not really close to "accurate." Chapter 8 describes the workings of power in Mozart's society and the ways those workings are depicted in the operas: rank and gender being the chief attributes that gave (or denied) people authority over others. This chapter raises the question of how we are to understand, and how performances are to communicate, the structural relationships between Mozart's characters in the modern world, whose class structures are radically different from those in eighteenth-century Europe, and where women, whatever the remaining inequalities of modern Western society, are no longer the property of their male relatives. I ask whether the operas are about particular social circumstances, anchored to particular historical periods and whether it is the job of productions to instruct audiences about them; or whether the works are essentially about "universals" (love, friendship, redemption, etc.) with little regard for particular structures of power. And I suggest that it is salutary to ask what is gained and lost with each of these positions.

There are no definitive answers to these questions. To ask them, however, is, to keep these operas alive, as productions argue with each other and appeal to different audiences. Chapter 9 proposes some ways to ask these questions about some particular modern productions available on video. It is not intended as a buying guide, since the choices available change almost from hour to hour; and the point is more to put these productions into an intellectual framework than to point the reader to any particular pattern of consumption.

I have deliberately avoided music-technical terms: where they are necessary I have defined them at their first appearances and they are included in the index. My basic approach to these works is as total theatrical experiences. At their point of origin they were the result of intensive collaboration between Mozart, his librettists, his impresarios, his patrons, his singers, his set-painters, his dancers, and others. Nowadays they involve just as much collaboration – between the written work, the singers, the conductors, the producers, directors, designers, and even the musicologists. This book is intended to be readable by the essential remaining collaborators in modern performances: namely, the audience. Although the "total theatrical experience" is the principal perspective of this book, I do, however, believe strongly in the rewards of close attention to the ways the characters, the plot, the verses and the individual words are articulated musically. Such attention is not at all beyond the capabilities of anyone willing to listen closely, especially now that live performances have surtitles, and most videos include quite adequate subtitles. To that end, I begin the book proper with a chapter on the "anatomy" of a Mozart opera, which describes the different kinds of music one is likely to hear in these works, and how each kind relates to the words and the action.

This is, then, a book centered on the works as such and on some practical, social, and aesthetic issues affecting their content and their lives in performance. It is neither an examination of Mozart's compositional circumstances nor a study of his operas in the context of his life – there are already several fine and varied examples of these available, by such respected authors as David Cairns, Daniel Heartz, William Mann and Jane Glover.[4] In addition, readers who would like more detailed information about particular operas can consult the fine series of Cambridge Opera Guides, put out by Cambridge University Press, which present basic historical information, a synopsis, and a series of essays about each of the mature operas.

CHAPTER 2

THE MUSICAL ANATOMY OF MOZART'S OPERAS

To a greater extent than any other composer with multiple operas still in the regular repertory, Mozart was also a successful instrumental composer. Perhaps because of that, his operas are often viewed as exceptions by people who don't like "opera," at least not of the metal bra and horned helmet variety. There is a tiny kernel of truth to the argument that Mozart's operas are somehow more "musical" than most operas in the standard repertory. The truth, of course, does not consist in the idea that nineteenth-century opera (the majority of the standard repertory) is not musical, but rather in the notion that the musical processes of Mozart's operas are more abstractly self-sufficient – that is, comprehensible and satisfying without reference to the words – than the musical processes of many other well-known operas. However, even though some of Mozart's operatic music may be independently comprehensible, its primary purpose is to articulate, emphasize, complicate, and sometimes even create the drama of his operas. This essay describes the different kinds of music in these works and shows how they contribute to the overall effect.

BASIC ANATOMY

Mozart's operas are "number operas," that is, works in which the different kinds of music are typically kept quite separate from each other and in which solo and ensemble musical statements tend to be self-contained and musically self-sufficient. The three fundamental kinds of music in a Mozart opera are recitative (talking music), aria (freestanding musical item for a single character and orchestra) and ensemble (freestanding musical item for between two and seven characters and orchestra). A fourth kind of music, the chorus, which occurs at least once or twice in most Mozart operas, is different from the ensemble by virtue of being sung by *classes* of participants in the drama – villagers, soldiers, the populace in general, etc. – rather than by identifiable characters. Choruses also tend to be musically simpler than ensembles, with everyone mostly singing the same words in more or less the same rhythm at the same time.

Composers of Mozart's era, including Mozart, did not have to decide which parts of the libretto to set as the different kinds of number; the text encoded those distinctions for them. Arias, for example, were clearly defined poems with rhyme, a regular meter, and shorter lines than the recitative, which, at least in Italian-language librettos, was often in a prose-like mixture of seven and eleven-syllable lines. Arias were often clearly *visible* to audience members who purchased the printed librettos; they were usually indented or marked off typographically in some other way (ill. 1). Ensembles were usually more like arias than recitatives, with respect to rhyme, meter, and visual distinction from the prose-like recitative, but librettists would indicate lines to be sung simultaneously by different characters with vertical brackets or other typographical signs. Simultaneous-but-different text for the different characters in ensembles also rhymed, so that phrases would end with the same sound from all singers. The rhymes would also be a visual cue to readers about who would sing what with whom.

To say that the text "dictated" the structure of the drama is not to say that composers did not make demands on librettists and make clear where they wanted arias or ensembles; Mozart in particular was very demanding about that kind of thing. Nevertheless, once those decisions had been made, whether by the librettist alone or by the composer or by some process of collaboration, the text was arranged in such a way that the alternation between the different kinds of numbers was both aurally and dramatically comprehensible and visually evident in the libretto itself.

RECITATIVE

Recitative is the music of "normal talk" in the Italian-language operas, whereas the German-language works use regular speech for this purpose. Most scenes in the Italian-language operas begin with recitative; the exceptions are act-openings and ensemble finales in the comic operas. The recitatives are where the plot typically moves most speedily and where the interactions between the characters are most like spoken drama. To simulate speech the words of recitative are uttered at a speed comparable to that of spoken stage declamation and each syllable is given only one, usually short, note. The words of recitatives are almost never repeated, which means that in many theaters and on all videos, sur- or sub-titles are particularly busy during these passages. The "melody" of recitative is essentially a heightening of speech – that is, an exaggeration of the normal rise and fall of a speaking voice rather than a hummable tune with a regular beat. As might be expected in a musical representation of speech, there are many repeated notes, especially in the middle of phrases. The vocal range for recitative is restricted on the whole, and not at the extreme end of any voice range. This vocal style encourages flexible pacing so that the singer can get through the words quickly or choose to drag out particular words or phrases for dramatic effect. Most recitative in Mozart operas is "simple," or, in Italian, *secco* (dry); in this kind the accompaniment is simply a keyboard instrument and a bass instrument (usually a cello), playing background chords to accompany and punctuate the phrases and give a sense of direction to the discourse. This extremely light and intimate accompaniment also contributes to the possibility of rhythmic flexibility in performance.

In addition to simple recitatives, Mozart also wrote accompanied ones. These occur in both the German and the Italian operas. In accompanied recitative the voice line is mostly as speech-like as it is in simple recitative, though it may have moments of more melodic writing; but it is punctuated (or, more rarely, actually accompanied) by the whole orchestra to emphasize the drama. Accompanied recitatives often include sudden and extreme shifts in emotional climate, usually announced or echoed by the orchestra in short but highly expressive phrases. Unlike simple recitatives, which keep the plot moving, accompanied recitatives are often moments of solo reflection, either by serious characters or by comic characters in their most serious moments; and in fact the presence of accompanied recitative often signals that a moment is particularly high drama. For example, in the fourth act of *The Marriage of Figaro*, Figaro, thinking that Susanna is about to betray him by having a rendezvous with the Count, sings an accompanied recitative before he sings his diatribe against women, "Aprite un po' quegli occhi" ("Open your eyes a bit"). The fact that Figaro is a comic character whose normal idiom would not include accompanied recitative tells the audience to take the moment seriously. Similarly, in *The Magic Flute*, where Tamino first meets the priestly gatekeeper of Sarastro's realm, their dialogue is conducted in accompanied recitative (though with an unusual number of genuinely tuneful vocal phrases). The use of this medium tells us not only that Tamino has high ideals in trying to rescue his beloved Pamina, but also that this encounter with the gatekeeper is dramatically and morally weighty. In the seria operas, where all the characters are, so to speak, "capable" of accompanied recitative, it is reserved for moments of particular intensity. Thus the first such recitative in *La clemenza di Tito* is sung by the lovesick traitor Sesto as he screws up his "courage" to attempt to murder the emperor Tito in order to keep the affections of his beloved Vitellia; and the second is sung by Tito himself as he tries to decide whether to condemn his friend Sesto to death for that attempt.

ARIAS

Arias are tuneful and elaborately accompanied solo numbers. They may be less than a minute or more than ten minutes long, they may be extraordinary displays of virtuosity or stunningly simple, they may be soliloquies or speeches addressed to onstage interlocutors. Some arias maintain the same emotional atmosphere throughout; others change mood or posture one or more times. Some arias solidify and elaborate a position that has already been reached in the recitative; others move the action forward, either by allowing the character to make psychological progress or by including stage action. However, even when the character is at a different place at the end of the aria than he or she was at the beginning, the music is always structurally coherent.

Aria texts

An aria's existence usually begins with a text. As with the shape of a whole opera, the words and form of a text may have been negotiated between Mozart and his librettist, but once an aria text was finalized, it affected the composer's options on a number of levels. Length, structure, consistency, and the presence or absence of dramatic or psychological progression were among the features that most immediately concerned any composer of this period. The aria texts in Mozart's operas range from as few as three or four lines to as many as thirty: Barbarina's little ditty at the beginning of the fourth act of *Figaro* is a simple four-line strophe, as is the Countess's entry-aria, "Porgi amor" ("Lend, O Love") in the same opera, while Leporello's famous "catalogue" aria in *Don Giovanni*, in which he describes the list of Don Giovanni's conquests to an appalled Donna Elvira, is an extravagantly long thirty-line disquisition, intended to leave no shred of doubt in Elvira's mind that she was nothing more to Giovanni than another one-night stand. Most texts lie somewhere in between these extremes in length. A short text did not necessarily mean a short aria, however. The texts of the notably long arias in Mozart's early seria operas, for example, typically consist only of two four-line stanzas. Extended passagework on some syllables, long orchestral introductions and interludes and multiple repetitions of the text could lengthen an aria considerably. The repetitions and syllable-extensions necessary to make a long aria out of a short text were a conventional signal of opera seria style partly because the redundancy of the words allowed the audience (and perhaps also the singer) to concentrate on tone, ornamentation, and other aspects of vocal technique that were very much on display in that genre. It was not that the words did not matter, but rather that with so many chances to have the audience understand them, the composer was freer to write vocal roulades and other pyrotechnic effects on any given iteration of the text. Thus if a composer chose to extend a short text in that way, he was usually committing himself to a set of conventions that would evoke the world of opera seria. With video subtitles and theatrical surtitles, short texts to long arias are usually indicated by long periods with no words on the screen, since each translated section usually appears only at the first iteration of the relevant text.

Just as short texts did not necessarily produce short arias, so longer texts also did not necessarily mean longer arias. The relative lack of repetition and the efficient delivery of the text necessary to make a short or at least not-long aria out of a long text, however, put a burden on the composer to make the words clear the first time around. Syllabic declamation (one note per syllable), lack of vocal display and general avoidance of notably tuneful music, all of which contribute towards clarity of diction, tended in this period to be signals of the comic style; and it was in fact the case that (as with Leporello's unusually long catalogue aria) long texts were more likely to be sung by comic characters than by noble or serious ones.

Essentially all of Mozart's arias, like those of his contemporaries, include some text repetition. It was obviously up to the composer to decide how he wanted to arrange the repetitions, but he made those decisions in part on the basis of formal conventions that had clear dramatic meaning at that time. For example, the da capo aria, which was a form used extensively in opera seria in Mozart's youth,[1] required that the first stanza (or occasionally the first two stanzas) of text be used for the A section of the music, and repeated as much as necessary to fill out that section. The second (or occasionally third) stanza would then be set to the (usually contrasting and always much shorter) B section of the music, and would typically be sung through only once, with perhaps some immediate repetitions of words or phrases. Then the A section would return, often embellished by the singer. A two-part text thus translated to a three-part aria.

For the drama of the da capo aria to be even remotely plausible, the text of the B section had to present a position or idea that did not render a return to the A section impossible, but that would nevertheless present another facet of the experience under consideration. In *Mitridate, re di Ponto*, for example, Mitridate's "good son" Sifare bids farewell to his beloved Aspasia, who is unhappily betrothed to Mitridate himself:

Lungi da te, mio bene,	Far from you, my love,
Se vuoi ch'io porti il piede,	I will remove myself, if you wish;
Non rammentar le pene,	forget the miseries
Che provi, o cara, in te.	that you feel, my dear.

Parto, mia bella, addio,	I leave, my sweet one, adieu;
Che se con te più resto	Were I to stay longer with you
Ogni dovere obblio	I would overlook all my duties
Mi scordo ancor di me.	and forget myself.

Here the second stanza shifts from an apparently selfless concern for Aspasia's wishes and feelings to a more direct statement of Sifare's own feelings of irresistible love. Mozart sets this as a graceful and lightly orchestrated tune in triple meter, while the A section (which repeats the first stanza no fewer than four times) is in a slow duple meter, with a prominent solo French horn part emphasizing the depth of feeling involved. The return to the first stanza after the more direct second one, then, allows Sifare to collect himself, and return to his concern for Aspasia rather than for his own self-control. The glimpse of a different angle on the subject afforded by the B section, moreover, makes the return to the A section not merely routine, but dramatically and rhetorically plausible as eloquent and heartfelt speech.

Compare this with the rage aria sung by Elettra, the spurned princess in *Idomeneo*, who thinks she is destined to marry Idamante until he falls for the captive princess Ilia. This aria is also a two-stanza structure, with the two stanzas expressing similar content, the second elaborating a bit on the objects of Elettra's fury, as one might expect in a da capo aria.

Tutte nel cor vi sento	In my heart I feel
Furie del crudo Averno.	all the furies of cruel Hades.
Lunghe à sì gran tormento	Far from so great a torment
Amor, mercè, pietà.	are love, mercy and pity.
Chi mi rubò quel core,	[She] who stole that heart
Quel, che tradito hà il mio,	which betrayed mine
Provin dal mio furore	will feel my fury,
Vendetta, e crudeltà.	vengeance and cruelty.

This is not a da capo aria, however. Mozart set the whole text through essentially twice, ending both halves of the aria with the second stanza. Even though the first stanza ends with the idea that love, mercy and pity are *far* from Elettra's heart, it would not do at all to end a rage aria with the words "amor, mercè, pietà." The text thus "tells" Mozart that it should end with the second stanza rather than the first. (And in fact da capo arias were decreasingly common in the last twenty years of the eighteenth century, giving way to forms that set the text "through.")

Aria types

As we have seen, aria texts dictate or suggest the particular formal and emotional structures of the music. But in many ways they also suggest in what larger category or "type" an aria may belong. The concept of aria type was enormously important in the eighteenth century, both in opera seria and in comic opera. The seria types included the virtuoso aria (*aria di bravura*), the song-like aria (*aria cantabile*), the declamatory aria (*aria parlante*), the Rondò (an aria which moves from a slow tempo to a fast one, but which returns to the opening section one or more times in its course), and the cavatina (a short songful aria in a slow to medium tempo with no tempo changes and little large-scale musical repetition). The Countess's "Porgi amor" is a cavatina, and "Dove sono" ("Where are [the beautiful moments]?") is a Rondò; her use of these aria types, along with her class and her emotional situation, mark her as a seria character.

The *aria di bravura* is easily recognizable by its vocal pyrotechnics. One example in the mature operas is Idomeneo's "Fuor del mar" ("Beyond the Sea"), in which he compares the state of his heart to being in a turbulent ocean with the imminent possibility of shipwreck. The vocal virtuosity in such arias usually emphasizes the nobility of the character or the high tone of his or her sentiments. In the comic operas the *aria di bravura* can have two kinds of functions. Most often it is obviously satirical and indicative of hysteria or pretension beyond capacity, as in the Queen of the Night's two arias in *The Magic Flute* or both soprano arias in *Der Schauspieldirektor*, but it can also be entirely serious and indicative of a noble spirit, as in Constanze's "Martern aller Arten" ("Tortures of all sorts") in *Die Entführung aus dem Serail*, where she tells both the audience and the Pasha at incredible length and with extravagant vocal technique to what lengths she will go to repel his advances. These two possibilities are not mutually exclusive, as in Fiordiligi's "Come scoglio" ("Like a rock") in *Così fan tutte*, where she, in all seriousness, swears stony immutability in her affections, but then proves true to comic type by falling for another man. The type itself has a strong dramatic function here because its clear dramatic and social associations lend it meaning beyond the particulars of a given situation or text.

The *aria parlante* was often used to express high-style rage (the kind felt by thwarted goddesses and princes), and typically had the singer spitting out the words in very short phrases and aggressive rhythms over a turbulent accompaniment. This type was as easy to mock as noble pride (Elvira's entry aria in *Don Giovanni*, "Ah chi mi dice mai" ["Ah who will tell me"] is a wonderful case of such a mockery). The other seria aria types, however, were less open to parody. In both Mozart's comic and serious operas, the *cantabile* (singing) style was a marker of tender feeling and sincerity. Ilia's opening aria, "Se il padre perdei" ("If I have lost my father") is an example of this kind of number. Thus when the normally pert and cunning Susanna uses something like this vocal style at the end of *The Marriage of Figaro* in "Deh vieni, non tardar," ("Come, don't delay"), even though she is playing a trick on Figaro by pretending to sing to the Count, we know there is a serious core to her utterance.

If seria aria types were categorized by vocal delivery, comic aria types were categorized more by who was singing and in what situation. The most common purely comic aria type is the buffo aria; this is sung most often by a bass (though sometimes by a comic tenor) to emphasize various characteristics of the buffoon. Such arias often start with a mock-heroic tune to a text expressing knowledge or pride, but move quickly to a more speech-like declamation, and often later in the aria include passages of patter (very fast delivery of the words, with a lot of repeated notes). They are usually addressed either directly to the audience or onstage interlocutors (and sometimes to several interlocutors with mutually exclusive demands on the singer) to enhance both the pride and the humiliation of the inevitable fall. Such arias often include many contrasting short phrases as the character moves through various positions, unable to maintain the kind of rhetorical focus characteristic of noble figures. Buffo arias almost always end with the character seeming to lose control, repeating a short phrase ad nauseam, or juxtaposing more or less unrelated text fragments in a case study of incoherence. In Mozart's mature operas, the classic buffo aria is Figaro's "Aprite un po'" ("Open [your eyes] a bit"), in which, thinking he has been deceived by Susanna, he advises the men in the audience to watch out for womanly wiles. He starts out with some self-possession and even learnedness ("weak reason pays tribute to the deceived senses"), but descends quickly to name-calling (witches, sirens, flirts, thorny roses, charming wolves, vicious doves are among the descriptions), which names get spat out with increasing speed as he works himself up. He finally has to finish by saying that the rest of his description of women is too awful to utter, which is an admission of defeat rather than of respect for the tender ears of his audience. The music of buffo arias is normally through-composed; that is, it does not have large sections of text or music return once they have been fully exposed. As with Rondòs like "Dove sono," though to very different effect, the composer works through the text from beginning to end. It was not unusual for buffo arias to have several tempos, ending as quickly as the singer could sing.

The other largely comic aria type did not have a consistent name in the eighteenth century, but it could be called the "serving girl" aria. It lies somewhere between cantabile and buffo in style, with a more ingratiating melody than most buffo arias, but less emotional intensity and richness than the typical cantabile aria. Such serving girl arias typically involve a lower-class woman – whether servant or peasant – explaining her amorous needs, which usually involve a lot of gifts, obedience from her man, and the possibility of moving up socially. Alternatively, the character may explain how to deal with men (usually by looking elsewhere at every opportunity, and using them as a convenience rather than a necessity). Despina's "Una donna a quindici anni" ("[Even] a fifteen-year-old woman") in *Così fan tutte* is a perfect example of such an aria. In her continued amazed reaction to the naiveté of her mistresses, who were at first prostrate with grief at the departure of their lovers, and are now in agonies about the possibility of being attracted to other men, Despina says that in the real world, fifteen-year-old girls know how to deal with men, by flirting, lying, and being entirely manipulative. The aria begins with a graceful melody in a moderate tempo (Andante) and continues in a sprightly jig-rhythm (6/8). The vocal range is not extreme, the text-setting is mostly one note per syllable so the words are extremely clear, there is very little vocal display, the melody is neat and mostly symmetrical, and the overall effect is both charming and slightly edgy.

Along with form and dramatic or emotional content, aria types are marked by particular textual vocabularies and literary devices. Seria texts often use similes or comparisons: Idomeneo's likening his heart to a potential shipwreck on a turbulent sea in "Fuor del mar" is a very characteristic example. Seria arias also tend to invoke the gods and to use extreme vocabulary for emotions, especially negative ones: "affanno," (grief), "tormento" (torment), "furia" (fury) are not uncommon. The mode of expression in seria arias tends, not surprisingly, to be somewhat abstract, and to invoke concepts like reason and wisdom. Comic arias, on the other hand, tend to use more everyday vocabulary; things rather than ideas are their currency. Enumerating the adorable (visible) body parts of a beloved – ruby lips, sparkling eyes, rosy cheeks – is a typical strategy in a comic love aria, and the list, as in Leporello's catalogue aria, is another well-used comic device.

In Mozart's theatrical world a clearly-typed aria could telegraph a lot of information to a barely-attentive audience. This technique is not foreign to us. Indeed, acting styles, costumes, sets and plot types work in exactly the same way in many movies and TV shows, as anyone who has recognized a sitcom from the domestic set with a sofa facing the camera and a staircase behind it knows. But eighteenth-century composers (like good sitcom writers) also combined the elements of different aria types in less obviously conventional arias. In the hands of so deft and knowledgeable a composer as Mozart, this matrix of meanings gives arias (as well as whole characters and plots) exceptional richness and depth. Figaro's aria battling the idea that the Count can have his way with Susanna, for example, uses the rhythm of the minuet (a noble dance) to tell us that Figaro imagines himself the Count's equal in asserting his right to his own beloved. Or when Zerlina mollifies Masetto by offering to let him beat her in the aria "Batti batti, bel Masetto" ("Beat me, beat me, sweet Masetto"), the tune is well within the confines of the "serving girl" aria type; however, Mozart's addition of a solo cello line in the accompaniment – a feature usually found in arias sung by more noble characters – complicates the merely coy connotations of this text and situation.

ENSEMBLES

Ensembles, like arias, are closed, or musically self-contained, numbers, but for more than one character. Many ensembles involve only two or three characters (these are duets and trios), but on occasion, as in Act III of *The Marriage of Figaro* or Act II of *Don Giovanni*, they may include up to six (sextets). Like arias, ensembles often occur at the ends of scenes, and can either crystallize the recitative-driven action to that point, or move the plot to the next stage. Because by definition the characters in an ensemble are at least aware of each other, if not actually interacting, these numbers are more likely to include dramatic action than are arias. But in addition to ensembles in the same structural positions as arias, Mozart's comic operas – both German and Italian – include ensembles at the end of each act (finales), and sometimes opening the whole opera (introductions). Comic opera included many more ensembles than opera seria, which was constructed primarily of arias alternating with simple recitative. It was, however, not unusual for an opera seria to include a love duet in the third act; nor was it exceptional for a seria opera to end with a short piece for the whole cast. The first act of *La clemenza di Tito* (1791) also ends with a trio, and there are several duets in the course of that act – a disposition not to be found in earlier seria operas. This reflects changing practice in the genre as a whole at the end of the eighteenth century, but also Mozart's extensive experience with ensembles, particularly in his Viennese operas.

The Viennese seem to have been particularly fond of ensembles; they are quite numerous in works written for that city and they were often encored and singled out for particular comment.[2] That preference seems in turn to have suited Mozart's temperament very well, since the ensembles in his mature operas are among the crowning glories of his entire oeuvre. Ensembles in general, and Mozart's ensembles in particular, do not fall into dramatic types in quite the same way as arias. They can, of course be categorized, but the criteria for categorization do not evoke the world of socially meaningful conventions in the way I have described above for arias. This is partly because most ensembles, especially the larger ones, are intimately tied to the progress of the particular plot and to the working out of particular relationships or intrigue. On the other hand, just as the minuet gesture in Figaro's "Se vuol ballare" ("If you want to dance") means something about

Figaro's imagined assumption of power over his master, so the use of particular rhythms, melody-types, and other musical devices is comparably meaningful in ensembles. But that kind of device in ensembles is often more momentary and fragmented than in arias.

Ensembles tend to be structurally as well as dramatically more flexible than arias, and there are no ensemble structures equivalent to the da capo aria, with conventional meaning apart from the specific content of the number. This does not mean that ensembles have "no form," but rather that the way they are organized tends to follow less codified principles than is the case with arias. The most readily-audible organizing principle in most ensembles, wherever they occur in the act, is the alternation between tuttis (the place where all the participants sing together) and solos or small-group singing. Mozart's ensembles essentially all end with tuttis, with all the characters uttering, if not the same words, then assonant ones, and if not the same tune then essentially the same rhythm. However, most of his ensembles do not begin that way. Most ensembles work up to the full tutti through a series of solos and (in larger ensembles) duets and trios. Intermediate tuttis may include everyone, but the music may not be unified – one or more characters may sing a line that conspicuously does not fit with the rest. Tuttis thus may or may not indicate substantive agreement among the characters, but they always represent a common understanding about the importance of the moment. To listen for tuttis is to listen for the essential dramatic as well as musical punctuation of an ensemble. Some ensembles simply coalesce into a final tutti; others have smaller ones along the way. Some ensembles indicate the final tutti by changing to a faster tempo. Each of these devices makes sense on its own terms within its particular dramatic context. Within the non-tutti sections, Mozart creates meaning in part by giving characters similar or different material, depending on their alignment with each other. For example, the quartet "Non ti fidar, o misera," ("Do not trust [him] poor woman,") in which Donna Elvira tells Donna Anna not to trust Don Giovanni, and Don Giovanni, eager to arouse no suspicion with Donna Anna, who still does not know who assaulted her, tries to persuade Donna Anna and Don Ottavio that Elvira is insane, begins with Elvira singing a noble tune alone. Don Ottavio and Donna Anna respond together, first of all in music that seems more declamatory, but which turns out to be a variant of Donna Elvira's tune. These three characters are thus very nicely aligned with each other. Don Giovanni's solo entry is a contrasting shifty or nervous downward motif; he is clearly the odd person out in this ensemble, even before the other characters know what he did to Donna Anna. This kind of musical articulation is the norm in Mozart's ensembles, (though of course there are exceptions) and it is one of the ways in which this kind of number contributes to the overall drama.

Mid-act ensembles

As with arias, mid-act ensembles can either solidify a moment already reached, or move the plot further. A well-known example of an ensemble in which plot furtherance happens is the trio "Cosa sento" ("What do I hear") in *The Marriage of Figaro*. Here, with the Count behind a chair hiding from the nosy music-master Basilio, and Cherubino on the chair under a dress to hide from the Count, Basilio makes insinuations both about the Count's interest in Susanna and Susanna's supposed interest in Cherubino; the Count leaps up from his hiding place and confronts Basilio (this is where the trio proper begins); Susanna faints from terror but revives in time to resist being put in the chair containing Cherubino; the Count says that Cherubino should be banished and complains about the young man's amorous activities around the house; he re-enacts a previous occasion when he found the page under a tablecloth, pulling the dress off the chair to illustrate and re-finding the wretched boy. This causes the gossipy Basilio untold delight, the Count great anger, and Susanna great consternation, all of which sentiments are expressed simultaneously to end the ensemble. The essential plot action in this ensemble is not enormous, but the Count's discovery of Cherubino is the trigger that pushes him into getting the page a military commission; the commission itself is a piece of business in the second-act finale, and the page's refusal to leave the household fuels material later in the opera.

As far as musical coherence is concerned, Mozart is careful to divide this trio into discrete "paragraphs," each with its own unmistakable ending. These paragraphs cohere into a structure that makes abstract musical sense, dividing the ensemble roughly into half, with the second half (beginning at "Onestissima signora") referring back to the musical events of the first half. He also invents short, highly expressive musical ideas to characterize either particular moments or particular characters; his larger or more action-packed ensembles rarely have extended melodies. In this trio, two obvious such ideas are the sliding-downward motif that Basilio sings in his first phrase in the trio to the words "In mal punto son qui giunto," and the little flurry of faster notes that Susanna sings in her first phrase. The first indicates Basilio's unctuousness, but is also used in the most wonderful way as the Count describes his previous discovery of Cherubino, and the second stands for panic. These highly expressive ideas return as needed to connect otherwise disconnected moments, and to provide "reassurance" that the ensemble hangs together. The overall effect of these devices is a delightfully tense balance between externally imposed order and internally motivated freedom of form.

Finales

The finales in Mozart's mature operas have long been considered monuments of Western civilization. Their combination of musical coherence and beauty with compelling action and human characterization is a testament both to Mozart's genius and to the musical style that allowed this mixture of rigor and flexibility. Finales had long been an element in opera buffa: Carlo Goldoni's mid-century librettos increasingly included them, and composers since the 1760s had been writing multi-scene, multi-sectional continuous music with a final tutti to end their acts. By the 1780s the general shape was quite conventional, as Lorenzo Da Ponte wittily pointed out in describing the effort required to make the libretto respond to the conventional sequence of "adagio (very slow), andante (moderate), amabile (ingratiating), armonioso (harmonious), strepitoso, (uproarious) arcistrepitoso (very uproarious), strepitosissimo (ultimately uproarious)."[3] In fact the steady sequence of speed-increases indicated by Da Ponte's list does not happen in Mozart's finales (nor in those of his contemporaries); however, the librettist's general message that the ending segments of finales moved inexorably towards a climax of excitement is true enough. Da Ponte continues, "It is a dogma of theatrical theology that all the singers should appear on the stage, even if there were three hundred of them, by ones, by twos, by threes, by sixes, by tens, by sixties, to sing solos, duets, trios, sextets, sixty-ets; and if the plot of the play does not allow of it, the poet must find some way of making the plot allow of it, in defiance of his judgement, of his reason, or of all the Aristotles on earth. . . ."[4]

Mozart's finales do fit the general model that Da Ponte describes (with the obvious exception of the sixty-ets), but the effect is not formulaic; rather the variety of kinds of singing, the introduction of all (or most) of the characters, and the move to the final tutti seem remarkably unforced and organic with the particular material of each opera. Even though the structures of finales are quite various, middles ones (usually at the end of the first act) typically build the plot to the point where everyone is at odds, and the imbroglio is at its tightest. The final tutti of these finales usually has the characters agreeing that things are pretty bad. The last finale of two-act operas, on the other hand, moves the plot to the dénouement and resolution so that the final tutti can have everyone agreeing that things are as they should be. (In earlier three-act comic operas, and also in Mozart's *La finta giardiniera* and *La finta semplice*, the second act finale only partly resolves things, and the more or less vestigial third-act finale ties up the final details, but is not particularly long or elaborate.)

Mozart's finales, like those of his contemporaries, cover several scenes as identified in the librettos, since they involve many entrances and exits. The first act finale of *Don Giovanni,* however, is quite unusual in changing stage sets in the middle, from outside to inside Don Giovanni's house. All of them involve significant plot movement; there are moments of stillness and reflection in all of them, but as a whole they are about furthering the narrative. They all have at least as much solo as simultaneous singing, so that when the ensemble moments happen, they punctuate the rapid fire dialogue. The solo singing on the whole is not especially tuneful; it tends to be syllabic and often almost recitative-like to get the words across. The orchestra usually provides the identifiable musical motifs in these moments, and is always responsible for continuity. The ensemble singing, however, is on occasion strikingly melodic: the hymn begging the Count to relent in the second-act finale of *Figaro,* the trio of the masked Don Ottavio, Donna Anna and Donna Elvira before they join Don Giovanni's party, and the "champagne" quartet in the second act finale of *Così,* where the "wrong" lovers (with the exception of Guglielmo, who grumbles through the whole thing) toast each other, are all famous examples of beautiful tunes in the midst of finales. The latter two of these are related to what musicologist John Platoff has memorably called "shock tuttis": that is, places where the activity stops for a moment, and the assembled characters reflect together on events either past or to come.[5] Such moments, which are quite conspicuous, serve in part to allow the engine of the action to move into increasingly high gear in the succeeding sections.

The finales all have many sections in different keys, tempos and meters. Some of these join seamlessly; at other places the contrast is the point. For example, when Susanna emerges from the closet in the second-act finale of *Figaro,* confounding both the Countess and the Count, the music changes to a minuet rhythm (echoing Figaro's use of the minuet in "Se vuol ballare" to indicate his desired control over his master), and the contrast with the previous duple meter is stunning. And in the first act finale of *The Magic Flute,* which differs from the opera buffa finales in including an enormous section of accompanied recitative as well as participation by the chorus, the changes from the comic music of Pamina and Papageno to the "folk-like" strains of Monostatos and the other slaves and to the ceremonial music announcing Sarastro and his retinue, serve to articulate the different social and narrative functions of the characters.

There was less burden on finales to exhibit tight musical construction than there was on mid-act ensembles. The coherence in these operatic segments is provided by the flow of the drama and by the way the music is deployed to articulate or intensify that flow rather than by the return or repetition of tunes or motifs. Mozart's finales do all begin and end in the same key, and the overall structure of keys in these very long musical numbers is often planned to maximize both the inevitability of the return to the home key, and the

possibility of surprise at particular dramatic moments. This underlying structure is something we may all feel even without the vocabulary to describe it.
Unlike in the mid-act ensembles, though, where a balance between audible
structure and narrative flow is the ideal, in finales a sense of plot progression
is more important than of watertight musical coherence.

Introductions

Introductions (or *introduzioni*) are less common than finales in Mozart's
operas, but like finales, they are commoner in comic than in seria operas,
perhaps because comic operas are profoundly "about" social relationships,
and the point of an introduction is to establish the relationships that will drive
the plot. Like finales, introductions may encompass one or more scenes, but
they more often finish at the end of the first scene of the opera. The most
"classic" introduction in Mozart's operas occurs in *La finta giardiniera*, where
the characters sing a jolly tutti, identify their individual miseries, resentments,
and desires in a series of solos, and then (somewhat unconvincingly) repeat
the jolly chorus. This number serves as the first member of a frame for the
whole opera, which also ends with a rejoicing chorus; the togetherness that is
only a gesture at the beginning has, by the end become a reality. *La finta
semplice* begins with a comparable tutti for the assembled characters, with
several solo interjections in the middle.

Among the mature operas, the only two that identify their opening
sequences as *introduzioni* are *Don Giovanni* and *The Magic Flute*. Unlike the
ones in the earlier operas, both begin with a solo: Leporello's "Notte e
giorno faticar" ("Working night and day") in which he complains about the
lousy life of a servant, and Tamino's "Zu Hilfe" ("Help!") in which he is
being attacked by a serpent. In the former, Leporello is interrupted by
Donna Anna struggling with Don Giovanni, and he joins them in a trio. The
Commendatore, Donna Anna's father, comes out to see what the noise is, and
Don Giovanni kills him. This introduction ends with a trio for the three men
in which the Commendatore announces his death, Don Giovanni watches his
death agony, and Leporello says that he's shocked and terrified. This trio moves
without an emphatic final chord into recitative. In *The Magic Flute* Tamino's
cries for help (and subsequent swoon) are answered by the Three Ladies, who
slay the monster in harmony and reflect on Tamino's beauty in a mixture of
ensemble and solo singing. The necessarily action-filled introduction to *Don
Giovanni* is extremely unusual (and effective) in its fluidity; it is much more
like most finales than the normal introduction. The opening of *The Magic
Flute* is less fluid than that in *Don Giovanni*, but also moves smoothly between
ensemble and solo singing. *The Marriage of Figaro* and *Così fan tutte* do not

designate their opening numbers as introductions, but in both the otherwise highly unusual juxtaposition of two ensembles using the same characters (in *Figaro* two duets between Figaro and Susanna, and in *Così* two trios between Don Alfonso and the young people) serves the introduction's normal purpose of framing the action with music that clarifies important relationships in the opera. In the remaining mature operas, *Die Entführung aus dem Serail* begins with an aria, and *Idomeneo* and *La clemenza di Tito* both begin with recitative.

THE ORCHESTRA

The role of the orchestra is quite different from that in much nineteenth-century opera, where it often serves as the opera's "subconscious," reminding us (and possibly the characters) of themes and ideas from earlier points in the story, and indicating to the audience what the character might "really" be thinking. Mozart's orchestral writing in the operas certainly provides atmosphere, but it does not function as the voice of the characters' souls, and with the well-known exceptions in the overtures to *Die Entführung aus dem Serail, Don Giovanni* and *Così* – the first anticipating the opening aria, the second foreshadowing the crashing return of the Commendatore in the Act II finale, and the third announcing the little motif to which Don Alfonso sings the opera's motto ("Così fan tutte"), the orchestra does not engage in the anticipation or repetition of significant tunes or motifs at crucial points in the drama.

The first role of the orchestra in Mozart's operas is to provide rhythmic and harmonic support for the singers. The second role is to do so in a way that communicates something about the character of the utterance under way. Seria arias often include a so-called "trommel" (drum) bass, often reinforced by the upper strings. This is a series of rapidly repeated notes that provide a kind of heartbeat for the longer-breathed melodic lines in the vocal part. This kind of accompaniment is especially common in Mozart's juvenile operas, and it was part of the pan-European seria style. This accompaniment gives life to the singer's lines, but does not compete with the voice at all. In the pauses between the phrases, where the singer breathes, the orchestra will often play a more interesting figure as punctuation, and then return to its throbbing once the voice re-enters. Another common accompaniment for the more sentimental seria aria is a "murmuring" pattern, often in the middle strings; this also moves faster than the voice line, but because of its smooth profile, it feels atmospheric rather than simply rhythmic. Again, in the pauses between phrases, it is usual for the orchestra to emerge from its background role and play something more melodic. Sentimental arias of this sort often use an obbligato (prominent and indispensable) wind instrument to play a melody which may function in counterpoint to the vocal line, or simply take turns being the centre of attention.

The French horn in Sifare's "Lungi da te" ("Far from you") in *Mitridate, re di ponto* exemplifies this, as does the same instrument in Fiordiligi's "Per pietà ben mio," ("Forgive me, my love") in *Così fan tutte*.

The orchestra is typically most interactive with the voice in comic arias. The vocal phrases in comic arias are shorter, and there is more space for the orchestra to comment or to suggest gestures that the singer can choose to enact. For example, in "Madamina, il catalogo è questo" ("Young lady, here's the list"), Leporello's catalogue aria, the bouncy downward scales in the violins once he starts enumerating the geographic spread of Giovanni's conquests evoke the kind of running around that Don Giovanni must have done. And in at the end of Figaro's "Aprite un po'" in Act IV of *The Marriage of Figaro*, the rude horn calls when he says "everyone knows the rest" (of women's many failings) play – not subtly, since the horns are completely alone, very loud, and not playing gracefully – on the idea of the horns sprouted by cuckolds. This meaning could easily be reinforced gesturally by the singer.

In ensembles, given the declamatory nature of the vocal lines in many cases, the orchestra typically provides the basic character or mood of a given section, wrapping the often very short vocal lines in an atmospheric "blanket." In the second-act finale of *The Marriage of Figaro*, for example, when Figaro is trying to claim that it was he who jumped out of the window and not Cherubino, and the (fortunately inebriated) gardener Antonio tries to dispute this, the orchestra plays a series of staccato triplets that lend a tense humor to the whole proceeding.

The orchestra also often plays a significant introduction (ritornello) to many arias, especially in the earlier operas, and especially to seria numbers. This introduction presents the main thematic material of the aria; it would have allowed the singer to get into position on the stage; and it may have served to get the attention of the audience. In the comic operas long introductory ritornellos are much less frequent, and when they occur (as in Constanze's "Martern aller Arten" ["Tortures of all sorts"] in *Die Entführung aus dem Serail*), they are, like da capo form, a signal of seria status. Short ritornellos, however, survive into the comic operas. Sometimes they are as short as a chord or two, just to give the singer the pitch; sometimes they start the accompaniment, and sometimes they present the first melody of the aria. The kind and size of the ritornello typically have to do with the degree of formality of the "speech" and the particular dramatic situation in which it occurs. Susanna's strikingly action-filled aria "Venite, inginocchiatevi" ("Come and kneel down"), for example, in which she dresses Cherubino as a girl, begins with a couple of orchestral flourishes – just enough time for her to get close to Cherubino. In contrast, her "Deh vieni, non tardar," at the end of the opera, which is a real set piece, and in any case represents her singing a song, has a full six measures of tune in the orchestra before Susanna starts singing. The other "song" in this opera, Cherubino's "Voi che sapete" ("You who know"), also has a noticeable ritornello introducing the main melody. Numbers that begin acts also typically have more orchestral material at the beginning, presumably to set the scene and settle everyone down before the action begins. Orchestral introductions to ensembles work essentially the same way as in arias, though no ensembles have the full-length ritornello found in the early and seria arias.

Mozart's deployment of the instruments of the orchestra is one of the miracles of his operas. His basic orchestra in Vienna, Munich and Prague comprised strings, flutes, oboes, clarinets, bassoons, French horns, trumpets and timpani. But he augmented this with "Turkish" percussion (cymbals, triangle and bass drum) for *Die Entführung aus dem Serail*, trombones for *Idomeneo* and *Don Giovanni*, mandolin for the serenade in *Don Giovanni*, and glockenspiel for *The Magic Flute*. These extra instruments dramatize the moments in which they occur: the electrifying trombones when the Commendatore appears at Don Giovanni's door (and in the overture, antici-pating this moment), as well as to accompany the voice of Neptune in *Idomeneo*, and the glittery percussion in the overture and janissaries' choruses in *Die Entführung* are particularly memorable. But more important than the special colors lent by unusual instruments is Mozart's use of the regular orchestra to underline the feeling and meaning of arias and ensembles. His use of wind instruments is (as in the piano concertos) particularly gorgeous. Wind instruments in the eighteenth century were strongly associated with the idea of the pastoral – shepherds, both literal and mythological, having conven-tionally played pipes of various kinds. Thus in Susanna's above-mentioned "Deh vieni, non tardar" the flute, oboe, and bassoon play figures that describe delicate curlicues around both each other and the rather plain voice line, which evokes a simpler and sweeter world far from the social divisions and deceptions of real life.[6] But colour and meaning are not only the province of the wind instruments. In this same short piece for Susanna, the strings begin by playing a plucked accompaniment, perhaps reminiscent of a guitar or mandolin, and thus of a lover's serenade. A bit more than halfway through the aria (to the words "Vieni, ben mio") the first violins use their bows to play a sighing figure over the still-plucked notes of the lower strings, and then for the last couple of phrases all the strings abandon the pizzicato and play smoother lines with the bow, partly doubling (playing the same tune as) Susanna.[7] The effect is of increasing warmth, sincerity and desire; what began as a ruse to make Figaro think she is serenading the Count ends as a full-fledged love song to her true love (not that he appreciates the gift at that moment); this is a wonderful humanizing effect achieved by deceptively simple means.

CHAPTER 3

MOZART AND OPERA SERIA

Of the three operatic genres in which Mozart worked (opera buffa, Singspiel and opera seria), opera seria is the least familiar and comfortable to modern audiences. It is the least apparently naturalistic, the most ritualistic and overtly conventional, and it is the genre whose content most directly reflects the patronage system that funded and supported it. On the one hand, Mozart's works in the genre can easily be appreciated for their range and richness of characterization and for the innumerable musical delights they contain. On the other, their dramatic rhythm and pace, and the worlds they invoke and portray do not always acquiesce to the kinds of default expectations we may bring to Mozart's comic operas, and it often takes some mental adjustment to enter their ethical and aesthetic universes.

THE ORIGINS OF OPERA SERIA, UP TO METASTASIO

In keeping with the generally self-conscious nature of opera in its early days, opera seria began around 1690 as a carefully thought-out response to what opera (understood to have been "invented" around 1600) had become at the end of its first century. During that century, comic and serious elements were mixed together, stage machinery and special effects were important aspects of the show, and arias, recitatives and ensembles were mixed together in relatively unregulated ways, with operas often containing as many as 50 short arias, "running on" quite directly from the recitatives. The plots were also quite often bawdy. The Arcadian Academy in Rome (an intellectual society comprised of learned aristocrats and other renowned men of letters) proposed that opera be re-imagined according to Aristotelian principles, filtered through the ideals of French classical drama as expressed in the works of such authors as Jean Racine and Pierre Corneille. These principles included the unities of time, place, and action: that is, plots were to take place over a period of no more than twenty-four hours, in a single general location, and with a single central narrative trajectory. The rules of *bienséance*, or decorum, were also crucial, as were those of verisimilitude, which involved the "natural" disposition of events and progression from one situation to the next.[1] In addition, the older plots deriving from myth were discarded in favour of stories based on history (usually ancient, often Roman); and endings involving a *deus ex machina* were exchanged for endings created by the internal energy of the story and the actions or dispositions of the characters themselves. *Idomeneo* is an obvious exception to this, but that work was in part the result of the next big reform of serious opera, in which librettists and composers followed the principles of French *tragédie lyrique*, which had always used mythological rather than historical material.

METASTASIO

The most famous and successful exponent of the opera seria libretto was Pietro Trapassi (1698–1782), who in early adulthood changed his professional name to Metastasio, perhaps in acknowledgment of his own transformation from the child of impoverished circumstances to a literary figure of significant ambition. Metastasio inherited and built upon the initial efforts of the first generation of opera reformers, whose chief representative was Apostolo Zeno (1668–1750). Metastasio's career began in Rome, but in 1730 he replaced Zeno as Caesarean Poet at the imperial court in Vienna, where he remained until his death. Mozart, who moved to Vienna permanently in 1781, does not mention him in person in his letters from this period, though he set the poet's *Il sogno di Scipione* in 1771, his *Il re pastore* in 1775, and a version of *La clemenza di Tito* in 1791; and his letters to his father during the 1779–80 composition of *Idomeneo* make it clear that he knew the older man's work well. Metastasio's works were instantly and universally successful; they were published in "complete works" series several times during his lifetime, and many of the individual dramas were set by numerous composers. These *drammi per musica* (dramas written for music) range from the early tragedy *Didone abbandonata*, in which the heroine commits fiery suicide, to elegant dramas of noble self-sacrifice happily thwarted, like his *Olimpiade*. He also wrote numerous smaller pastoral, or less heroic, works, often for particular occasions at the Habsburg court; *Il re pastore* is one of these, despite being designated *dramma per musica*.

METASTASIAN AESTHETICS

For most of the second half of the eighteenth century Metastasio's texts provided the basic template for opera seria across Europe – that is, not only in

Italy and countries, like Austria, Spain and France, with interests in Italy, but also in places like Denmark, Russia, Portugal and England. These texts were typically based on stories from the ancient world: Rome, Greece, North Africa and the biblical lands were the most frequent venues, and Metastasio often prefaced his text with an "argomento" (part back story and part analysis of the motivations of the characters) which asserted the historical veracity of the characters and at least some of the work's narrative episodes. The settings were typically quite splendid: courtyards, palaces, battlefields, great halls. The ambitions of the main (male) characters, which formed the context for the action, were usually commensurately grand: adversarial countries or empires were to be vanquished, kingships to be assumed, great personal sacrifices to be made, and family relationships subordinated to the affairs of state. At the same time, the animating force of most of these works was romantic love, and the arena of the primary emotions essentially domestic and personal.

La clemenza di Tito, which Metastasio wrote in 1734 for the name day of Habsburg Emperor Charles VI, and which was the last seria libretto Mozart set, is a good example of the mixture of what we would now describe as public and private. (See the note on the opera, pp. 67–75, for a plot synopsis.) The public political context involves a never-explained discontent with, or incipient rebellion against, the Roman emperor Tito that is easily ignited into action by his favourite, Sesto, at the behest of the jealous would-be empress Vitellia. Two scenes, one in the first act and the other in the third, take place in large, public, and important places in Rome, with a chorus singing Tito's praises. Tito's soliloquies also spend considerable time pondering the nature of absolute power and its burdens. The private dimension of the plot involves Sesto's fascination with Vitellia, her jealousy of Tito's choices of bride, both ultimately unsuccessful, and Tito's fatherly friendship for Sesto. In contrast to some Metastasian dramas, where the public and private dimensions are relatively separate until the end, in *Tito* the two are inextricably tied to each other: Tito takes the plot against him as a most personal insult; Vitellia's jealousies are as much about becoming empress as about her love for Tito, and Tito's eventual dispensation of mercy to Sesto is an expression both of his friendship for the young man and of his political philosophy.

One of the fundamental characteristics of opera seria is a play of binary oppositions that turn out to be harmonious, such as public vs. private, duty vs. love, or mercy vs. justice. On the largest level this play of oppositions helps engineer the *lieto fine* (happy end) which completes almost every work in this genre: if, for example, events lead to the revelation that an apparent shepherd is in fact of royal blood, then he can both rule and marry his beloved. Or, as in *Tito*, if justice is in fact determined to consist of mercy, then the emperor can pardon his close friend without appearing to be weak. The opera seria happy end is precisely not a result of sudden divine intervention (the *deus ex machina*) at the moment of unresolvable impasse, but rather of the trajectory of events leading logically – if to modern sensibilities, somewhat improbably – to the resolution.

The notion of harmonious opposition is deeply embedded in both the music and the texts of most arias. The much-used da capo (ABA) form, for example is a perfect example of both textual and musical harmony through opposition. In such arias (see also Chapter 2) the first stanza of a two-stanza text is set to a coherent package of musical material, the second stanza to another, often contrasting package, and then the first one repeats, either in full or in large part, thus demonstrating the essential compatibility of the two segments. The text of Servilia's aria to Vitellia in Act III, scene 10 of Metastasio's *Tito* (it is in Act II, scene 13 in Caterino Mazzolà's revision of the text for Mozart), exemplifies all these characteristics. Servilia, the *seconda donna* of the plot, has just heard that her brother Sesto (Tito's favourite), is about to receive his punishment from Tito for attempting to murder the emperor, and she addresses Vitellia as the empress-to-be, in the belief that she could (and would want to) persuade Tito to act mercifully. In fact Vitellia put Sesto up to the plot and is weeping because the plot failed and she is likely to be caught and punished:

Se altro che lagrime	If you do no more for him
Per lui non tenti,	than shed tears,
Tutto il tuo piangere	all your weeping
Non gioverà.	will have no effect.
A questa inutile	This useless
Pietà che senti	pity that you feel,
Oh, quanto è simile	oh, how similar it is
La crudeltà!	to cruelty.

The theme of the text involves the opposition between pity and cruelty, and mere tears and action. But it is the elegance of the text as well as the presence of oppositions that so beautifully exemplifies the Metastasian aesthetic. It presents itself as simply and symmetrically constructed: alternating lines of 6 and 5 syllables with "piano" ("feminine") endings lead to final four-syllable lines with "tronco" ("masculine") endings; and internal assonances ("altro/lagrime", "lui/tuo" "lagrime/piangere") maintain a mellifluous sound. It is also quite restrained: given the extremity of Servilia's pain, and the urgency of the situation, it is striking that Metastasio leaves the most direct word ("crudeltà" [cruelty]) for the very end, and that the first verse is an elaborate dependent clause rather than a straightforward first person or accusatory expression of anguish. But the elegance and restraint serve high emotion and serious characterization. The obliqueness of the expression intensifies the underlying feeling by squeezing it into an obviously "undersized" verbal container; at the same time, Metastasio's delaying of the word "crudeltà" until the very end of the text exaggerates the effect of this direct and passionate word precisely because of the strained moderation and rationality of the context. Metastasio's letters show him to have been extremely interested in the persuasive communication of character, and the stage directions in some of his librettos suggest that on occasion (and the whole issue here is "on occasion" rather than "constantly") he wanted acting and blocking that would convey intensity.[2] For example, when Sesto keeps refusing to tell Tito the reason for his treasonous behaviour, in order to protect his adored Vitellia, Metastasio indicates that he is to deliver a line "con impeto di disperazione," or "with a rush of desperation," which would be all the more affecting in the context both of Sesto's unwillingness to identify Vitellia as the real culprit and of the generally rather static and formulaic acting style which was the norm in this genre. (See Chapter 7 for more on eighteenth-century acting styles.)

Metastasian operas are structurally elegant overall; this serves dramatic efficacy. They are normally configured as a series of units which begin with recitative, often involving several characters in dialogue, and culminate in an aria for one of the characters, followed immediately by that character's departure from the stage (the "exit aria"). Scenes are defined by entrances and exits – each time the number of characters on stage changes a new scene is indicated in the libretto; a single period of recitative, then, might encompass several scenes. It was generally thought desirable to have some continuity in personnel from one scene to the next; this was called the *liaison des scènes*. The effect of this is that when all the stage personnel changed simultaneously it made an important moment of punctuation, often also marked by a change of set – of which there were usually two or three per act. Arias were distributed among the characters according to the singers' place in the dramatic hierarchy: the *primo uomo* (first male soprano) and *prima donna* (first female soprano) would get the largest number of arias and usually one duet; after that, the second-rank characters would get one or two arias fewer, and so on down the ranks. The roles would be designed from the beginning with their place in this hierarchy already planned. The arias would normally fit into a well-understood system of vocal and expressive conventions: bravura arias, singing-style arias, declamatory arias, for example (see Chapter 2 pp. 12–14). Each of these vocal and expressive types was associated with a specific emotional range, and the more important singers, who were reflected in the importance of the characters, would be asked to sing a wider variety of expressive types, thus allowing a richer and more complex characterization to develop over the course of the opera.

SINGERS

Although the texts of opera seria contained the essential ethics and the intellectual aesthetic of the genre, and were, indeed, read as independent works of literature, singers were integral to the genre as a whole. The voices of opera seria were either those of women, of castrati (castrated men) or of tenors; there were almost no bass roles in the central repertory of the genre, and tenor roles were usually restricted to one or two of the normal six or seven characters, even though there were usually at least four male roles. Until the middle of the century the castratos were the highest-paid and the most artistically celebrated but after about 1740 the prima donnas began to usurp that role, in part because of the numerical decline of castratos due to the increasing unacceptability of the practice of castration.[3] A heroic and central role like Mozart's Tito would in the first part of the century usually have been written for a castrato; indeed, in the first setting of La clemenza di Tito, by Antonio Caldara in 1734, that was the case. And whereas Mozart's Publio, the faithful retainer in Tito, is a bass, such roles would earlier have been played by tenors, as is Idomeneo's confidant Arbace in Mozart's earlier opera seria. Mozart did, however, write the role of Sesto for a castrato, as he did for Idamante in Idomeneo; the high male voice now being used to signify youth rather than power and majesty.

The singers also made enormous creative contributions to the genre; operas were written with particular voices in mind, and the owners of those voices often made their desires and demands known to the composers, who equally often had to revise what they had written to please the singers. On the one hand, this represented some compromise of what we now think of as the composer's autonomy; on the other, since the success of the work depended to a large degree on the singers being satisfied and sounding good, it was clearly in the composer's interest to accommodate them to the extent possible. Mozart's concern to have the music fit the singer "like a well-made suit of clothes" is well known. It is somewhat less well known that Metastasio himself seems to have had an equally detailed conception of the casts of his works as he was writing. In the cases where he did not have particular singers in mind we do not know whether he considered vocal style, but he was certainly concerned to communicate the way his performers moved and comported themselves on stage; there are, for example several letters in which he describes his very particular wishes in this domain.[4]

Singers also had some creative control once the work was written. The da capo aria was designed to encourage the addition of ornaments during the return of the first stanza (the second A section of the ABA form). Singing manuals of the time – two of the most famous by castrati (Pier Francesco Tosi and Giambattista Mancini) – devoted considerable ink to teaching singers how to improvise in this way; and a completely unornamented rendition of an aria was in most circumstances considered unacceptably naked. Singers also exercised some choice about which arias they sang in an opera; if they did not respect the composer, or if they simply preferred to sing arias that they knew would show them to advantage, they simply substituted their preferred numbers for the composer's. Today this seems to many like an abominable impertinence (and our attitude was not unknown in the eighteenth century); however, in a world where "the work" was not a fixed entity separate from its performances, and where every new production of an opera required significant rewriting for the new circumstances, the singers' energetic claims to creative prerogative were not out of line.

CIRCUMSTANCES OF PRODUCTION AND PERFORMANCE

Mozart's composition of new seria operas for the carnival period in Milan in the 1770s, in Munich in 1780, and then for the coronation of Emperor Leopold II as King of Bohemia in 1791, were entirely typical of the kinds of occasions for which these works were written. The carnival period in Italy (the intensely festive period between Christmas and Lent) was the most regular occasion for the production of new operas, though some cities in Italy would have new operas for the spring and autumn seasons as well.[5] The singers would normally be hired for the whole carnival season; thus the two or occasionally three new operas for a given season would be written for essentially the same cast. The first opera would be given every evening except Friday for some weeks, depending on its success and perhaps the readiness (or not) of the second work, and then that second, more prestigious, opera would be given every evening except Friday until the beginning of Lent.[6] The singers were often hired before the libretto was chosen, and it was not unusual for the subject of the libretto to be established without consultation with the composer. This was the case with all of Mozart's seria operas, with the possible exception of *Idomeneo*, and we do not know Mozart's input on that choice. The audience would stay essentially the same for all performances: aristocrats typically rented, or in some places bought, boxes at the theater for the season, and used them as extensions of their homes, entertaining company, eating, talking, playing cards, and sometimes engaging in other less respectable activities. Gambling areas were quite common in many theaters, and helped the theaters break even. The audience would thus pay relatively good attention at the beginning of an opera's run, but then probably listen more intermittently as the work became more familiar. Daily tickets to the parterre (the seats of benches on the floor of the theater directly in front of the stage) and to the highest balconies were available, so presumably the audience in those places varied somewhat more than the boxholders. But the boxed aristocrats were the staple audience for opera seria in most places, and it was around their interests and pleasures that most operatic systems were organized.

Librettos were almost always printed and sold before the opening performance of an opera, so audience members could acquaint themselves with the general story and some of the texts to be sung, and follow along if they were so inclined. Nevertheless, especially after the initial performances of a work, the other pleasures of the opera house mounted a stiff competition with the content and performance of the opera, and singers were compelled to keep outdoing themselves in inventiveness of ornamentation and expressivity of delivery in order to keep the audience's attention.

REFORMS

The pleasure-filled, performance-centered, highly ornamented and generally celebratory ethos of mid-eighteenth-century opera seria was essentially rococo. Nevertheless, the classical origins of many of the stories, the restraint of Metastasio's language, and the emphasis on noble behaviour contained the seeds of a more neo-classical art, and indeed, as noted above, an invocation of the classics had been part of the intention of the reformers at the turn of the eighteenth century. "Noble simplicity" was part of this early conception of the genre, and taken simply as texts, Metastasio's libretti in many ways exemplify that ideal.[7] But in performance, the audience's expectation, and the singers' delivery, of florid vocal display to the point where the words were barely comprehensible, the dramatic fragmentation resulting from substitute arias and other circumstantial expedients, the frequent improbabilities of plot required by the *lieto fine*, and the rigidity of the recitative-followed-by-exit-aria formula, came to be seen almost immediately as problematic aspects of the genre. Various kinds of "re-reform" were tried by a variety of composers and librettists: the librettist Mattia Verazi and the composer Niccolò Jommelli, who worked in Mannheim, for example, experimented with more melodramatic stories and tragic endings, and with more choruses, ensembles, accompanied recitative, and a generally wider variety of musical number, linked together in more ways.[8]

But the most famous of all the mid-century reformists was the writer and librettist Ranieri Calzabigi, who worked in Vienna from 1761 until 1773, and whose preface to the reform opera *Alceste*, set by Christoph Willibald Gluck, sets out a clearly anti-Metastasian agenda. This preface (which Calzabigi

essentially ghost-wrote for Gluck)[9] starts by identifying the "abuses" introduced "either by the mistaken vanity of singers or by the too-great complaisance of composers."[10] This was a clear signal that the power relations
between singers and composers was thought to need change, towards a
model with the composer more firmly and comprehensively in charge of
what the singers did, which Gluck himself certainly exemplified. These
reformists also wanted to shift the balance between the words and music, so
that the music served the words more obediently and subserviently. This
involved drastically cutting the amount of vocal coloratura (virtuoso display)
so that the words didn't get lost in "pure voice," reducing orchestral passages
in arias so that singers would not have to wait around for implausibly long
periods with nothing to do, decreasing the importance of the repeat of the
A section for the da capo aria, and generally subordinating any sense of
difficulty or learnedness, whether vocal or compositional, to the "natural"
declamation of the text. Topics for librettos were to be taken from Greek
myths rather than history, in one of opera's repeated attempts to emulate
Greek tragedy. At the same time as this model required composers and librettists and certainly singers to strip away certain sorts of ornamentation,
Calzabigi and Gluck, much influenced by French opera, introduced more
choruses, more ensembles, and more dancing into their operas, thus moving
"ornamentation" from an individual and improvisatory phenomenon to
something collective, non-improvised, and arguably more integral to the
drama. Metastasian opera seria had often had dancing in between the acts,
at least in opera houses with companies of dancers, but the music for the
dances was usually by a different composer from the opera, the stories of the
intermediate ballets were usually unrelated to that of the opera, and in
general the dancing was a largely separate phenomenon.

These reforms affected all of opera seria in the latter part of the century in
various ways and to various extents. The greater variety of kinds of musical
number, the increased flexibility in linking those numbers and defining
scenes, the corollary move towards a more integral conception of "the work,"
the increased dominance of the composer, the move away from coloratura as
the vocal norm, and the increase in emotional and moral solemnity, all led
towards something more like "grand opera" as we may know it now. More
pertinently and immediately, these reforms also affected Mozart. *Idomeneo* is
their obvious beneficiary, with its scene-complexes in addition to recitative-
plus-exit-aria units, and its much-expanded use of the chorus. However, even
La clemenza di Tito, which is in many ways a traditional opera seria, not least
in being based on a libretto by Metastasio, has a variety and flexibility of forms
and dramatic construction that would have been unthinkable without the
reforms of Calzabigi and Gluck and their peers. *Tito* also owes something to

Mozart's experience writing comic operas, and it must be said in conclusion that while the "demise" of opera seria in the last two decades of the eighteenth century has been much exaggerated, the enormous popularity of opera buffa, along with its relative inexpensiveness to produce, did make inroads into opera seria's previously unchallenged dominance.

Mitridate, re di Ponto (*Mitridate, King of Pontus*) Dramma per musica. Libretto by Vittorio Cigna-Santi, after *Mithridate* by Racine. Milan, Teatro Regio Ducal, 26 December 1770.

CHARACTERS

Mitridate, King of Pontus and other kingdoms, Aspasia's lover	Tenor
Aspasia, betrothed to Mitridate, already declared queen	Soprano
Sifare, younger son of Mitridate and Stratonica, Aspasia's lover	Soprano
Farnace, older son of Mitridate, also Aspasia's lover	Alto
Ismene, daughter of the King of Parthia	Soprano
Marzio, Roman tribune, friend of Farnace	Tenor
Arbate, Governor of Ninfea	Soprano

SUMMARY

Before the opera begins, Mitridate has been at war with the Romans and has lost. The basic plot outline concerns the three-way attention to Aspasia by the father and his two sons, one of whom (Farnace) is also a political traitor, and consequently already at odds with his father. The true love in the story is between Aspasia and Sifare, who do not confess their love for each other until quite late in the opera, but who are noble enough to understand that they may need to sacrifice their personal desires to the larger social order.

SYNOPSIS

In Act I, in a city square in Ninfea, Sifare tells Arbate that he and Farnace are quarrelling over Aspasia; Arbate swears allegiance to Sifare. Aspasia asks Sifare's protection from Farnace: he gives it gladly and says that he will show his good faith by disappearing from her sight once Mitridate returns. She, however is not entirely happy at the prospect of marrying Mitridate. Sifare is given hope by this and decides to declare his own love. In the second stage-set, a temple of Venus, Farnace demands that Aspasia marry him. He is about to force her at swordpoint, when Sifare interrupts him and the brothers quarrel. Arbate tries to reconcile them, and they call a temporary truce. Aspasia sings of her misery at being betrothed to Mitridate.

Farnace's political treachery is revealed. Mitridate, battered but unbowed, enters onto a stage set representing a port within sight of Ninfea. He gives Ismene to Farnace. She, however, senses that Farnace is no longer interested in her. Mitridate is angry with both his sons for their apparent political disloyalty, but Arbate persuades him that only Farnace is disloyal. Mitridate is relieved that Sifare, his favoured son, is also the more loyal; he swears to kill Farnace if he finds out that Aspasia loves him.

Act II begins indoors as Ismene and Farnace quarrel; she threatens to tell Mitridate about his inappropriate advances to Aspasia, and Farnace says it will cost her dearly to do so. Mitridate comforts Ismene, then accuses Aspasia of loving Farnace. When Sifare arrives, Mitridate tells him to tell his brother that Mitridate's wrath will descend upon him. It seems that Mitridate is about to announce his marriage to Aspasia, who tells Sifare to go away so that she will not be tempted by him; he unwillingly bids her a heartbreaking farewell. Aspasia sees her duty and laments her fate. The scene changes to a battlefield, where Mitridate tells Ismene that Farnace is a traitor, and that he himself has to go to war with the Romans again. He offers Farnace a military assignment that reveals Farnace's nefarious plans. Ismene rejects Farnace as unworthy of his father, and tells Mitridate not to sacrifice the good of his country to his distaste for his son. Farnace then reveals to his father that Sifare has also betrayed him by falling in love with Aspasia. Mitridate wrings the truth out of Aspasia while Sifare watches from a hiding place. Aspasia offers to die to rectify the situation, but Sifare tells her to marry Mitridate and forget him. She refuses and they resolve to die together.

Act III opens in a hanging garden. Ismene tells Mitridate that she still loves Farnace, and that it would be better for him to try to change Farnace's mind than to kill him. Aspasia remains constant to Sifare in the face of Mitridate's promise that he'll spare Sifare if she changes her heart. Seeing her constancy he threatens to kill her. Mitridate is suddenly called off to war, and a servant gives Aspasia a cup of poison, which she welcomes but somehow cannot bring herself to drink. Just as she is about to put it to her lips, Sifare runs in and knocks it away, explaining that Ismene had freed him from the prison where Mitridate has evidently put him. In an attempt to regain his father's favour he has decided to go and fight with him, however evil he may be. Imprisoned in a tower in the walls of Ninfea, Farnace agonizes over his fate. When Farnace's co-conspirator Marzio enters to free him and lead him back to the Roman armies, he sees the error of his ways and rejects the opportunity. The final scenes are set in a courtyard with a view of Roman ships burning on the ocean. Mitridate returns, mortally wounded, but lives long enough to designate Sifare and Aspasia the next rulers and to see Farnace reconciled to him. The final chorus notes that no war is won solely on the external front.

COMMENTARY

Mozart won the *scrittura*, or commission, for this opera from Count Karl Joseph Firmian, the Governor-General of Lombardy and the brother of Count Firmian, the Chief Steward to the Archbishop of Salzburg. Karl Joseph had hosted a soirée for Leopold and Wolfgang in Milan in March 1770; Wolfgang had composed several arias for the occasion, and it seems that these arias gave rise to Firmian's interest in having an opera written by the teenaged composer. Mozart was not told what the libretto of the opera was to be until July, at which point he was also informed about the singers. The libretto by Vittorio Cigna-Santi that Mozart eventually received had first been set to music in 1767 in Turin by Quirino Gasparini; the version printed for Mozart's operas is very close to the Gasparini original; two aria texts are substituted for the originals (Sifare's "Parto" ["I leave"] and Aspasia's "Nel grave tormento" ["In terrible torment"]), one is added where there was no aria before (Farnace's "Son reo" ["I am guilty"]), and the text to Aspasia's and Sifare's duet at the end of the second act is altered a bit. Other than that, Mozart omitted some of the recitative text, and composed only one verse of several two-stanza arias. In a world where librettos were often completely overhauled for each new setting, these changes are extremely minor, and may speak to Mozart's inexperience with, and lack of standing in, this genre, and also to the haste with which this work had, in the end, to be written. He was considerably more demanding of librettists in his later career.

Despite Mozart's complaisance, composition did not go entirely smoothly. As was the custom of the time, he waited to hear the singers before writing their arias; it was important both to the composers and to the singers that the former "fit the costume to [the] figure" of the latter.[11] But the latter were not always easy to please. The prima donna, Antonia Bernasconi, was at first furnished (by whom it is not known) with a set of arias which she was to sing in place of Mozart's (it was not unusual for singers to substitute their preferred arias into operas), but then, according to Leopold's letters home, once she heard how well-written Mozart's were, she was quite delighted with them. The evidence of the autograph, however, suggests that she was more demanding than that. Mozart wrote a complete version of her opening aria, and then produced a new one which shows off her wide vocal leaps closer to the beginning, and has coloratura passages that are slightly less mechanical than in the original version. Mozart did not set one third-act aria text for Aspasia that exists in the libretto; it is possible that Bernasconi sang another setting of that text.[12] Bernasconi, however, was evidently no more demanding than Guglielmo d'Ettore, who played Mitridate himself; Mozart sketched at least four versions of his entrance aria before he managed to please him, and his aria "Vado incontro al fato estremo" ("I go to meet my destiny") is in fact by Gasparini.[13] And there is evidence that other singers made similar demands on Mozart. But in the event, the opera was a huge success, with many numbers being encored; in fact it was so successful that the ballets, which were put on between the acts of the opera, and which added two hours to the length of the evening, had to be shortened, in part to accommodate the encores, since a six-hour-long show was evidently just about enough.[14]

The subject matter of the libretto is entirely characteristic of mid-eighteenth-century opera seria, with its characters drawn from epic ancient history, but with an essentially domestic plot delineating a conflict between love and duty and prescribing the proper behaviour of its noble characters. Mithridates the Great was in fact a ruler of ancient Pontus (Asia Minor) in the first century BCE. He spent his reign at war with Rome. For many years Mithridates made conquest after conquest. His last battles, however, were lost to Pompey. The final insult was that his son, Pharnaces II, led Mithridates's own troops against him, at which he ordered a Gallic mercenary to kill him.[15] The eighteenth century saw two general types of Mitridate narrative in opera; one, exemplified by Alessandro Scarlatti's *Mitridate Eupatore*, turned Farnace into the husband of Mitridate's mother, who had murdered his father. The other, based on the 1673 play *Mithridate* by Jean Racine, and obviously taken up by Cigna-Santi, focused on the three-way rivalry between Mitridate and his two sons for Mitridate's beloved. Racine's drama has no character corresponding to Ismene, but Monime (the Aspasia equivalent) does have a female confidante. *Mithridate* also lacks Farnace's repentance and conversion at the end; Pharnace remains a traitor and his just deserts lie in the future.

Mozart's setting of *Mitridate* is an astonishing advance over the comic operas of his childhood. There is a much greater variety of mood and intensity, and the characters seem much more human, in part, surely, because the situations in which they find themselves are more meaningful than those in the earliest comic operas. Nevertheless, in Sifare's show-stopping second-act aria "Lungi da te," with its solo horn obbligato (a particularly prominent part for a solo instrument), it is the music as much as the situation that compels our attention. The melody itself is relatively conventional, but the murmuring accompaniment in the strings, and the dialogue between the voice part and the solo horn gives the impression of a kind of inner life. Obbligato instruments and murmuring accompaniments at moments of introspection or emotional intensity were not unusual in this repertory, but one feels, listening to this aria, that the young composer was really exploring the meaning of this formula and not applying it mechanically. This is one of the arias that cost Mozart the most work: there is one almost-complete sketch of a largely different version, and a complete version of the final aria but without the solo horn part. Scholars have surmised that the singer (the castrato Pietro Benedetti) demanded the first rewrite and that the orchestral players suggested the addition of the solo horn part.[16] If these suggestions are correct, we should thank the performers – who, as a class, are often portrayed as interfering egomaniacs – for pushing Mozart beyond his original ideas.

Another opera seria formula was the da capo aria.[17] This formula was on the wane by 1770, and Mozart reflects this often in this opera by not repeating the first (A) section of the da capo form exactly, but rather presenting a very much abbreviated version. The consequent restrictions of the singers' embellishments seem not to have been a point of contention between Mozart and his performers; indeed, Mozart's inclusion of significant vocal passagework or other virtuosic vocal devices (like extremely large leaps) in the first long section of many arias may have compensated for the abbreviated opportunities to improvise.

Like most seria operas, *Mitridate* includes a significant amount of accompanied recitative, which is used at moments of particular emotional intensity, usually preceding an important aria; the vocal lines in this kind of recitative tend to be quite like those of secco, or simple, recitative, but the orchestral interjections between the (usually) short vocal phrases have to capture and convey a kaleidoscope of changing, usually strongly-felt emotions. As such, they are a wonderful opportunity for composers to engage in unusual changes of key and to write immediately apprehensible emotional vignettes. The orchestral interjections are only a couple of seconds long in most cases. Mozart clearly relished these opportunities, and these recitatives are among the most engaging moments in this opera.

In short, then, *Mitridate* shows the young Mozart engaging fully with an extremely formulaic genre, setting a libretto pretty much as it was given to him, and negotiating with renowned singers who evidently did not hold back on their demands out of respect either to his youth or his genius. But one could argue that these constraints were in fact stimulating rather than inhibiting. Mozart found the heart of the drama in the noble and self-sacrificing love between Sifare and Aspasia, and he makes that story sufficiently compelling on a musical level that Mitridate's rather repetitive and unmotivated pride, and Farnace's somewhat pro forma conversion fall into place as effective foils to the central emotional energy of the story.

Mitridate is sometimes considered the best of Mozart's early operas. It is certainly more often staged than most of the others, and whether significantly abbreviated, as in Jean-Pierre Ponelle's striking production, set in the Teatro Olimpico in Vicenza,[18] or done essentially complete, as in Graham Vick's production at Covent Garden,[19] the existence today of singers who can carry off the coloratura with power and elegance, and the willingness of designers to marry the visual extravagance and ritualistic quality of this genre with a more emotionally immediate modern sensibility has meant that this opera has come into its own in this era for the first time since Mozart's lifetime.

Ascanio in Alba Festa teatrale. Libretto by Giuseppe Parini. Milan, Teatro Regio Ducal, 17 October 1771.

CHARACTERS

Venus	Soprano
Ascanio [her son]	Alto
Silvia, nymph, descended from Hercules	Soprano
Aceste, priest	Tenor
Fauno, one of the main shepherds	Soprano

Choruses of spirits, shepherds and shepherdesses

SUMMARY

The libretto begins with the following background: Ascanio was the son of Aeneas; he left Rome and established the city of Alba, whence come Albanians. Hercules was said to have visited there as well. The libretto continues, "From such historical and poetical foundations comes the allegorical fable of the present representation." The story concerns the wedding of Ascanio and Silvia, and Venus's fomentation of a "natural" attraction between them.

SYNOPSIS

Part I: Venus praises the beauty of the countryside in which the action takes place, relates it to Aeneas, and tells Ascanio that he should reign here as her representative. She says the population will be eager to see him. He is anxious to meet Silvia, his destined bride, who already loves him because Venus made him appear to her in a dream. Venus tells Ascanio not to identify himself to Silvia until he is sure that he wants to marry her. Venus leaves, assuring Ascanio that his parents are proud of him. Left alone, Ascanio laments not being able to tell Silvia of his love, but realizes that his mother knows best and looks forward to meeting Silvia, praising her virtue and modesty.

Fauno and the chorus of shepherds enter, praising Venus. They note that Ascanio looks like a god, and praise Venus further. According to Fauno she bestows everything on the place, and guides the industry in the cabins; her favour is their very dew and her eyes are like the sun's rays. Ascanio accepts these praises with delight.

Silvia arrives with Aceste; Fauno tells Ascanio she's too modest to talk to a stranger, so Ascanio hides among the chorus to watch her. The chorus and Aceste praise Silvia and her lineage, in conjunction with more praise of Venus. Silvia is sad because she is to marry Ascanio despite being already in love with a youth she's seen in her dreams. Aceste explains that Venus placed that image of Ascanio in her mind, at which she rejoices.

Ascanio calls on Venus to tell her how happy he is with what he's seen of Silvia. Venus wants to test Silvia's virtue one more time, by having Ascanio not talk to her. In the meantime, she calls on her spirits to make a new city rise up from the plain.

A ballet (for which only Mozart's bass line survives) connects the two acts.

Part II: Silvia sees the city rising, and comprehends that only Venus could have done this. Ascanio comes in looking for Silvia. They see and recognize each other but he may not speak to her. Each thinks their union is not to be. Fauno praises Silvia to Ascanio and Silvia faints among her nymphs.

Ascanio sees her sorry condition, and realizes that she thinks he is not her husband. He asks Venus to appear and end the trial. Silvia keeps being drawn to Ascanio, only to remember that she's supposed to be waiting for her husband to be. Ascanio realizes that her capacity to resist desire in favour of duty will make her an exceptional wife. Aceste assures Silvia that the gods will arrange things as they should be. The chorus invokes the goddess, who descends onto the altar. Venus reveals Ascanio as the husband, and Aceste, as the representative of his people, assures her of the adoration of her subjects.

COMMENTARY

The wedding of the Archduke Ferdinand, third son of the Empress Maria Theresia and her late husband Francis I, to Beatrice Ricciarda d'Este, only daughter of Prince Ercole III d'Este, was a major affair of state because it consolidated Habsburg control over northern Italy. As befitted its political importance, the celebrations were extraordinary; the temporary effects on Milan were akin to a modern city hosting the Olympics. Leopold Mozart's letters describe the city possessed with its frenzied preparations: dancers rehearsing constantly, painters and designers working day and night, important city buildings being given facelifts, and so on.[20] It was for this massive occasion that the fifteen-year-old Mozart was invited by Maria Theresia, probably through Count Karl-Joseph Firmian, who had the previous year commissioned *Mitridate, re di Ponto*, to write a *festa teatrale*. Mozart's contribution was not the only new musical work at the wedding; the renowned composer Johann Adolf Hasse (1699–1783) composed his last opera, *Ruggiero*, for this occasion, and there was newly composed ballet music as well.

The libretto, like that of Mozart's *Mitridate* (1770), was given to the composer quite late – at the end of August for a performance in mid-October. It was by the celebrated poet Giuseppe Parini (1729–99), who had long worked as a literary figure and teacher in Milan, and who was patronized by Count Firmian. It is an undisguised allegory (indeed Parini himself described it as such)[21] whereby Venus stands for Maria Theresia and Ascanio himself for Ferdinando; his bride, the daughter of Ercole d'Este, is the nymph Silvia, a descendent of Hercules (Ercole in Italian). The libretto makes it clear that while it would be desirable for the bridal couple to find each other attractive, the real mover and shaker in this union is the empress. (In the event, Ferdinando and Beatrice did evidently find each other sufficiently attractive to produce nine children.) Almost the first words out of Ascanio's mouth when he first sees his intended bride are "Oh madre, oh diva" (oh mother, oh goddess). And although this refers to the difficulty of keeping his promise to Venus not to reveal himself to his bride, the words do encapsulate the hierarchy of his relationships with the two women. The work ends with a chorus praising not the beauty or happiness or good fortune of the young couple, but the dominion of the goddess herself: "The goddess of the soul governs the whole world so that the earth will be happy; your descendants will propagate eternally, so that the ages will be happy."

The production, as befitted the occasion, was highly elaborate, and the music only a portion of the whole entertainment. The single stage setting, by the renowned Galliari brothers, is probably the most complex in any Mozart opera, with the possible exception of the trial scene in *The Magic Flute*: "Spacious area, intended for solemn pastoral assemblies, bounded by a rim of very high and leafy oak trees, which, loosely distributed around the space, provided a fresh and holy shade. Far from the row of trees a natural green rising landscape is visible, with variously formed slopes made for the shepherds to sit on, distributed with graceful irregularity. In the middle, a rustic altar, in which is sculpted the prodigious animal from which, it is said, the city of Alba takes its name. In the gaps between the trees is visible a charming and pleasant landscape, scattered about with a few cottages, and bounded at the middle distance by lovely hills, down which run copious and limpid streams. On the horizon are the bluest mountains, whose peaks merge with the purest and calmest sky." This vision represents not only the lovely place where this most "natural" of rituals – a wedding – was to be celebrated, but also the human world (the little cottages full of happy peasants) over which Maria Theresia ruled, as well as the larger universe in which her territories and power were a central part. Venus descends from the heavens twice in the course of the opera; the stage machinery required for this would also have added to the occasion.

Dancing was also an integral part of the entertainment, and particularly unusual for Mozart's operas was the addition of dancing to the choruses. Leopold Mozart described it as follows:

The Andante of the symphony [overture] is danced by eleven women, that is, eight genii and three graces, or eight graces and three goddesses. The last Allegro of the symphony, which has a chorus of thirty two voices . . . is danced by sixteen persons at the same time, eight men and eight women.

In the last scene all the singers and dancers appear, genii, graces, shepherds and shepherdesses, and they dance the last chorus together. This does not include the solo dancers, Mr. Pick, Madame Binetti, Mr. Favier and Mlle Blache. The short solo dances, which take place during the choruses, sometimes for two sopranos, sometimes for alto and soprano and so forth, are interspersed with solos for male and female dancers.[22]

Thus with splendor and unimpeded celebration the purposes of the occasion, it is not surprising that Parini's libretto, even set to Mozart's music, fails to develop any real dramatic tension. We do not even think to wonder whether Ascanio and Silvia might not be made for each other. This overall atmosphere in part explains the profusion of remarkably long arias, remarkably full – even by opera seria standards – of coloratura, with the virtuosity distributed in ways that do not necessarily correspond to the dramatic importance of the characters. Fauno, the chief shepherd, for example, has the most striking passagework, ascending to high Cs and Ds several times, and finally to a high E flat, in an aria praising Silvia. Perhaps it makes sense of the occasion for a subject to work harder in admiring his superior than the superior works to rule him. In any case, the proliferation of stunning vocal display certainly added to the sense of the occasion. The one exception to this is the arias for Ascanio, sung by the alto castrato Giovanni Manzuoli, a particular friend of Mozart. His arias avoid coloratura on the whole; Manzuoli's gift was more in his tone and delivery than in his passagework, and this was in any case his last public performance, for which he came out of retirement.[23] This lack of display did also allow Mozart to represent Ascanio as a slightly more neoclassical (as opposed to rococo) hero, which, in the age of Gluck, would have lent him a measure of seriousness appropriate for his future responsibilities.

This work has more choral writing than most of Mozart's other operas; only *Idomeneo* rivals it. The choruses, as Leopold Mozart notes, represent the shepherds living in this pastoral utopia (i.e. the citizens of the Habsburg lands), but also spirits and graces adorning Venus/Maria Theresia. Three of the choruses are sung more than once, punctuating the occasion with increasingly familiar music and dance, and emphasizing the ritual nature of the occasion. The opening chorus announcing Venus' arrival, "Di te più amabile" ("More beloved than thou"), is repeated at the end of the first scene, and then again to close the first act. The chorus "Scendi celeste Venere" ("Descend heavenly Venus") is sung twice towards the end of the second act to bring Venus down to bless the union of the young couple, and the shepherds' chorus "Venga de' sommi eroi" ("May [honor] arrive from the highest heroes") in which they welcome love and honor to their domain, occurs no fewer than six times over the course of the work. It is worth noting here that these repeated moments of punctuation emphasize the lack of dramatic or psychological development, which is a virtue when the occasion is about the ruler's ability to predict the future of this young couple.

Mozart's music – especially for the arias – is understandably not at the level of his *Mitridate, re di Ponto*, written the previous year for Milan. The characters are not particularly clearly distinguished, and there was very little to excite his dramatic imagination. Nevertheless, at the moment of greatest misery, in the second act, where Ascanio and Silvia both believe they have lost each other, Mozart writes two touching arias, Silvia's using the slow melody and murmuring accompaniment beloved by composers of this period and here turned to good effect. The multiply-repeated shepherd's chorus is of musical interest for its woodwind-heavy orchestration (there are no violins or violas) and drones (repeated or held notes in the bass), both of which paint a vivid picture of conventional rusticity.

Il sogno di Scipione (*Scipio's Dream*) Azione teatrale. Libretto by Metastasio. Written probably summer 1771; probably performed spring 1772.

CHARACTERS

Scipione	Tenor
Costanza	Soprano
Fortuna	Soprano
Publio [dead], adoptive relative of Scipione	Tenor

Emilio [dead], Scipione's father   Tenor
Licenza   Soprano

The work is in one act, set in Africa, in the kingdom of Massinissa.

SUMMARY

Metastasio's "argomento" (narrative background) to this libretto refers to Cicero, *Somnium Scipionis* [The sleep of Scipio], from the book *de Republica VI*: "Few can be ignorant of Publius Cornelius Scipio, the destroyer of Carthage. He was the adoptive nephew of the other man who had rendered it a tributary of Rome (and whom we, to distinguish, always call only by his first name, Publius), and the son of that Aemilius who led Perseus, the king of Macedonia, in triumph. Our hero united in himself thus miraculously the virtues of the uncle and of the father, such that the most eloquent Roman wanted to perpetuate his memory in the famous dream that he felicitously invented; this is what served as my companion in the present dramatic work."

SYNOPSIS

The work begins as Fortune and Constancy appear to Scipio in the eponymous dream, and ask him to choose between them. He asks for time to think, and is taken to Elysium, where Constancy explains the harmony of the spheres, and where he meets the ghosts of Publius, his adoptive uncle, and Aemilius, his father. Publius tells Scipio that though Scipio may think they are dead, their essentials live on, as will Scipio's if he follows the noble path set by Publius, Aemilius, and the other heroes who gave themselves for Rome. Aemilius explains the heroes' altruistic omniscience. Scipio wants to stay with the heroes, but Publius reminds him that he has work yet to do for Rome. It is now the moment to choose between Fortune and Constancy, each of whom tries to persuade Scipio to choose her. Scipio chooses Constancy and rejects Fortune as the goddess of base men. Fortune sends storms and turbulence as vengeance. Scipio wakes, realizing that despite these events occurring in a dream, Constancy is a true beacon for him. The work ends with an *homage* to Archbishop Hieronymous (Girolamo) Colloredo of Salzburg.

COMMENTARY

Metastasio wrote this libretto in 1735 for the birthday celebrations of Emperor Charles VI. The message, that Scipio should stand firm in his attempts to conquer parts of Africa, was a transparent reference to Charles' campaigns in Italy and elsewhere as part of the war of Polish succession. The applicability to Salzburg is unclear at best. It is fairly clear from the sources that Mozart wrote this work to honor Archbishop Sigismund von Schrattenbach, who was to celebrate the 50th anniversary of his ordination on 10 January 1772. However, this archbishop died in December 1771, and in March 1772 Hieronymous Colloredo was elected the new archbishop. This change is evident in the *Licenza*, or epilogue, which comes at the very end of the work, and where the allegory is explained. The honoree is announced as "Girolamo" (Hieronymous), but close examination of the autograph shows that the word "Girolamo" is actually written over an erasure, under which reads "Sigismondo."[24] In other words, Mozart first wrote this to praise the first archbishop, and then made the necessary change when the person holding that office was replaced.

The human characters in the opera are true to history, as the "argomento" suggests. Scipio himself is Scipio Africanus the Younger (185–129 BCE); Emilio is Lucius Aemilius Paullus Macedonius, who was indeed Scipio's father, and Publio was indeed Publius Scipio, who adopted Scipio probably after his father divorced his mother.[25] According to Cicero, the dream took place in Africa, two years before the Carthaginian campaign that would earn Scipio his own right to the title "Africanus," which hitherto had only been inherited from his father. The relevance to Charles VI probably operated on two levels; the first one being the general desire to identify a living emperor with any Classical conquering hero, and the second being that Scipio had had considerable military success in Spain, a country with which Charles VI had had, and continued to have, both military engagements and diplomatic quarrels over the further-flung elements of the Habsburg empire. Cicero's text is largely devoted to explaining the eternal life of souls, the harmony of the universe, and the need for virtue if a man is to return to this heavenly realm after death. All of these elements find their way into the Metastasio text, but through the more operatic device of the competing seductions of the two female allegorical figures.

Even less than *Ascanio in Alba* – Mozart's other early occasional opera – is this one dramatic. Not only is it a foregone conclusion that Scipio will choose Constancy over Fortune, or, in more modern terms, persistence over luck, but the choice is more philosophical than interpersonal, and part of the message of the opera is the eternal existence of the soul, which is not an obviously operatic topic. Mozart's music is in the opera seria format of recitative followed by arias, which are arranged so that Emilio's is at the centre, and each of the other characters has one on each side of it, with Scipio singing first and last. At the beginning of the opera, Constancy is distinguished from Fortune by her more graceful and cantabile aria, but her second aria matches Fortuna's for martial bombast and extravagant coloratura.

For all three operas written for Milan during this period, Mozart waited until meeting the singers before writing the arias out in full. For this work we must assume that he knew the singers of the Salzburg musical establishment well enough that he felt comfortable writing this very taxing music for them, even several months before a performance could possibly have been scheduled. Unfortunately, because he was at home, neither he nor his father needed to communicate by mail with his mother or sister, and so any expectations nurtured or arrangements made remain without record.

Lucio Silla Dramma per musica. Libretto by Giovanni da Gamerra. Milan, Teatro Regio Ducal, 26 December 1772.

CHARACTERS

Lucio Silla, dictator	Tenor
Giunia, daughter of Caius Marius and betrothed to	Soprano
Cecilio, banished senator	Soprano
Lucio Cinna, Roman patrician, friend of Cecilio and secret enemy of Lucio Silla	Soprano
Celia, sister of Lucio Silla	Soprano
Aufidio, tribune, friend of Lucio Silla	Tenor

SUMMARY

The plot centres on the faithful love between Giunia and Cecilio in the face of Lucio Silla's attempts to win Giunia for himself. Silla's sister, Celia, and Cecilio's friend Cinna play important roles in convincing Silla not to abuse his power and to allow destiny – the couple's love for each other, and Giunia's late father's desire for this match – to take its proper course.

SYNOPSIS

Act I begins in a remote place on the banks of the Tiber. Cecilio and Cinna meet and discuss the fate of Giunia, whom Lucio Silla has carried off. Cinna tells Cecilio that if he takes a secret route he can visit the grieving Giunia, who thinks Cecilio is dead, and who is also mourning the loss of her father, Caius Marius. Cecilio, left alone, looks forward intensely to seeing his beloved again. In Silla's apartments Silla, Celia and Aufidio discuss how to make Giunia submit to him, preferably immediately. He threatens violence, but Celia says he should be more cunning. Aufidio regrets seeing Silla brought low by a woman. Giunia enters, and Silla tries to persuade her, first by tenderness and then by threat, to love him, but she remains true to the memory of Cecilio, who was also her father's choice of spouse for her. Silla is embarrassed that he is still fond of her, and decides on violent revenge. In the last scene of this act, set in a sepulchral place with monuments of Roman heroes whom Silla has killed, Cecilio, who has found his way there with Cinna's help, sees Giunia approaching and hides behind a funerary urn. Giunia enters accompanied by a sadly singing chorus of maidens. She tries to conjure forth the spirits of her dead father and her lover, whom she believes to be dead. Cecilio announces himself and they sing a joyful duet.

Act II opens in a portico decorated with military trophies, where Aufidio suggests that rather than killing Giunia, Silla should propose to her in public, with troops and the Senate there to compel her to respect the apparent will of the Roman people. Silla agrees. He tells Celia that he will have Giunia and that she will marry Cinna, which pleases her. Alone, he says he has no remorse; he will not vacillate. Cecilio is ready to murder Silla, in part because he hears Caius Marius's voice from the grave calling for vengeance, but Cinna restrains him, reminding him that Giunia's life depends on him as well. Cecilio is torn by conflicting emotions, but decides to save Giunia at whatever cost. Cinna and Celia converse: she tells him that she is to be his wife. Left alone Cinna says he doesn't think he's capable of love, and if he were to be, the object of his affections would not be the sister of a horrible dictator. Giunia enters, and Cinna tries to persuade her to pretend to accept Silla's hand and then kill him, but she wants to leave that to the gods. She asks Cinna to tell Cecilio she still loves him. Cinna decides to kill Silla himself. The preparations for the public betrothal are complete: Silla says that when he thinks of Giunia, he is no longer the proud dictator, but ready to forgive her sins. Giunia comes in; he tries to convince her that he is capable of love, but she spurns him again and says she'd rather die. Silla replies that she will indeed do so, and not alone; nevertheless he still feels a nagging doubt about this course of action. Giunia realizes that the other person to die will be Cecilio. They meet; Giunia persuades Cecilio to flee; heaven will take care of her. Cecilio says that if he dies his shade will look after her. Celia tells Giunia to be happy and not to pine after an already dead lover; she herself is about to be wed to Cinna. Giunia replies it would be easier to die than to suffer like this. In the Capitol, Silla appears with his senators, subjects, and troops, all singing his praises. He says it is time to heal the old enmity between him and Caius Marius by marrying the latter's daughter. Giunia refuses and tries to stab him. Cecilio arrives, sword drawn, and Silla says he will die before daybreak. Then Cinna arrives with his sword drawn, but seeing the situation, pretends to be defending Silla. Giunia persuades Cecilio to throw down his sword, and the two of them sing a duet preparing for death together.

Act III begins in an atrium of a prison, with Cecilio in chains. Cinna apologizes for his turncoat behaviour at the Capitol and promises to save both Cecilio and Giunia. Celia arrives, and Cinna tells her to ask Silla to come to his senses and give up his desire for Giunia. If Celia succeeds, Cinna will marry her. That persuades Celia. Cecilio thinks the enterprise is hopeless, but Cinna thinks Silla may change his mind. Giunia arrives; Silla has unchained her long enough to bid Cecilio a final farewell; she is happy they are dying together, and her death fulfils her obligations both to Cecilio and to her father. Aufidio comes for Cecilio; the lovers bid farewell. Giunia is left alone to lament. In a great hall, Cinna and Celia try to persuade Silla that murderous revenge is not worthy of him, and not wise. Giunia is brought in, protesting; Silla tells her she will watch his cruelty and see what is in his heart. In the final scene, Silla presents the two traitors to the population and then forgives them. Cinna confesses his treachery, and Silla forgives him and gives him Celia as a wife. Silla announces that he is no longer a dictator, but rather the equal of the rest of the population. He announces that it is better to rule by justice and mercy than by fear and grandeur. General praise results.

COMMENTARY

Mozart received the commission for *Lucio Silla* in 1771, on the heels of his successes at the same theater – the Regio Ducal in Milan – with *Mitridate, re di Ponto* (1770) and the wedding serenata *Ascanio in Alba* (1771). Although Ferdinand, the young Archduke of Lombardy, third son of the Empress Maria Theresia, was passionately interested in the theater, and eventually gained some control over the choice of repertory and performers there, it seems that the commission was made simply by the theater director on the basis of Mozart's previous successes, rather than for potentially political reasons.[26] The opera was ordered as the first opera for the carnival season, which lasted from just after Christmas 1772 until the beginning of Lent 1773; in Italy this was the traditional time for the presentation of new seria operas. Just as in other Italian cities, in Milan the tradition was to present two new operas during this time, the second usually being more prestigious than the first. Mozart's work, befitting a very young non-Italian composer with little operatic experience, was the first of the season. Leopold and Wolfgang arrived in Milan in early November, with some recitatives already composed, because these numbers did not need to be fitted to the particular singers as intimately as the arias. Mozart also wrote the choruses early in the process for the same reason. The singers arrived one by one; the prima donna, Anna de Amicis, whom the Mozarts had heard in Venice in 1771,[27] and who was to sing the role of Giunia, was not expected until early December; on the other hand, the least famous singers – Felicità Suardi, the *seconda donna*, who sang Cinna (a male role), and Giuseppe D'Onofrio, the *ultimo tenore*, who sang Aufidio, were already there.[28] On 5 December, 21 days before the premiere, it turned out that the tenor who was to sing Lucio Silla himself was too ill to perform, and so a new one, Bassano Morgnoni, arrived on 18 December, and Mozart wrote at least two arias in one day for him.[29] It seems more than probable that Mozart had a fairly good sense of the general shape and thematic material of the arias before he actually met the singers; nevertheless, the speed with which he could produce whole arias is still remarkable. The capacity of the singers to learn enormous amounts of new material in stunningly short order should also not be forgotten.

The libretto, by the young (b. 1743) Giovanni De Gamerra, employed by the Teatro Regio Ducal, is one of several eighteenth-century treatments of Lucius Cornelius Sulla, the Roman dictator who won the first civil war in Roman history, and who was in fact opposed by Lucius Cornelius Cinna, and gave up his throne and power a year before he died.[30] Aufidius and Caius Marius (the father of Giunia) were also historical figures, as were the Caecilii, from whose clan Cecilio comes.[31] The story Gamerra tells, of an amorous competition over a woman (Giunia) is, as far as we know, fictional, and bears only the slimmest relation to that of the opera *Silla*, set by Handel in 1713; the most important common element is Lucio Silla's conversion to virtue in the finale. De Gamerra's libretto for Mozart was a significant success, being set not only by Mozart, but also in the next few years, by Johann Christian Bach, Pasquale Anfossi, and Michele Mortellari.

De Gamerra uses many of the conventions of Metastasian opera seria, of which Mozart's *Mitridate, re di Ponto* is a fine example. These conventions include a preponderance of arias featuring the singers' virtuosity, a basic dramatic rhythm of alternating recitatives and arias, a happy end, a conflict between love and duty, and a setting in the ancient or near-mythical world. But De Gamerra was also interested in the various "reforms" of opera seria taking place in the mid-eighteenth century, which in aggregate tended to shift the focus slightly away from the solo arias, and to create both a more multi-layered and in some ways a more dramatically focused experience. Thus in *Lucio Silla* the chorus plays a somewhat larger and more varied role than in much opera seria, and for particularly dramatic scenes, like Cecilio's lament and surprise meeting with Giunia in a crypt, the regular alternation of recitative and exit aria is suspended, and the scene seamlessly connects accompanied recitative, orchestral interludes, a choruses and an aria. De Gamerra was also interested in greater "spectacle" in the genre,[32] which fit quite well with the splendid stage sets designed by the Galliari brothers, the resident set designers at the Regio Ducal.

De Gamerra was one of the first to produce a more Romantic style of libretto; this partly had to do with his interest in Revolutionary politics, but was also partly an aesthetic stance, manifested in scenes of darkness and supernatural suggestions.[33] This is not especially evident in *Lucio Silla*, but the scene in the crypt at the end of the first act – not a normal venue for opera seria – does exemplify this trend, as does the looming presence of the dead Caius Marius, invoked and addressed several times by his daughter Giunia and also by Cecilio.

Mozart responded to De Gamerra's relatively modest innovations especially in his newly various and inventive use of the orchestra, calling for instruments and instrumental combinations rare in opera seria of the time. Trombones give the crypt scene an unearthly atmosphere, and incidentally foreshadow Mozart's use of them in *Idomeneo*, *Don Giovanni*, and, unsurprisingly, the Requiem. Trumpets and timpani appear in the overture, the final chorus, and in the heroic arias, and Giunia's accompanied recitative soliloquy after Cecilio has been dragged off, apparently to his death, is accompanied by a pair of flutes, doubled by divided violas, contrasted with pizzicato strings. The bassoon is also periodically liberated from its normal bassline-doubling functions. There is also somewhat more music in the minor mode than this normally relentlessly major-mode genre permits; Giunia's aria following the soliloquy just mentioned is a good example, but significant portions of the chorus in the crypt scene use the minor mode for tempestuous effect.

In keeping with Metastasian aesthetics, however, the arias are long, many of them in a version of opera seria's signature da capo form, and with considerable amounts of very virtuosic passagework. Giunia's arias in particular, written for the spectacular Anna De Amicis, are extraordinarily demanding. The Metastasian model is also evident in the way accompanied recitatives are reserved for the most passionate or introspective moments. These recitatives often employ quite jarring harmonies to express the often conflicting and always strong emotions of the texts they set, and Mozart's use of short orchestral interjections is always dramatically telling.

One of the most striking moments in the opera is Cecilio's farewell to Giunia. They both think he will be executed, and that this is their final moment together. Rather than either a heroic defense of his political position or (more likely in opera seria) a passionate account of how duty calls despite love, De Gamerra wrote an intimate text about how Giunia's beloved eyes would make him die (of love) before he was killed. Mozart set this as a remarkably plain and graceful minuet – the dance most associated with the nobility. After the miles of amazing coloratura in this opera, this simple and relatively brief number is moving in no small part because it shows Cecilio's gentlemanly restraint, which makes a timely and powerful contrast with the vindictive and power-hungry Silla.

Il re pastore *(The Shepherd King)* Serenata. Libretto by Metastasio; adapted into two acts for Pietro Guglielmi (Munich 1774); this libretto re-revised, perhaps by Mozart and Giambattista Varesco. Salzburg, 1775.

CHARACTERS

Alessandro, King of Macedonia	Tenor
Aminta, shepherd, beloved of Elisa, who, unidentified even to himself, is discovered to be the sole legitimate heir to the throne of Sidon	Soprano
Elisa, noble nymph of Phoenicia, of the ancient race of Cadmus, beloved of Aminta	Soprano
Tamiri, fugitive princess, daughter of, the tyrant Stratone, dressed as a shepherdess, beloved of Agenore	Soprano
Agenore, nobleman of Sidon, friend of Alessandro, beloved of Tamiri	Tenor

The opera is set in Sidon.

SUMMARY

The opera celebrates the virtues of simplicity and fidelity in a ruler. Aminta (the shepherd king of the title) is tested, first by being elevated to kingly status, and then by being accidentally given a wife who is not the woman he already loves. His preference for love over status wins the day and turns out to be compatible with ruling.

SYNOPSIS

Act I begins as Elisa and Aminta discuss Alessandro's liberation of Sidon and the rumor that the true heir to the throne of Sidon is living incognito somewhere. They rejoice in their love; Aminta worries that he is not worthy of Elisa's noble heritage, but Elisa assures him that she would give up everything for him, and wants to ask her parents for permission to marry him. Alessandro and Agenore arrive and ask Aminta about his life and condition. His modest and contented answers delight Alessandro, further convincing him that Aminta is indeed Abdolonimo, the proper ruler of Sidon. Aminta sings of his happiness as a shepherd, but Alessandro is delighted at the prospect of having a good ruler for the country that he liberated. Agenore and Tamiri meet; she is in disguise as a shepherdess following what she believes to have been the murder of her father, the tyrant Stratone, by Alessandro. Agenore tries to persuade her that Stratone actually killed himself before Alessandro could show mercy, and that she should expect justice and compassionate treatment from this conqueror. Agenore reminds Tamiri of his love for her. She comments that her fate could be worse; despite her material deprivations, she is still beloved. The scene returns to Elisa and Aminta, who rejoice in Elisa's father's approval of their marriage. Their celebration is interrupted by Agenore, who swears fealty to Aminta as the new king of Sidon. Elisa is willing to give him up as beyond her rank, but he will not leave her; if the price of the throne is losing Elisa, he is not willing to pay it. The lovers end the first act with a duet.

At the beginning of Act II, Elisa, looking for Aminta, tries to enter Alessandro's tent. Agenore stops her, saying that she does not belong there. He has also been trying to intercede with Alessandro on behalf of Tamiri, but has not yet had the opportunity. Elisa is furious and grief-stricken at being separated from Aminta. When Aminta arrives, and learns that Elisa has come and gone, he is disappointed, and is about to go and find her when Alessandro arrives. Alessandro declares that Aminta's pastoral virtues will make him a great ruler, but to complete the perfection, he tells Agenore that he will give Tamiri to Aminta; that way he will restore her to her rightful place as queen of Sidon. Agenore tries to hide his horror, and Alessandro is very pleased with himself. Agenore and Aminta talk at cross purposes; Aminta says that he who receives a kingdom from a hero should not oppose that hero's wishes, meaning that he will refuse the throne for Elisa, but Agenore thinks that he intends to accept Tamiri as his wife, and tells him to love her. Misunderstanding again, Aminta says he doesn't need to be told this, and sings the most famous aria from this opera, "L'amerò, sarò costante" ("I will love her, and be faithful"). Elisa is distraught at the news; Tamiri tells Agenore that he should not expect sympathy from her if he has donated her to Aminta. Agenore sings of his misery; Alessandro follows this up with another aria of self-satisfaction. The women explain their misery to Alessandro, and Aminta returns the royal cloak in favour of staying with Elisa. Alessandro allows the two pairs of lovers to stay with their hearts, and proclaims Aminta a Shepherd King. General rejoicing ensues.

COMMENTARY

Two opportunities converged in the commissioning and creation of this work. The larger of the two was the brief visit in April 1775 to Salzburg of Archduke Maximilian Franz, youngest son of the Empress Maria Theresia, and Mozart's exact contemporary. For this occasion, Archbishop Colloredo, the ruler of Salzburg and Mozart's employer, commissioned two stage works, one from Mozart and one from court composer Domenico Fischietti. Fischietti's work was also a serenata.[34] The other opportunity that Mozart was able to capitalize upon was the engagement, for the royal visit, of two renowned musicians from the court at Munich, namely the soprano castrato Tommaso Consoli, and the flutist Johann Baptist Becke. The Salzburg musical establishment did not include castrati, so both Mozart and Fischietti leapt at the chance to write a nobly virtuosic part. The work was performed only once as far as we know, but Mozart had individual numbers of it performed at various points later in his life: during his 1778 sojourn in Mannheim, for example, he had his then-beloved Aloysia Weber (sister of Constanze, Mozart's eventual wife) sing four of its arias.

This libretto was originally written by Pietro Metastasio for the imperial court in Vienna in 1751. It was set to music by the court composer Giuseppe Bonno, and performed at the imperial summer palace of Schönbrunn. Like most of Metastasio's texts, it was taken up by numerous composers, and Mozart could have heard the setting by Felice Giardini, given in London in 1765.[35] However it was the abbreviated two-act version, set to music by Pietro Guglielmi, and performed in Munich in 1774 which was the main source for Mozart's text. Mozart was in Munich in December 1774 for the premiere of his opera buffa *La finta giardiniera*; there is no indication that he saw the Guglielmi (or that he did not). Nevertheless, he may at least have picked up the libretto of that version during the visit. The text for Mozart's setting is very close to that of the Guglielmi, with a few lines of the original Metastasio re-inserted (Mozart owned a book of Metastasio texts). In addition, the Abbé Giambattista Varesco, the court librettist at Salzburg, and future librettist of *Idomeneo*, added some lines of recitative.

Metastasio's original text was designated *dramma per musica* and had three acts. Nevertheless, its function as a private entertainment, its cast of five rather than the usual six or seven, and its purely pastoral subject matter bring it closer to the *serenata* than to the grander *dramma per musica*. There was also a strong tradition of such semi-staged works in the Viennese court, the point of origin for both the work and the Archduke Maximilian.[36] In addition to being a favorite kind of entertainment at the Viennese court, the *serenata* was an important genre more broadly in the seventeenth and eighteenth centuries. A work with that designation would normally be written for private performance at court, rather than in a fully set up theater.[37] The designation *serenata* could also indicate that the work was relatively short (often in two acts rather than an opera seria's normal three) and that it presented itself as half-way between a cantata and an opera. The pertinent differences between these two genres are that cantatas did not necessarily have persistent characters or a strong narrative, and were quite likely to be unstaged or semi-staged and performed from the sheet music, while operas would have had characters who lasted the length of the story, a more or less coherent plot, and would have been fully staged and sung from memory. *Il re pastore* is obviously operatic with respect to its internal construction, but it seems probable that the performance in Salzburg was at most semi-staged: there is no printed libretto, the score includes no scene settings, and two contemporary accounts refer to it as "cantata" and "serenada."[38]

Opera seria was always a political genre, always tightly connected to the general institution of court patronage and often to the specific court or family either sponsoring a given production or underwriting the theater. "Occasional" or private genres like the *serenata* made the connection between the sponsor and the work even more immediate. Pastoral topics were particularly favoured for this kind of "domestic" aristocratic entertainment, perhaps to persuade the rulers in part that they were at heart "natural" people, in line with the growing Enlightenment celebration of the union of humans and nature. The "English" gardens of Capability Brown, the writings of Jean-Jacques Rousseau, the radically simplified melodies of Christoph Willibald Gluck's "reform" operas, and the growing interest in comic opera across Europe are all examples of this taste for the natural – which was, of course, in every case just as constructed as the elaborate artificialities of French style gardens and opera seria. Pastoral plots may also have functioned to reinforce the rule of aristocratic families; if they did in fact display natural virtues, then it was surely equally natural that they should exercise power.

The text of *Il re pastore* is, from a political point of view, unusually bald, even for this genre. Metastasio indicates numerous times that the pastoral virtues of humility, care for one's flock, and fidelity are also the virtues of a good ruler; and Alessandro's kindness to Aminta, as well as his quick capitulation to the lovers' desires to stay together are examples of these virtues in action. As often, Metastasio cites historical sources as his justification: in this case Quintus Curtius Rufus's *History of Alexander* and Marcus Junianus Justinus's *Epitome of the Philippic History of Pompeius Trogus*. He writes in the preface to his libretto: "Among the most luminous actions of Alexander of Macedonia was that of having liberated Sidon from its tyrant, and then, instead of ruling it himself, having re-established on the throne the only scion of the legitimate royal line, who, unknown to himself, was living a poor and rustic life in the country." Such assertion of historical truth lends weight to the ideological content of the work.

There is nothing in Mozart's biography or in the setting of this work, however, to prove (or, indeed, to disprove) Mozart's agreement with or interest in this ideological program. Alessandro is a relatively conventional seria hero, with martial music, enough coloratura to reinforce his power, and no moments of self-doubt or deep reflection. If we can judge by the relative liveliness and freshness of the music, it was clearly the sweet love story of Elisa and Aminta, in combination with the opportunity to paint musical pictures of the pastoral world, that stimulated Mozart's imagination. At the very beginning of the opera, for example, the overture leads directly into Aminta's first aria with a little duet between the oboe and the flute, which has hitherto been completely silent. This emphasis on winds was a clear signal of the pastoral mode, reminding the audience, probably quite remotely, of the outdoors piping of a variety of rustic characters. The first flute, as mentioned above, was played by the visiting Johann Baptist Becke, so this was also a clever way of introducing him. Aminta's first aria is also utterly pastoral; it is a short song with a simple lilting melody in 6/8 time (two groups of three in each measure) rather than the more elaborate march-tempo coloratura that would normally open an opera seria. 6/8 was often used to indicate a pastoral setting. Played slowly it would remind listeners of the Siciliana, a melody type often used in songs and arias about the natural world, and played fast it would remind them of the gigue (jig), a dance thought to be particularly associated with peasants. Mozart's medium tempo song is precisely neither a Siciliana nor a jig, but it is closer to the former than the latter. The murmuring accompaniment in the second violins is an obvious reference to the burbling of the brook to which Aminta is addressing himself, and the rather odd offbeat accents right at the beginning of the aria suggest a kind of clumsiness thought characteristic of rustics – which Aminta thinks himself to be.

When Elisa sings her first aria very shortly after Aminta's opening song, it makes a clear contrast with his naturalness and simplicity. Elisa's aria is a much more typical opera seria aria, in 4/4 (march time) with a thrumming bass line and quite extravagant vocal passagework. This contrast illustrates their apparent social standing relative to each other; she from the line of Cadmus, and he merely a shepherd. But the relative brevity of some of her phrases, the marked contrasts between one musical idea and the next, and the lively interaction of her line with the orchestral melody instruments (winds and first violins) gives this aria an almost opera buffa-like aura that suits Elisa's vivacious sweetness.

The music of this opera does not continue to present this degree of contrast between characters. Aminta follows Elisa's vocal extravaganza with an elaborate da capo aria of his own, with a full, contrasting middle section, and coloratura at least as elaborate as Elisa's, which suggests that despite his rustic dress and occupation he is fully her equal, da capo arias of this sort being the normal currency of noble characters.[39] His third aria (he is the only character to get three), the famous "L'amerò, sarò costante," with solo violin obbligato, is in yet a different style; it is a "rondeau" – an aria with a repeating refrain – which is the opening music of the aria. Rondeaux (also spelled 'Rondòs') were typically written for characters in serious love situations; they might or might not include extravagant vocal display, but their most salient feature in the latter part of the eighteenth century was a slow or medium-tempo particularly heartfelt, opening tune. Rondeaux were usually given to only one character in an opera, and they usually represented a moment of unusual psychological insight, whether directed by the character to him or herself, or by the audience into the soul of the character. Aminta's rondeau is of the latter sort; he is only saying what he has been saying all along, but the intensity of this music is surely intended to convince the audience that he means it with all his heart. We should also note that Agenore, onstage during this aria, believes Aminta to be singing about Tamiri, so the heartfeltness is as painful to him as it is reassuring and delightful to the audience.

The other characters do not have this expressive range – nor should they; Tommaso Consoli was the star of the evening, and the plausibility and persuasiveness of the work as a whole rests almost entirely on Aminta's capacity to be both noble and simple, high-flown and heartfelt. Mozart used the traditional opera seria means of different arias to show the different facets of Aminta's character, but the musical conviction of each of these facets, in combination with the subtlety of Elisa's music, which mixes the highest style with touches of something more middling, suggests a composer poised to move on to more complex and ambiguous characterizations. And indeed, *Il re pastore* was the last opera Mozart wrote before *Idomeneo*, generally acknowledged to be the first of his inarguably great operatic works.

Idomeneo, re di Creta (*Idomeneo, King of Crete*) Dramma per musica. Libretto by Giovanni Batista Varesco, based on *Idoménée*, by Antoine Danchet. Munich, Residenztheater, 29 January 1781.

CHARACTERS

Idomeneo, King of Crete	Tenor
Idamante, his son	Soprano

Ilia, Trojan princess, daughter of Priam	Soprano
Elettra, princess, daughter of Agammemnon, King of Argus	Soprano
Arbace, confidant of the King	Tenor
High Priest of Neptune	Tenor
[Voice of Neptune]	Bass

SUMMARY

The mainspring of the opera is Idomeneo's promise, during a dreadful storm at sea, to sacrifice to Neptune the first person he sees if he is permitted to live to reach his homeland. This person turns out to be his son Idamante. Neptune's power over the people of Crete and Idamante's selfless nobility are demonstrated as the plot unwinds. Idamante's beloved, Ilia, proves herself worthy of him, while his betrothed, Elettra, proves quite the opposite.

SYNOPSIS

Act I opens in a hall in the royal palace in Sidon, capital of Crete, and close to Ilia's quarters. Ilia laments her situation; she has been taken prisoner in the endless battles between Greece and Troy. Furious and ashamed at being a captive, she also finds it impossible to hate Prince Idamante. Idamante enters with his retinue. Knowing that his father Idomeneo is in a storm at sea, he hopes for his safety; he also confesses to Ilia his attraction to her, saying that his affections are under the control of the gods. He breaks her chains, wishing he could do the same for himself. The Trojan prisoners enter, and he frees them as well, to a chorus of praise from both sides. Elettra, however, who has been promised to Idamante, finds this action treasonous. The confidant Arbace enters with the terrible news that Idomeneo has drowned at sea. Idamante rushes off in despair; Elettra is also in despair, not out of grief for Idomeneo, but because Idamante's now clear path to the throne will allow him to marry Ilia. She swears vengeance.

On a storm-wracked seashore, a chorus of shipwrecked sailors pleads for mercy. Neptune appears, disperses the storm in mime, and threatens Idomeneo with a look. Idomeneo is grateful for the cessation of the storm, but horrified to be stranded on this shore. He is so desperate to be home that he promises Neptune a sacrificial victim – the first mortal he encounters. Idamante arrives at this desolate place. They do not recognize each other. Idamante tells Idomeneo that he has come there to mourn the loss of the hero Idomeneo; Idomeneo hints that he is still alive, and Idamante explains that his inordinate joy at hearing the news is due to the fact that Idomeneo is his father. Idomeneo reveals himself, with enormous grief, and runs away.

Idamante cannot understand why their mutual rediscovery seems to have affected his father so badly.

In an intermezzo, the Cretan troops arrive back home with Idomeneo, and the Cretan population celebrates the occasion in choral singing and dance.

Act II begins in the royal quarters. Idomeneo reveals to Arbace his bargain with Neptune, hoping that the latter will say that his past bravery will excuse him from obedience. Arbace does not oblige. When Arbace hears that the victim is Idamante, however, he suggests that the prince be sent away, and Idomeneo resolves to have him accompany Elettra back to Argos. Ilia has an audience with Idomeneo in which she reveals that Idamante has set her free and that she has given him and Idomeneo her loyalty; they will be a new family for her. Left alone, Idomeneo realizes that this loyalty may have something to do with romance, and he is sent into agonies at this thought. He informs Elettra of his plan to send Idamante away with her; she is blissfully happy.

At the port, the chorus and Elettra bless the coming journey. Idomeneo sends Idamante on his way, and the three sing a trio expressing their very different responses to the moment. However, before anyone can embark, a sudden storm arises, obviously due to Neptune's disfavor. Idomeneo cries out, requesting to be the sole victim of this eruption, but to no avail.

Act III begins in a royal garden, where Ilia asks the breezes to send her loving wishes to Idamante, who unexpectedly appears. He says he has come to bid his final farewell; he may die fighting the evil forces that seem to have beset the kingdom. Ilia reassures him of her love even to the point of being willing to die with or for him, and they sing a duet. Elettra and Idomeneo arrive; Idomeneo tells Idamante that he must leave; Neptune has hardened the paternal heart against him, and he must rule elsewhere. The following quartet combines the different psychological states of the protagonists at this moment. Arbace arrives to announce that the populace is in revolt and that the High Priest of Neptune demands his presence; Idomeneo rushes off to deal with this, and Arbace is left alone to lament the demise of great Crete.

The final segment of the opera opens in a great piazza in front of the palace. The High Priest tells Idomeneo that his people are suffering under the scourge of Neptune's rage, and that he needs to know the name of the victim in order to set the wheels of restitution in motion. Idomeneo announces that Idamante is the intended victim, to which the populace responds in horror.

The scene changes to the exterior of Neptune's temple. Idomeneo and the chorus sing Neptune's praises; Arbace rushes in to say that Idamante has slain the monster that was attacking the population; he learns, however, that Idamante is due to be sacrificed. Idamante arrives, telling his father that he is happy that his father's displeasure was due to no fault of his own, and that he is happy to die under these circumstances. The two bid an impassioned farewell. Ilia rushes in to offer herself in Idamante's place; Idamante will not hear of it. The Voice of Neptune himself interrupts this argument to say that love has won the day, that Idomeneo should leave the throne as punishment for failing to keep his promise, and that Idamante and Ilia should rule in his stead. Elettra departs in a rage, and everyone else celebrates.

COMMENTARY

Origins

Because Mozart wrote most of the music of *Idomeneo* in Munich and his librettist Varesco was in Salzburg, and because Leopold Mozart was both an eager go-between and a hoarder of his son's letters, Mozart's compositional choices and methods are better documented with *Idomeneo* than with any other opera. Mozart wrote copiously to his father on the subject, and Leopold communicated the relevant messages to Varesco, but often contributed ideas of his own.

Mozart was familiar with the Munich court personnel, as they were largely the same as those at Mannheim, which he had visited at length in 1778. In the meantime, the elector Karl Theodore had become Elector of Bavaria and had moved the establishment (including the Mannheim orchestra, probably the best in the world) to Munich. Count Seeau, the Intendant of the court theater was of particular interest to Mozart. It was probably he, in consultation with other court officials, who chose the subject of the opera, and also the particular French text to be adapted – namely, Antoine Danchet's 1712 libretto *Idomenée*. Mozart and his father probably then chose the Abbé Giambattista Varesco as the librettist, since he was conveniently located in Salzburg, where Mozart was at the time of the opera's commission. The basic chronology of the composition was that Mozart spent from early November until February in Munich, but before traveling there he seems to have written the first scene for Ilia, and to have had some overall ideas. Rehearsals began on 1 December with much diminished forces (no full orchestra), and the second act came into rehearsal a week after that. By 16 December the whole work was being rehearsed in Count Seeau's apartments, and by 19 December two acts were ready and rehearsals were taking place in front of an audience, with the Elector listening incognito in a side room. The third act was largely finished in the first week of January. The opera was eventually performed on 29 January, after a postponement by the court. In the interim, Mozart never ceased to revise and cut.

To say, then, that composition proceeded at breakneck speed is no exaggeration. Nevertheless there is nothing routine about this work, partly because it is not a "pure" opera seria of the sort the Mozart had written for Milan, but rather a mix of French and Italian elements, and partly because, in contrast to his early teenage years, Mozart was now desperate for permanent employment, and hoped that *Idomeneo* would be his ticket out of Salzburg and into a more prestigious, interesting, and opera-filled position.

Two big compositional issues seem to have occupied Mozart's mind as he worked on this opera. The first, and in some ways the most immediate, was working with the singers. Some, like Dorthea Wendling, who sang Ilia, were easily pleased and caused few difficulties for Mozart. Others, like the castrato Vincenzo dal Prato, who sang Idamante, were unalloyed agony. The letters repeatedly describe his stupidity, his bad musical training, his unappealing vocal production, and in particular, the amount of time Mozart had to spend teaching him the part by rote. In one letter Mozart refers to him with his typical verbal spritz and bite as the "molto amato castrato dal Prato."[40] The most interesting case was the tenor Anton Raaff, then 66, who played the title role. Raaff had had a distinguished career in Italy and Germany, and had a wide range and easy coloratura.[41] Mozart clearly respected Raaff's age and experience, but complained that he acted like a statue.[42] He also worried about the singer's capacity to "show off" in the virtuoso aria "Fuor del mar," in Act II.[43] On the other side, Raaf was not hesitant to express his preferences; in particular he wanted an aria that would allow him to show off his legato (the smooth transitions from note to note) and he and Mozart together rejected a text for his third-act aria sent by Varesco on the grounds that it would not permit him to display this effect.[44] There are a few other comments in the letters about the effect of the vowel sounds in arias for more than one singer: this is clearly something both the singers and Mozart worried about. On the whole, though, it seems that Raaff and the composer had a very healthy working relationship, at least as chronicled by Mozart; he recounts that Raaff did not like the Act III quartet "Andrò ramingo e solo" ("Alone I shall wander") when he first encountered his part in it, because it was not grateful to sing. Mozart, however, insisted on keeping it as written because although he was willing to accommodate singers in arias, when they were on show, in ensembles "the composer must have a free hand,"[45] and he was (rightly) very satisfied with this number. Eleven days later, Mozart reports that Raaff "was delighted to be mistaken" about the quartet, and could now understand the effect it made. At this historical distance it is difficult to gauge the extent and probability of Raaff's delight, but at the very least it suggests that the old

singer respected the young composer's craft; and if we put the story in a somewhat broader context, it suggests the growing importance of the composer, as
operatic music became less about the singers and more about the overall effect
of the drama.[46]

The second issue which recurs again and again in Mozart's letters about
writing this opera is the question of theatrical effect. This takes a number of
forms, and affected a number of places in the opera. One aspect of effect has
to do with the emotional engagement of the audience; the appearance of "the
subterranean voice" (Neptune) at the moment of dénouement is a chief
example of this. Quite early in the compositional process, Mozart wrote to his
father that the voice must be "terrifying" and that "the audience has to believe
[the voice] really exists," both of which qualities would be better achieved by
brevity.[47] He wrote four versions of this appearance, and fought with Count
Seeau over the trombones, whose only appearance this is, placed so they
appear to emanate from the same place as the voice. It appears that Mozart
may have lost that battle, and a trombone-less voice from beyond was what
the first audiences experienced.[48] Mozart also worried about the length of the
first dialogue between Idomeneo and Idamante, one of the most wrenching
scenes in the work. It clearly needed to be long enough to make the point, but
short enough to carry no risk of boring the audience, and the unimpressive
acting abilities of Raaff and dal Prato argued for brevity. Mozart also thought
seriously about the stage logistics, to allow entries and exits to be seemly and
to allow characters their proper space. For example, he extended the Act III
introduction to the High Priest's entry to allow Arbace time to exit after his
aria and return directly if he needed to. Theatrical effect also included the
question of the proprieties involved in representing a royal personage. At the
very beginning of the process, Lorenzo Quaglio, the stage designer, had
pointed out that in Idomeneo's first (non-singing) appearance, enduring a
shipwreck, he should not be alone in the boat – presumably no sailors would
abandon their ruler to the vagaries of the ocean.

Finally, the letters demonstrate yet again the depth and variety of collab-
oration required to mount an opera. Very early in his stay in Munich,
Mozart met with Christian Cannabich, the orchestra leader, Lorenzo
Quaglio, the set designer, and Le Grand, master of the court ballet, as well as
Count Seeau, to plan the opera. He and Le Grand evidently worked together
quite closely on the action and grouping of the characters on stage.
Obviously he and Varesco had a lot of dialogue (through Leopold, once
Mozart was in Munich), not least about how much of Varesco's unused or
cut text would be printed.[49] The singers also collaborated in a variety of
ways, some more helpful than others. Such pervasive collaboration does not
in any way detract from the idea of Mozart's creative genius; indeed, to have

been able to welcome (or simply adapt to) the needs of so many constituencies and write a work of such consistent depth and interest is surely a sign of creativity at its height.

REPUTATION

As far as we know, *Idomeneo* received only one post-Munich performance during Mozart's lifetime; a private, probably unstaged, one in Vienna's Auersperg palace, in 1786, with amateur singers. Mozart made more cuts and added two new items for this performance: the aria with violin obbligato "Non temer amato bene" ("Fear not, well beloved") for Idamante, and a new duet for Idamante and Ilia. There is no record of audience reaction to this performance. The opera was published in various versions, including several reduced for voices and piano, during the late eighteenth and early nineteenth centuries, and it was clearly well known among experts and Mozart enthusiasts throughout the nineteenth century. Its first public performance in Vienna took place in 1806. Indeed, it had a higher profile among scholars and critics than it did among audiences for all of the nineteenth and much of the twentieth centuries. Although the first twentieth-century performance in the English-speaking world was in Glasgow in 1934, and the 1951 Glyndebourne production is sometimes taken as the beginning of the work's reinstatement in the canon, it was still possible for opera critic Owen Lee, writing in *Opera News* in 1977, to lament that *Idomeneo* was still not part of the repertory,[50] and for Jean-Pierre Ponelle's 1982 production for the Metropolitan Opera, with Luciano Pavarotti in the title role, to make a major splash.

There are some common themes in the commentary about this opera in the many years before it became a standard part of the repertory in both Europe and America. One of the most pervasive is the extraordinary quality of the music, and especially Mozart's exploitation of the resources of the marvelous Mannheim orchestra, famous throughout Europe in the later eighteenth century for its precision and virtuosity. As early as 1832, for example, a report in *The Harmonicon* noted that "the accompaniments are universally full, the wind instruments being kept in almost continual employ."[51] And in 1849, G. A. MacFarren commented that "This opera is interesting in the history of the art as being the earliest example of what may be esteemed the modern school of instrumentation, distinguished from that which preceded it by the general difference in the relative treatment of the wind and string instruments."[52] By 1859 Macfarren's relatively modest comment about the use of the orchestra had expanded to include many other things about the music: an anonymous commentator reviewing a London performance of seven selections from the opera said "The novel phraseology, the unused combinations of harmony, the original forms of construction, and the wholly untried resources of instrumentation, are the technical points which mark *Idomeneo* as the initial work of what may be styled the modern school of music."[53] Some version of this commentary continued well into the twentieth century, though the later writers mostly avoided the *Harmonicon* author's implication that the richness of the instrumental writing was due to the work being written in Germany for German taste, with Mozart thus liberated from the shackles of the Italian addiction to "certain forms of melody" and "the simplest harmony."[54]

The music of *Idomeneo* is indeed extraordinary, and the work is rightly considered to be the first opera, and perhaps even the first work, of Mozart's true maturity. But the common praise of the music in the writings of the nineteenth and early twentieth century also complements the equally common queasiness about the libretto and about the work's stageworthiness. The work's genre was for a long time a discouragement; it was often described simply as "opera seria," which was (wrongly) understood as superannuated by 1780, and (equally wrongly) interpreted as undramatic. *Idomeneo* is, of course, an opera seria, but its expanded use of choral music and dance, and the emotionally intense mythological topic connects to the French *tragédie lyrique,* and to Italian operas on the French model written for Mannheim in the mid-eighteenth century. In line with the idea that *Idomeneo* is "only" an opera seria, the anonymous author in the above-mentioned 1859 *Musical World* article notes the "paucity of action in the drama and the conduct of what little there is, chiefly in recitative; [and] the prevalence of episodical songs, the effect of which has now become tedious upon the stage." Even in 1951, in an otherwise sympathetic and intelligent essay, Hans Gal writes, "The problem of this opera, however, is how to make it convincing on the stage, and this problem is rooted in the style and structure of the libretto. . . . But [the libretto's] weakness is . . . not peculiar to this individual opera: it is inherent in the constitution of the baroque opera seria, of which this is a late offspring at a time when the whole species had already become obsolete. . . ."

However, in addition to the genre, the libretto itself was also panned (this is a theme in the history of Mozart opera criticism more generally). The renowned Viennese music critic Eduard Hanslick wrote in 1879, "First comes the libretto! That is the source of all mischief. The book of *Idomeneo* is in bad taste, empty, wearisome, and all in the indescribably antiquated garb proper to the mythological opera of gods and heroes."[55] Only very recently has it been possible to celebrate the size and pace of this work as staged, including the danced divertissements at the ends of Acts I and III. In a 1990 review, for example, Hilary Finch points out that the dance music, which would as recently as twenty years before have fallen squarely into the "undramatic" and therefore problematic, category, "substantiate[s] the public dimension of the opera, filling out the celebratory and hieratic context in which the private emotional drama is played out, and with which it is inextricably linked."[56]

Another common thread about staging in the writings from the nineteenth and earlier twentieth century involves the voice types of the cast: three sopranos (Ilia, Elettra and Idamante) three tenors (Idomeneo, Arbace and the High Priest) and one, very briefly appearing, bass (Voice of Neptune). The anonymous 1859 *Musical World* article quoted above commented on the difficulty of engaging three sopranos, with a slightly acid comment about Idamante's part being written for one of the "'*uomini*' [castratos] so much in esteem at the time." Many productions in the nineteenth century and well into the twentieth used a tenor for this role: Hans Gal strongly supported this: "This part is unsuitable for [a female soprano], not only on dramatic grounds – Idamante is not a youngster like Cherubino, but a man and a hero – but also for musical reasons. We know from many contemporary descriptions that the castrato voice sounded strikingly different from the female voice, much more strident and metallic." One justification for making Idamante a tenor is that, as some commentators note, Mozart "altered the part for a tenor in the 1786 Vienna production." But Julian Rushton authoritatively points out that the alteration is by no means unambiguous.[57] And in any case, this 1786 performance, done by noble amateurs, was unlikely to have had a castrato available to play the part. Most present-day performances use female singers, on the grounds that the music wants the close intertwining of the parts in the ensembles, and that many female singers can act the role convincingly.

A work's reputation obviously rests in part on what counts as integral to it. This is a somewhat vexed issue in most of the Mozart operas, but it is particularly so with *Idomeneo*. Mozart wrote considerably more music than was performed in the first production: not only was the Voice of Neptune section written in four versions, but it seems that Arbace's second aria, and (more crucially), Elettra's departing howl, "D'Oreste, d'Ajace" ("Of Orestes and Ajax"), as well as Idomeneo's final aria, "Torna la pace" ("Peace returns"), were omitted in 1781 in order to leave room for the dance music. Idamante's "No, la morte io non pavento" ("No, I do not fear death") was also on the chopping block, though it seems as though it probably included.[58] These omissions were clearly not made because these arias were substandard, or because Mozart himself necessarily saw these arias as dramatically superfluous. Thus even if a director or conductor decides (as most do) not to include the extra numbers from the 1786 performance, on the grounds that doing so would be "outside" the initial and essential conception of the work, the 1781 material does not present a single coherent version of the opera. Modern productions have tended to include at least some of the main characters' final arias while omitting the dance music (as "undramatic"); the principles on which these decisions are made tend to have more to do with the audience's presumed capacity to sit still for over three hours, and the director's sense of the crux and nature of the drama than with Mozart's presumed intentions or desires, which are not really knowable.

MUSIC AND DRAMA IN *IDOMENEO*

Mozart's operas have often been accused of having music "too good" for the libretto – or conversely, have been praised because Mozart "overcame" or "transcended" the perceived inadequacies of the librettist's work. The "trivialities" of *Così* are said to be redeemed by the music, for example, as is the "nonsense" of *The Magic Flute* and the "episodic structure" of *Don Giovanni*. *Idomeneo* has had a similar "problem," but the issue with this work is not so much that the music transforms an inadequate text into a transcendent artwork, but rather that the music has been thought to be too much of a good thing given both the genre and the particular qualities of this libretto. And indeed, this is a young man's opera to the extent that one gets the impression that, offered an emotionally intense story, the incomparable Mannheim orchestra, great singers and real rehearsal time, Mozart could not restrain himself from using every musical device at his disposal. The sheer variety of kinds of music is quite stunning: marches, dances, accompanied recitatives, choruses of various sorts, arias in all the emotional types, supernatural moments all co-exist, each type represented with stellar examples.

The drama is emotionally strong stuff, with an ill-advised bargain between Neptune and Idomeneo, the possibility that Idomeneo will kill his son, Ilia's heroics, and Elettra's towering rages. But there is no denying that it moves slowly. As we have seen, Mozart was intensely aware of this, and he was probably not the only one so aware, given the radical cuts he made for the first performance. Even with the cuts it is not action-packed, and in that respect it accords with both courtly genres that fed into it, namely opera seria and *tragédie lyrique*. But unlike in opera seria, the focus is not primarily on the performers' prowess, and unlike in *tragédie lyrique*, the focus is not strongly on spectacle and barely-relevant divertissements. Rather, one of the primary foci in this work is the composition itself – its craft and its art. One way in which the audience's attention is drawn to Mozart's compositional prowess is in the many striking effects he wrote into the work. Among these are the offstage sailors singing in answer to the onstage ones in the shipwreck scene in Act I; and the elaborate writing for woodwind instruments, especially in places like Ilia's aria "Se il padre perdei," where they act as dialogue with the voice rather than just accompaniment. Other unavoidably noticeable compositional effects include the ending of the great quartet "Andrò ramingo e solo," where Idamante, all by himself, repeats the phrase with which he opened the ensemble, and exits, thus subverting the traditional tutti (everyone singing) ending, and bringing his utter desolation into stark relief. The subterranean voice accompanied by trombones is another obvious effect, as is the pizzicato accompaniment in the violins against the long lines of the winds and the voices in Idomeneo's third-act aria with chorus, "Accogli o re del mar" ("Receive, O god of the sea").

The choruses also throw Mozart's compositional craft into relief. As he himself pointed out to Raaff, in ensembles (and by extension, choruses) the composer ruled; these were pieces "about" what the composer wrote, not about the singers' capacity to interpret them. *Idomeneo* has more choruses than any other Mozart opera, and they express a remarkably wide variety of circumstances and states of being, from the disappearing "Corriamo, fuggiamo" ("Let's run, let's flee") and the grand and terrifying "Pietà, Numi, pietà" ("Have mercy, O gods") to the gorgeously tranquil "Placido è il mar" ("The sea is calm").

To the extent that each of the choruses captures a single mood or response with striking immediacy, highlighting the composer's ability to paint a vivid picture, these numbers should be included among the compositional "effects" of the opera. But the chorus – usually representing the population of Crete – is also a vital participant in the drama, setting the celebratory mood in "Godiam la pace" ("Let us enjoy peace"), warning the audience and the main characters of impending danger in "Qual nuovo terrore" ("What new terror"), confirming the happy conclusion in "Scenda Amor, scenda Imeneo" ("Let Love and Hymen descend"), and so on. To that extent, then, the choruses point not only to Mozart's craft on the local level, but also to the larger narrative and political thread of the work. Indeed, this opera overall is characterized to an extraordinary degree by a combination of contrast or chiaroscuro (created largely by the juxtaposition of different effects), with a kind of seamlessness and flow in the telling of the story.

Moments of contrast are everywhere. The ubiquitous accompanied recitatives, for example, are replete with sudden juxtapositions of different moods and gestures as the characters come to terms with situations, make decisions, and react to the latest circumstances. The moment in Act I when Idamante and Idomeneo have recognized each other, and Idamante is desperate to reach out to his long-lost parent while Idomeneo, knowing Idamante's fate and his responsibility for it, is equally desperate to leave, moves in rapid succession from excitement to regret to panic to chilly formality as Idomeneo tells his son to fear seeing him again. There are also contrasts of various sorts between movements: both Marches, for example (in Acts I and III), emerge directly out of moments of private contemplation, and the trombone sounds surrounding the slow diction of the subterranean voice follow on the heels of a rhythmically lively, string-accompanied recitative. These contrasts isolate the dramatic moments from one another, combining with the striking effects that characterize particular moments to "freeze" them in memory.

At the same time, however, this opera is by far the most continuously constructed dramatic work that Mozart ever wrote. On the largest level, he linked many numbers musically, so that they form scene-complexes rather than the more usual opera-seria series of exit arias. One example concerns Elettra's first rage aria, "Tutte nel cor vi sento," which connects without pause to the following chorus, "Pietà, Numi, pietà." Another is Idamante's "No la morte non pavento," which dissolves into the recitative which introduces the next segment of the plot instead of ending with a firm cadence. On a more local level, this opera is shot through with musical motifs (little melodic or rhythmic ideas) that recur throughout the opera, linking otherwise perhaps discrete moments. For example, a longish note followed by a rapid descending run to four repeated notes is associated with Idamante and the idea of sacrifice throughout the work: it appears first in the overture, but is perhaps most easily identifiable in Ilia's "Padre, germani" ("Father, brothers") in the accompaniment to her words "D'ingrata al sangue mio" ("Of ingratitude to my relatives").[59] Ilia herself may be identified by a syncopated motif (both "Padre, germani" and "Se il padre perdei" begin in this way), as well as by a little winding melodic figure. These motifs, as Rushton writes, do not stand out from the surrounding music to act as "calling cards" for the characters or ideas with which they are associated; rather, the experience of listening to this opera is of continuously hearing fragments that sound curiously familiar, if not exactly the same, and that seem almost mysteriously to make dramatic sense.[60]

Thus although the time-scale of this opera is grander than that of the other mature operas, and in the hurried modern world the work may suffer somewhat from the barely restrained burgeoning of Mozart's musical skills, it should also be remembered that the extraordinary music of this work does in fact articulate the drama, both as a series of unprecedentedly vivid moments, and as a continuous web of narrative connections.

La clemenza di Tito Dramma serio per musica. Libretto by Metastasio, revised for Mozart by Caterino Mazzolà. Prague, National Theater, 6 September 1791.

CHARACTERS

Tito Vespasiano, Emperor of Rome	Tenor
Vitellia, daughter of the Emperor Vitellius	Soprano
Servilia, Sesto's sister, beloved of Annio	Soprano
Sesto, Tito's friend, in love with Vitellia	Soprano
Annio, Sesto's friend, beloved of Servilia	Soprano
Publio, Prefect of the Praetorian Guard	Bass

SUMMARY

The opera plays the emperor Tito's great-heartedness against the ambitious scheming of Vitellia, who desires to be empress, and the weakness of Sesto, who is willing to burn Rome and kill Tito to retain Vitellia's love. The subsidiary couple Annio and Servilia demonstrate nobility by being willing to sacrifice, respectively, love and status – Annio is willing to give up Servilia to Tito, and Servilia is willing to refuse Tito's hand to stay with Annio.

SYNOPSIS

Act I begins in Vitellia's quarters. Vitellia is eager to put her plot to kill Tito into action through Sesto. She is primarily angry that Tito has robbed her of her dynastic right to the throne by proposing to marry Berenice. Sesto tries to persuade her against the plot; she makes as if to break off their engagement; they sing a duet about their conflicted feelings. Annio comes in to tell them that Berenice has given up her claim to Tito's hand; Vitellia is delighted, but Sesto fears for Vitellia's fidelity to him. She responds that he who expects deception will entice people to commit it. Left alone with Sesto, Annio celebrates the near completion of his arrangements to marry Servilia and the two young men sing a duet of friendship.

In a magnificent part of the Roman Forum, a chorus praises Tito. He announces that he will give their tributes to help the victims of a recent erup-tion of Vesuvius. He regrets privately to Sesto and Annio that Berenice did not love him, and says he will marry Sesto's sister Servilia instead, since she is of noble blood. Sesto is thunderstruck on Annio's behalf, but Annio nobly rescues the situation by praising his choice. Tito expresses the thought that being able to dispense benefits on the deserving and the virtuous is the only pleasure in ruling. Annio informs Servilia of her change in rank, and apologizes for treating her with insufficient humility now that she is practically empress. She replies that he is the only one she ever loved.

In a lovely retreat in the Palatine hills, Publio is beginning to tell Tito of the plot against him when Servilia interrupts to tell him that she cannot be his wife because she loves Annio. Tito's noble response is gratitude for her sincerity and boldness in telling him this: an aria praising these qualities follows. Servilia and Vitellia meet briefly; Vitellia is scornful and does not learn that Servilia has renounced the possibility of being empress. She humiliates Sesto into agreeing to set the Capitol on fire and murder Tito. He sings an aria describing his complete helplessness in the face of his love for her, and runs off to do the dreadful deed. Publio and Annio arrive to tell Vitellia that Tito has chosen her as his consort. She is overcome with horror at what Sesto is about to do: Annio and Publio misinterpret this as joy.

Right before the first act finale, Sesto is revealed alone in the Capitol, agonizing about his traitorous assignment. The scene shows the Capitol in flames. The finale begins as Sesto prays for Rome to be saved. Annio accosts him, but Sesto runs away in shame. Everyone expresses their horror at the destruction, and amidst the confusion, Sesto tells Vitellia that he has stabbed Tito in the heart, for which she roundly condemns him.

Act II begins in the Palatine hills again. Annio tells Sesto that he cannot have killed Tito, for the emperor is still alive. Sesto confesses his role in the plot, and Annio begs him to throw himself on Tito's mercy; his grief at his betrayal is clearly a sign of virtue. Vitellia has also heard that Tito did not die and importunes Sesto to keep quiet about his and her roles in the plot. Publio, however, arrives, ordering Sesto to surrender his sword. They sing a trio in which Sesto asks Vitellia to remember his love for her, Vitellia is possessed by grief, horror, and fear, and Publio sees that a judgment has to be made, despite his sympathy for their misery.

In a great audience hall, Tito receives the blessing of his people, and tells Publio that he is confident that the Senate will find Sesto innocent of treason; how could a faithful heart commit a traitorous act? Publio delivers the Senate's verdict to Tito: Sesto is guilty. Annio apologizes for defending him and pleads for him to consult his heart in deciding on a judgement. In a solo scene, Tito agonizes about Sesto's betrayal and his own obligations as emperor, and yearns for the simple life of a peasant. Publio brings Sesto in; the three men sing a trio of anxious expectation. Tito and Sesto are left alone: Tito is appalled that his friendship for Sesto has reaped this reward, and tries to get Sesto to confess why he betrayed him. At enormous cost to himself, Sesto refuses to name Vitellia, and tries to remind Tito of the bonds that united them, begging for mercy in an aria. Alone, Tito first resolves to execute Sesto, and then decides that mercy is a more powerful legacy than vengeance; if successful rule is dependent on violence, he would rather not be in power. Vitellia anxiously awaits news of Sesto's fate. Servilia begs her to intercede with the emperor, but Vitellia is paralysed. In a soliloquy she comes to the realization that she cannot let Sesto die for her treasonous demands; she will confess to Tito and sacrifice her hopes of marriage and power.

Near a vast amphitheater, Tito's entry is again lauded by his subjects. He refuses Servilia's and Annio's pleas for mercy, and starts to pronounce what seems to be a condemnation of Sesto when Vitellia rushes in and confesses. Tito wonders whether any loyal souls are left, but forgives both of them to gratitude and praise from all his followers.

COMMENTARY

Origins

Metastasio's libretto was written originally for the Habsburg Emperor Charles VI in 1734, and set to music by Antonio Caldara. Between Caldara and Mozart the libretto was set by about forty different composers in cities all over Europe, from Naples to London, Lisbon, and St. Petersburg; it was one of Metastasio's most successful works. Mozart could thus count on many members of his audience knowing the text, whether in a setting by another composer, or as an autonomous drama, since Metastasio's complete works were published in multiple editions. Written for the coronation of the Habsburg emperor Leopold II as King of Bohemia, Mozart's setting was commissioned by the Bohemian Estates (the representative body of the Bohemian aristocracy), via the impresario Domenico Guardasoni, rather than by Leopold II or his representatives. As was the norm on such occasions, the Metastasio text was submitted to another librettist for the necessary alterations. In this case the reviser was Caterino Mazzolà, court poet in Dresden, and briefly, in 1791, in Vienna. In his own catalogue of his works, Mozart described the text he set as the Metastasio "ridotto a vera opera" – "reduced to a true opera" by his collaborator. What Mozart meant by "vera opera" is subject to speculation, but Mazzolà certainly did reduce the original from three acts to two, write ensembles for the middle of the acts, and provide the first act finale, all of which were operatic conventions by this time. Most of the solo arias remained either exactly as Metastasio had written them, or were adapted from Metastasio's texts. The exceptions are Annio's "Tu fosti tradito" ("You were betrayed") and Vitellia's "Non più di fiori" ("No more flowers"), which are completely new.

Mozart's work on this opera is traditionally thought to have been extremely compressed, in part because of the short time he was in Prague, and in part because he was composing *The Magic Flute* at the same time. The first performance of *Tito* was 6 September 1791; he entered the work in his own catalogue on 5 September, composing up until the evening of that day, having arrived in Prague on the evening of 28 August. However, it seems likely that the impresario Guardasoni actually traveled to Vienna in mid-July to bring Mozart the commission and the libretto, and that most of the ensembles and some arias, including those for Tito, who was sung by Antonio Baglioni, the same tenor who premiered Don Ottavio in *Don Giovanni*, were written before the journey. Vitellia's great Rondò, "Non più di fiori" seems to have been sung in April 1791 as a concert aria: the singer on that occasion was Josefa Duschek, a longstanding friend of Mozart, but not the first Vitellia; this may explain why the range and tessitura (predominant vocal range) of the aria are different from Vitellia's other music. Mozart and Guardasoni had also had contact in 1789 and 1790; while the particular libretto is unlikely to have been discussed, Mozart may also have been cogitating for quite some time about themes, structures and devices for a serious opera. The shortness of time, however, is evident in the fact that Mozart outsourced the secco recitatives, most probably to Franz Süssmayr, his student and assistant.

The original singers included, in addition to Baglioni, the castrato Domenico Bedini playing Sesto, the female soprano Carolina Perrini as Annio, a Signora Antonini as Servilia, the well-known buffo bass Gaetano Campi as Publio, and the much-admired soprano Maria Marchetti-Fantozzi as Vitellia.

Reputation

Prague was the city that most fervently loved Mozart during his lifetime, and it is probably telling that the commission for *Tito* came from the Bohemian Estates and the Prague-based impresario Domenico Guardasoni rather than from the Vienna-based Habsburg Emperor Leopold. Its first performance was evidently not universally beloved: the ubiquitous Count Zinzendorf described it as "a most boring spectacle," and whether or not the Empress Maria Luisa, Leopold's wife, actually called it a "porcheria tedesca" ("German rubbish"), she did certainly find it tedious.[61] The opera began to catch on in Prague, however, and at the beginning of October Mozart reported to his wife, through the clarinetist Anton Stadler, who stayed in Prague to play the important solo clarinet parts in the opera, that the last performance, on 30 September (the same day as the premiere of *The Magic Flute*), had gone very well and had been well received. The opera may have benefited from Mozart's death in the years immediately following its premiere, assisted by his wife Constanze's promotion of it as a last musical memento of her husband: it was performed unstaged, in several musical "academies" (concerts) during the decade after Mozart's death, and the notices and reviews never fail to describe it as his last opera – which, compositionally, it was, though *The Magic Flute* was premiered last. Franz Xaver Niemetschek's 1808 biography of Mozart describes the composer's sickliness during his time writing this opera in Prague, and his tears on leaving his friends there.[62] This echoes a review written shortly after the first performance, and surely added to the opera's mystique. Whether because of, or despite, the weight of sentiment attached to it shortly after Mozart's death, *Tito* was the first opera by Mozart to be performed in London, in 1806, and it continued to enjoy somewhat regular performances there. It also spread across Europe in the first two decades of the nineteenth century, waning in popularity thereafter.[63] Certainly reviews from London in the 1820s suggest that it was not a novelty at that point. John Rice has pointed out that whereas in early nineteenth-century Germany it was the dramatic power of the opera, and the acting capacities of the singers that were particularly valued – even to the point of permitting easier music to be substituted for Mozart's if that allowed competent actors to play the parts – in London, it was viewed as a vehicle for great singers.[64]

Although as the last opera of a great composer *Tito* continued to be known by musicians and music critics, it was not widely performed after the 1820s, and indeed, did not really rejoin the standard repertory until the second half of the twentieth century – arguably, until the 1970s. It suffered from several related disadvantages, some biographical, some performance-related, and some generic. Biographically, the story (publicized by Niemetchek's 1808 biography) that the work had been written in 18 days (starting in the coach on the way to Prague) in response to a commission for an occasion which critics presumed meant nothing to Mozart – reinforced by the fact that the secco recitatives seem to be by Süssmayr (see above) – was cited as evidence of Mozart's lack of interest in the work. With respect to performance, this opera has always raised problems of the gender-casting of the role of Sesto (and to a lesser extent, Annio). Mozart's early biographer Otto Jahn, writing in the 1850s, was disgusted at the idea that woman would play this role: "True characterization is impossible when a woman in man's clothes plays the lover."[65] The role of Tito, with its sententious arias and action confined to the recitatives, was long thought to be a problem, and Vitellia's and Sesto's arias, with their elaborate coloratura (and the enormous range of Vitellia's "Non più di fiori") demanded a kind of vocal training that fell out of fashion in the mid-nineteenth century, when projection and declamatory power began to be valued more than agility. These performance problems are also related to the fact that it is an opera seria, a genre wrongly thought to be defunct in the 1790s and rightly thought to embody both political and aesthetic values at odds with the values of the bourgeois and democratic milieu of the nineteenth and twentieth centuries. The continuing dismissal of *Tito* on the grounds that it is a relic of a bygone genre contrasts strikingly with the late twentieth-century embrace of *Idomeneo* as a fascinating and powerful essay in reform opera.[66]

Tito's reputation has certainly grown over the past forty years. Nevertheless, as recently as 1997 it was described in *Opera News* as "one of Mozart's lesser efforts," hopelessly confined by its superannuated genre.[67] Almost all productions cut the recitatives, often drastically, assuming that audiences will not have the patience to let the story take its own time, and also that no-one wants to listen to Süssmayr. The availability of sur- and sub- titles may have mitigated the extremity of the cuts. Productions have typically made reference to the classical world in which the action takes place, whether elaborately and quite literally, as with the toga-clad characters in the Tanglewood production of 1952,[68] or more allusively, as with the laurel wreaths in the Paris Opera production of 2005.[69] The Drottningholm production of 1987[70] situated the work definitively in the late eighteenth century, suggesting parallels between Tito and the Swedish king Gustav III; a 1974 production in Berlin similarly turned Tito into the Emperor Leopold himself.[71] Some kind of political allegory has been quite usual in other modern productions; in the recent Paris Opera production, for example, Tito looks remarkably like the Ingres portrait of Napoleon on his throne. This may be making a point by negative allusion, since Napoleon was not a famously merciful ruler. But regardless of the political references, which, of course, were part of the original circumstances of the work, the most successful modern productions have been those in which impeccable singing has been conjoined to acting that conveys both the human emotions of the protagonists and the high political and ethical stakes of the arena in which these emotions play out. Such productions combine the dramatic power appreciated by German audiences in the early nineteenth century with the musical delights that drew contemporary London audiences to the opera.

Justifying Tito

One of the reasons that this opera has had a harder time in the repertory than Mozart's other mature works is because of the perceived "stiffness" of Tito himself. Regardless of his historical veracity (and it is the case that Titus Vespasianus was one of the best loved and most generous rulers of his time), Tito's absolute commitment to the principle of clemency in the face of the most appalling betrayals – by his closest friend, and by the woman to whom he is willing to give his hand – can seem implausible and undramatic. And his arias about the burdens of power seem cool exercises in rhetoric rather than deeply-felt personal statements; they do not progress from one state of mind to another, and the sentiments he expresses are more political than intimate. His dispensation of mercy is God-like, in part because it involves ignoring the recommendation of the Senate. His explicit reference to the biblical story of the Prodigal Son once he has pardoned the conspirators only intensifies that reference: in the final ensemble of the opera he sings "The true repentance of which you are capable is worth more than a truly constant fidelity."[72] Nothing about this is comfortable to a modern Western audience; we do not like to think of our rulers as above the law, we are generally uncomfortable with the rule of pure ideology, we are suspicious of disinterested generosity, and in an age of instant contact, we seem to want out rulers to be recognizeably like us rather than beings on a different plane of existence.

But Metastasio, Mazzolà and Mozart were not working in an age of folksy democracy, and barely in an age when rulers mingled with their subjects (Joseph II's attempts in this direction in Vienna did not earn him the love of his people). The character of Tito was created by Metastasio as undisguised homage to the magnificent Emperor Charles VI, and adapted by Mazzolà as an equally unveiled reference to Leopold II. Nicholas Till has interpreted Mazzolà's *Tito* (which, as noted above, was commissioned by the Bohemian Estates, not the emperor) as a plea from the aristocracy to the emperor to circumvent the law and look mercifully on their objections to the taxes Joseph II had levied on them rather than as simple sycophancy.[73] Regardless of the subtext, however, *Tito* provided at that time a plausible, recognizeable, and pertinent, if also somewhat exaggerated, example of imperial rule. One way to comprehend the figure of Tito, then, is as a glimpse of eighteenth-century political philosophy, or as a window to the concerns of a particular population at a particular time.

Tito is also, self-evidently, an exercise in neo-classicism: the revival and refurbishing of Classical Greek and Roman genres, figures, and ideals as models for a later age. The Metastasio text has for many critics recalled the elegance and power of Racine, perhaps the most classical of French authors. It is thus doubly neo-classical, recalling not only ancient Rome but a much-admired past epoch of French literature. The first setting of the text, by Antonio Caldara, would have diverted the libretto's severe elegance into a spectacle of elaborate scenery and limitless vocal display – a "classic" rococo opera seria. But by 1791, after the French Revolution, the mid-century oper-atic reforms of Calzabigi, Gluck and others, the uncompromising paintings of Jacques-Louis David (e.g. *The Oath of the Horatii* [1784], or *Brutus and his Dead Sons* [1789]), and especially after the essays on Classical art by Johann Joachim Winckelmann (1717–68), the ideal of "noble simplicity" was even more central to neo-classicism than it had been before. Winckelmann's famous statement on the "noble simplicity and quiet grandeur" of the Classical statue of Laocoon and his sons attacked by a giant serpent is the central articulation of this ideal:

> The pain is revealed in all the muscles and sinews of his body, and we ourselves can almost feel it as we observe the painful contraction of the abdomen alone without regarding the face and other parts of the body. This pain, however, expresses itself with no sign of rage in his face or in his entire bearing. He emits no terrible screams like Virgil's Laocoon, for the opening of his mouth does not permit it. It is rather an anxious and troubled sighing. . . . Laocoon suffers, but he suffers like Sophocles' Philoctetes; his pain touches our very souls, but we wish we could bear misery like this great man.[74]

"Noble simplicity," then, is precisely *not* the absence of pain or passion, but the mind's and the psyche's mastery over those states. Tito's bare acknowledgement of pain at his loss of Berenice and at Servilia's rejection of him, and his ability to conquer the fury caused by Sesto's and Vitellia's betrayals, are very much of a kind with Laocoon's mastery over his agony, and the calm of his arias in contrast with the high emotion of his recitatives, both accompanied and secco, could well have been understood at the time as part of the new neoclassical aesthetic.

These historical explanations may clarify the central characteristics of Mozart's Tito, but they do not necessarily work to convince a modern audience to warm to either the character or the opera. Sesto and Vitellia, the other central characters, have suffered from a related but different problem; Sesto's dog-like devotion to Vitellia and Vitellia's towering jealousy and rage have not infrequently been seen as evidence of "weak" and implausible character, but Mozart's music for them (especially their arias) has with comparable frequency been seen as too "sweet" for these possessed figures. Their more obviously passionate recitatives, by contrast, have often been praised. The implication here is not only that direct and robust expression of passion is more human, but also more suitably operatic, and thus that while Tito himself is not really a plausibly operatic figure because his position is fundamentally undramatic, Sesto and Vitellia would be properly operatic if Mozart had calculated differently. The historical record both about opera seria in general and about *Tito* in particular, even into the nineteenth century, suggests that when the singers acted with sufficient conviction and plausibility in the recitatives, the transition to vocal display in the arias was not problematic. However, once again, the historical record does not necessarily change modern minds about the effect of a work.

One way to approach this work that involves, but is not limited to, historically contextual justifications is to think of the conventionality of both the characters and the genre as a necessary frame for the unruly passions that desperate love and high treason generate. Opera seria was profoundly about social order: the need for hierarchy to be maintained and for nature in all its manifestations to be subdued or mastered by reason, or at least shown to be compatible with it. From this perspective, the perhaps surprising sweetness of Sesto's and Vitellia's music (note especially the lovely tunes in the faster sections of both of Sesto's big arias) is a kind of rationality imposed on otherwise dangerous emotions, and the confinement of Tito's most anguished moments to recitative is a way of containing them; the words in recitative do not repeat, the strong emotions reflected in the orchestral interjections in the accompanied recitatives are fleeting, and the glimpse of his agony is perhaps all the more moving for being only a glimpse. In that sense, the opera *Tito* is as close an heir to *Così fan tutte* as the character Tito is to *The Magic Flute's* Sarastro, with whom he is often compared. In both *Così* and *Tito* the characters experience both the wonderful delirium and the difficult consequences of passions that exceed or transgress against the socially acceptable or morally ideal norm. Sesto, Fiordiligi and Dorabella all fall prey to intense sexual/romantic attractions that undo their identities to some degree; Vitellia is seduced by the promise of power; Tito nearly falls prey to overwhelming vindictiveness. The message of both operas is quite clearly that society can only operate when laws or conventions are marshaled to keep those intensities in check. *Così's* message is surely more sophisticated overall, since it seems to endorse the notion that exposure to, and exploration of, extraordinary passions and desires lead one back to a more clear-eyed acceptance of the norm. For Sesto and Vitellia, in contrast, giving in to waves of powerful emotion is simply destructive. The message for Tito himself is perhaps more like that in *Così*: namely that to face the irrational side of both oneself and others and to contain rather than destroy it leads to a kind of enlightenment. The venue and manner in which this plays out is deeply unfamiliar to most of us, but the underlying message, if presented in a convincing performance, is not merely historical.

CHAPTER 4

MOZART AND SINGSPIEL

During the eighteenth century there were two distinct regional cultures of German-language opera sharing the designation Singspiel, which term simply indicates a dramatic entertainment with song. The more ideologically single-minded kind was that existing in northern Germany, shepherded into public consciousness chiefly by composer Johann Adam Hiller and librettist Christian Felix Weisse, who were concerned to give the German public, and especially the bourgeois, a kind of musical drama that would validate the use of the German language in opera, present an edifying view of middle-class life, provide a model for German-language song, and help to improve the miserable state of German singing. Partly because of these aims, and partly because the company in Leipzig, where they worked, was not well-endowed with virtuosic singers due to the condition of German vocal education, their Singspiels tended to have musical numbers of modest pretensions and dimensions.[1] Despite their German-oriented ideology, however, Weisse's librettos for Hiller were quite often adaptations of French or English plays, as he noted in his preface to an edition of his works.[2] In addition to the works of Hiller and others in the same mold, there were a variety of other attempts at German language opera; these were sometimes grander and more oriented towards the neoclassical spirit of French and Italian operatic reforms especially as executed by Christoph Willibald Gluck and his librettist Raniero Calzabigi. The poet and writer Christoph Martin Wieland, for example, working at the court in Weimar before Goethe's arrival there, collaborated with Anton Schweitzer in a version of the classical story of Alceste, in which the ideals were of a kind of stripped-down "noble simplicity," and in which there were some long passages of declamatory accompanied recitative to reflect the immediacy of the emotions undergone by the characters.[3] The Weimar milieu also produced Georg Benda's *Ariadne auf Naxos* and *Medea*, works full of intense and high-minded emotion, largely in accompanied recitative. These were enormously successful beyond Weimar, and admired by Mozart, among others.

The desire to create a German-language repertory for a German-speaking audience, and the need to do so in part by translating works from other languages, were also part of the second regional culture of Singspiel: namely, that in Vienna. But this tradition also had a wider variety of other influences, and was in various ways more performatively virtuosic. Since it is the Viennese Singspiel tradition to which Mozart is most connected, the rest of this discussion will concentrate on that.

ORIGINS

The Viennese Singspiel as Mozart knew it grew out from at least four main roots. The first was the tradition of Jesuit drama, which was particularly strong in Southern Germany and Austria. These operatic dramas on religious or morally edifying subjects were a mixture of sung numbers and spoken dialogue in Latin, though from 1665 there were also comic interludes in German. They were typically performed by students in the schools run by the Jesuits, but (at least from 1655 on), not in a classroom or cobbled together setting, but rather in a "lavish hall accommodating 3000 and with a musicians' gallery."[4] To enhance their educational function (and no doubt also to make them more appealing to more people) these dramas used all kinds of stage machinery and other special effects. Their influence on the Viennese Singspiel included the comic interludes in German, the mixture of speech and song, and the propensity towards spectacle. But perhaps more important than the direct similarities, some of which Jesuit drama also shared with French *opéra comique* and other operatic genres, was the relation Jesuit drama bore to the long Viennese tradition of *Stegreifkomödie*, or improvised comedy, itself a crucially important influence on Singspiel.[5]

This improvised comedy was certainly the most direct antecedent of Singspiel. In Vienna it usually centered on the character of Hanswurst (Jack Sausage), a servant quite determined not to be motivated by high ideals despite numerous opportunities; his driving force was, rather, his own physical needs. This character was embodied in Vienna by three men successively, all of them performing in the Kärntnerthor Theater. The first was Joseph Anton Stranitzky, who in 1710 or 11 established a company at this theater, and adapted Italian libretti to his needs, which involved removing arias and adding comic scenes for himself.[6] Stranitzky died in 1726 and was succeeded by Gottfried Prehauser. The Prehauser company was joined some years later by Joseph von Kurz, known as Kurz-Bernardon, from the name he gave his own Hanswurst-like character. A selection of titles of the works starring Bernardon and/or Hanswurst give some sense of the kind of entertainment they provided: *Bernardon, the Stupid Successor to Doctor Faustus, The Fourfold*

Marriage Bond with Hannswurst the Fashionable Beggar, French Baron and disguised Messenger from Naples, Hanns Wurst and Bernardon, the two heroic sons of the great knight Sacrapans, and bold liberators of Queen Leorella on the island of Lilliput, The Enslaved Actors, or Hanns Wurst the Strange Theater Director in Barbary, and *The Bewitched Apothecary, or Hanns Wurst the Dismembered Corpse.*[7] These titles suggest some salient features of the genre, many of which survived in Singspiel. Announcing a character as "stupid," for example, would have primed the audience to expect pratfalls, and the multiple disguises involved in a fourfold marriage (or betrothal) created another obvious opportunity for silliness. Impersonating a French baron and claiming to be the son of a great knight nobly off to rescue a queen are clear examples of the way these works parodied aristocrats and their culture. Setting scenes on the island of Lilliput or in the Barbary region allowed for exotic or fantastic scenery, and the bewitched apothecary allowed for the demonstration of magic effects on stage. Also, the idea of a "dismembered corpse" could permit some risqué dialogue and action. And finally, the way the system was organized by and around a theatrical figure whose only or primary role was a clown, continued into Emanuel Schikaneder's reign at the Theater auf der Wieden in the late 1780s and '90s. By Schikaneder's time, however, the Singspiel consisted of considerably more than a series of excuses for clowning.

These Hanswurst comedies seem to have had quite a lot of music, both instrumental and sung, and the sung music was evidently quite elaborate, including not only solo numbers, but also duets and ensemble numbers. One such entertainment from the 1730s included four choruses, five duets and twenty-four arias, for example.[8] Very little of the music survives, and it is quite likely that many numbers (especially the solos) were *contrafacta* (new words set to well-known tunes).

The North German Singspiel was known in Vienna. Unlike North German spoken drama, which had found a secure place there, it was not universally admired.[9] On the other hand, the cultural nationalism of the North German Singspiel was shared by Joseph II and his circle, and the more experimental works of Wieland and his followers were known and admired in Viennese intellectual circles. Mozart's "meologhi" for Gomatz and the Sultan in his unfinished Singspiel *Zaide* of 1780 was surely a response to these forward-looking works. (A melologo is like an accompanied recitative, but the voice part is spoken.)

Finally, Vienna had long been a place where English, French and Italian culture were available and celebrated (to different extents at different times, to be sure). Thus, the plays with music put on by the traveling English players,[10] the visiting commedia dell'arte troupes, the French plays and *opéras comiques*, and Italian opera buffa form the fourth kind of influence on the Viennese Singspiel, since they all supplied that genre with plots, comic riffs, and opportunities for ridicule. This variety of influences may account for the striking eclecticism of the music in the Viennese version of this genre.

THE FOUNDING OF THE NATIONAL THEATER SINGSPIEL IN 1778 AND THE PRESENCE OF SINGSPIEL IN VIENNA UNTIL MOZART'S DEATH

When Joseph II started his plan to improve the customs and morals of his people by showing German-language theater in the newly named Deutsches National Theater, he may already have had it in mind to start a Singspiel company. His determination was evidently bolstered by a visit to the Paris of his sister, Marie Antoinette, where he could observe the highly successful French musical establishment.[11] He sent the theater director Johann Friedrich Müller on a trip to hire singers, and he put together a solid, if very young company: the spectacular coloratura soprano, Caterina Cavalieri, was only 17, as was the other soprano, Therese Teyber. Aloysia Lange (née Weber), Mozart's former beloved, and the sister of his eventual wife Constanze, was hired in the second year of the company's existence, and the excellent male singers Valentin Adamberger and Ludwig Fischer joined in 1780. All of these except Lange sang in the premiere of Mozart's *Die Entführung aus dem Serail.*

The burning question was what kind of Singspiel to promote. It was clearly going to have to be vocally entertaining, and neither severely neo-classical nor conspicuously "unpretentious." State Counselor Philipp Gebler, for example, wrote to a colleague "We must, however, have (in the about-to-be-founded German Singspiel), real musical virtuosos, not [just] songsters; and the composers must be employed in writing the kind of music we're used to, like that of Piccinni, Anfossi, Paisiello, and, in part, Grétry."[12] In other words, opera in German was fine, but it had to be recognizeable as opera.

The first Singspiel performed in the Burgtheater under this new regime was a setting by Ignaz Umlauf of Paul Weidmann's libretto, *Die Bergknappen* (The Miners), a story of thwarted and then satisfied young love, involving a gypsy for exoticism and a mine-shaft collapse for spectacle. It included some coloratura fireworks for Cavalieri and was a great success, in part, surely, because of the cultural weight of the event. Umlauf started as a violist in the Burgtheater orchestra in 1772, and evidently made a good enough impression to be made Kapellmeister (music director) of the Singspiel enterprise, thus earning himself the commission for the first opera. He wrote four more Singspiels for this establishment before it shut down in 1783. Of these, *Die schöne Schusterinn* (The Beautiful [female] Shoemaker) of 1779 and *Das Irrlicht* (The Will o' the Wisp) of 1782 were by far the most successful.

Umlauf's style is pleasant; many of his arias are in a highly singable "folk-like" style with regular phrases and a limited range, but he also wrote more operatically when necessary, resulting in a stylistic eclecticism that Mozart exploited with particular virtuosity in *The Magic Flute*.

Despite Umlauf's stalwart services, the Singspiel needed more repertory than he could reasonably be expected to supply, and given the Viennese distaste for most North German Singspiel, the administrators quickly realized that the best expedient would be to present German translations of successful and appropriate French and (to a lesser extent) Italian works. In addition to being expedient, these translations had the additional advantage of steering away from the crude comedy of Viennese popular theater. Hence the majority of the repertory of the National-Singspiel was not in fact native, despite Joseph's nativist aims.

The writer Gottlieb Stephanie the younger (the librettist for Mozart's *Die Entführung aus dem Serail* and *Der Schauspieldirektor*) translated many of the French and Italian texts; he also wrote the texts for many of the new works produced at the Burgtheater, becoming, in 1781, director of the National-Singspiel. His activity on his "original" librettos was also often akin to translation: his "new" text for Umlauf's *Die schöne Schusterinn* was by his own admission a very lightly worked-over version of a French play, and even his libretto for *Die Entführung* relied heavily on a recent work by Christoph Friedrich Bretzner. Nevertheless, over the course of his time as director, Stephanie accumulated considerable experience with respect to what worked and what did not in this genre, and he wrote up his recommendations in 1792. These tread a fine line between aesthetic ambition and realism. For example, he liked acts to begin and end with action-ensembles, finding choruses stiff and unhelpful to the action, but he also recommended that the number of characters be kept to the absolute minimum to keep the performance quality as high as possible. He was also concerned with the relation between spoken dialogue and music: crucial plot events were to occur in the dialogue so as not to confuse the audience. Nevertheless, he recommended between 18 and 24 musical numbers, properly distributed among the singers and satisfactorily spaced in relation to the dialogues.[13] Mozart's two complete full-scale Singspiels adhere to the letter of this "law," with 21 musical numbers and relatively few choruses, but their musical ambitions may have been beyond what Stephanie was imagining as the norm.

The process of translation and adaptation that occupied Stephanie was not limited to the texts. Among the new works written by "native" composers was *Der Rauchfangkehrer* (The Chimney Sweep) by Antonio Salieri, Joseph II's Kapellmeister, and the director of the Italian opera. Salieri was evidently importuned to write something to an original German text for Joseph's pet project,[14] but the result is an opera buffa in all but name. The chief character is in fact an Italian, Volpino (Little Fox), who outwits his German employers (a widow and her daughter) in part by singing Italian music to make them fall in love with him. In this context, it is interesting to note that even Mozart's *Die Entführung aus dem Serail*, written for the National-Singspiel in 1782 has less Germanic "folk-like" music than *The Magic Flute*, written not only nine years later than *Die Entführung*, but also for a suburban theater with a larger bourgeois element in the audience.

The National-Singspiel of 1778–83 was not a sustainable enterprise. The problem lay largely in the above-mentioned lack of appropriate repertory, but also in the aristocrats' desire for Italian opera, which Joseph acceded to in 1783, dissolving the Singspiel company, and dropping the "National" designation from the theater. Singspiel was then found only in the suburban theaters until 1785, when Joseph installed a company in the Kärntnerthor Theater (the other court-controlled theater in Vienna) for three years, hoping it would provide stimulating competition with the buffa company.[15] After 1788, however, the suburban theaters were once again the genre's only home in Vienna.

SINGSPIEL IN THE SUBURBAN THEATERS

When Joseph II declared the Burgtheater a national theater, he also issued an edict of *Schauspielfreiheit* (Entertainment Freedom). That meant that entrepreneurs and artists were welcome to set up their own places of public entertainment without a court license. Not surprisingly, several did so. They set up new theaters in the suburbs where rents were lower and where their target audiences lived. The first such theater, founded in 1781 by Karl Marinelli, was in the Leopoldstadt, now the second district of Vienna, just north-east of the central city. The second, founded in 1787 and taken over by Emanuel Schikaneder in 1789, was the Theater auf der Wieden, in what is now the fourth district of the city, to the south-west of the centre. The last such theater founded in Mozart's lifetime was in the Josefstadt, now the eighth district. It was founded in 1788. The Josefstadt theater was the smallest of the three and the most restricted in its repertory, relying as it did mostly on low farces. But the Leopoldstadt theater put on a rich mixture of spoken theater (including "Kasperl" farces – Kasperl being a reincarnation of Hanswurst) and, especially from 1786, Singspiels of notable scale and ambition, directly comparable to *The Magic Flute*.[16] Schikaneder's Theater auf der Wieden was thus in direct competition with the Leopoldstadt theater and it is hard not to see the size and ambition of *The Magic Flute* (not to mention the coup of having Mozart as its composer) as an aggressive business move on Schikaneder's part.

The suburban repertory also included German translations and adaptations of the buffa operas playing on the Burgtheater stage. Such adaptations made the works available to a public not able to afford the Burgtheater. Nevertheless, the patrons of these theaters were by no means all penny-wise burghers. Joseph II and his family patronized the Leopoldstadt theater,[17] as did other aristocrats. Count Zinzendorf, the relentless diarist, recounted that he went to the 24th performance of *The Magic Flute*. "At 6:30 to the Starhemberg theater[18] in the Viennese suburbs, in the box of Monsieur and Madame Auersperg, to hear the 24th performance of *Zauberflöte*. The music and scenery are pretty, the rest an unbelievable farce. Enormous audience. Mesdames de Seilern and de Kinsky were in our box." Zinzendorf was generally sour about German opera, and he was not alone among his class. Nevertheless, by the end of Mozart's life it was a deeply embedded and essential feature of Viennese musical life.

Bastien und Bastienne. Singspiel. Libretto adapted by Johann Schachtner from a translation by Friedrich Wilhelm Weiskern and Johann Friedrich Müller of *Les Amours de Bastien et Bastienne* by Monsieur and Madame Favart and Harny de Guerville, after Jean-Jacques Rousseau's *Le devin du village*. 1768. First performance possibly at the house of Franz Anton Mesmer in Vienna.

CHARACTERS

Bastienne, a shepherdess	Soprano
Bastien, her lover	Tenor
Colas, a supposed magician	Bass

The work is in one act.

SYNOPSIS

Bastienne thinks Bastien has abandoned her. Colas enters, playing the bagpipes, and sees immediately from Bastienne's lovelorn demeanour that his "magic" will be easy to exercise. Bastienne asks Colas to help her, but since she has no money, he asks for kisses as payment instead. That goes nowhere, but Colas tells her that Bastien is not really unfaithful; he's just interested in the finery that a richer woman (the "lady in the castle") has given him. Colas advises Bastienne to be cunning to win him back. He is struck by Bastienne's innocence. She leaves, and Bastien arrives, telling Colas that he's decided to reject the trinkets offered by the richer woman for the constancy that Bastienne offers. Colas, however, tells him that Bastienne has already broken off their engagement; indeed, she already has a lover. Bastien implores Colas to help win her back, and the latter sings a gibberish "magic" incantation to assist in the process. The lovers finally meet; she pretends not to know him any more, at which he threatens to go back to the richer woman. Things get worse until Bastien threatens suicide, and in the course of a duet they realize that they do in fact still love each other. Colas comes in and credits his magic powers with this reunion, and they all sing his praise.

COMMENTARY

The origins of *Bastien und Bastienne* are quite unclear. The autograph, which might answer some of the questions, was lost during World War II. Mozart may have begun the work in Salzburg before the family's 1767–9 visit to Vienna; in favour of this idea is the fact that the German translation of the French text was adapted by Johann Schachtner, a close friend of the Mozarts in Salzburg; his version is extant in a manuscript copy.[19] It is possible that he made these adaptations (which include the addition of "Diggi daggi," the magic incantation text) specifically for Mozart. There is no mention of this work in the Mozart family correspondence, and so even the private perform-ance at Anton Mesmer's house in Vienna is not fully confirmed; it was mentioned by George Nikolaus Nissen, Mozart's widow's second husband, in his 1828 biography of Mozart, but no other source substantiates this perform-ance. A further confusion concerns the recitatives. These seem to have been written later than the rest of the opera: the texts would originally simply have been spoken, as in Mozart's later Singspiels *Die Entführung aus dem Serail* and *The Magic Flute*. However, the occasion that produced the recitatives is unknown. Additional confusion is provided by the recitatives for Colas, which are in the alto clef (implying a contralto singer), though the rest of his part is for a bass.

The text is a kind of grandnephew of *Le devin du village* by Jean-Jacques Rousseau, which was premiered in Paris in 1752. Shortly after its premiere, Monsieur and Madame Favart and Harny de Guerville performed and published a "parody," *Les amours de Bastien et Bastienne* which, far from making fun of Rousseau's original, adapted it as a piece for "real" rural char-acters as opposed to Rouuseau's aristocratic pastoral fantasy. This version was then, at the request of Giacomo Durazzo, administrator of the Viennese court theaters, translated into German in 1764 by actors Friedrich Weiskern and Johann Müller.[20] This text was taken up by the Berner traveling troupe of child actors, who played a version with songs by Johann Baptist Savio. They visited Salzburg in 1766, when Mozart was present there. However, it is not known for certain either that they played *Bastienne* in Salzburg or whether Mozart saw them.[21] Finally, as noted above, the Mozart family friend Johann Schachtner re-adapted this text to singing, and Mozart set a text that was a combination of the Weiskern/Müller translation and Schachtner's adaptations.

Rousseau's original *opéra comique*, strongly influenced by the Italian opera buffa troupes visiting Paris in the 1750s, was an enormous success in France, and was kept in the Parisian repertory until the nineteenth century. Mozart, however, could not have heard it on his 1763–4 or 1766 visits to Paris because it was not playing at any of the times he was there.[22] He could, nevertheless, have seen a score, since Rousseau published it in 1753. Although Rousseau's work was influenced by the small scale, contemporary settings, and approachable and appealing melodies of the Italian opera buffa he heard in Paris, which contrasted strikingly with the elaborateness, mythical settings and more involved melodic style of the French fare heard at the *Opéra*, many of the songs in Rousseau's work are actually more French than Italian. That is, they are often quite short and in a style that we might now call "folk-like" (tunes that go up and down the scale quite plainly, mostly syllabic [one note per syllable of text], no coloratura to speak of, and pretty regular phrase-lengths). Mozart's music is also closer to this *opéra comique* style than to opera buffa, as a comparison with his full-length opera buffa *La finta semplice*, written later the same year, shows. The arias in *Bastien und Bastienne* are much shorter than those in *La finta semplice*, much easier to sing, and are typically not organized into the repeating forms that we find in the bigger work: the music typically gets where it is going and stops. This could not be attributed simply to the influence of Rousseau even if we knew (which we do not) that Mozart had seen that score or heard a private performance of the work. Rather, this self-consciously simple style was characteristic of North German Singspiel, itself strongly influenced by *opéra comique*. We do not know for certain which works of these types Mozart may have heard or learned, but his sojourn in Paris could have afforded him opportunities to hear *comédies mêlées d'ariettes* (another term for *opéra comique*), which may have influenced his sense of the genre.

Many of the songs in *Bastien und Bastienne* convey the pastoral tone and setting of the text; graceful triple meters with the first two notes of three slurred, and some wide melodic leaps, cross the aristocratic minuet with the country-dance Ländler – a perfect blend for this text (the Intrada, or overture exemplifies this, too). "Folk-like" tunes in duple meter – anticipating numbers like Papageno's "Ein Vogelfänger bin ich ja" ("A birdcatcher am I") in *The Magic Flute* – also delineate Bastien's and Bastienne's status. Colas, the so-called magician, participates in this pastoral style, but Mozart's music for him also provides some contrast. His entry, which is illustrated by a short instrumental number, illustrates his bagpipe playing not only in the drones (single notes played continuously underneath the tune), but also in the occasional use of the Lydian mode – that is, a scale with the fourth note a half step higher than it would be the normal major or minor. And Colas' ridiculous incantation is set to wonderfully stormy music in the minor.

Die Entführung aus dem Serail (*The Abduction from the Seraglio*) Singspiel. Libretto by Christoph Friedrich Bretzner, adapted by Gottlieb Stephanie the Younger.Vienna, Burgtheater, 16 July 1782.

CHARACTERS

Selim, Pasha	Speaking role
Konstanze, beloved of Belmonte	Soprano
Blonde, Konstanze's maid	Soprano
Belmonte	Tenor
Pedrillo, Belmonte's servant and overseer of the Pasha's gardens	Tenor
Osmin, in charge of the Pasha's country house. A coarse fellow.	Bass

SUMMARY

The opera concerns the noble Belmonte's attempted rescue of his betrothed Constanze and her servant Blonde from the clutches of the Pasha and his buffoonish servant Osmin. Constanze demonstrates noble fidelity by not submitting to the Pasha's desire for her; in the end the Pasha demonstrates nobility by letting her go.

SYNOPSIS

Act I takes place in a square in front of the Pasha's palace, on a seashore. Belmonte arrives in the Pasha's realm to rescue Constanze, who, along with Blonde and Pedrillo, has been captured by pirates and sold as a slave. The first person Belmonte meets is the irascible Osmin, the keeper of the harem and inveterate hater of all things Western, who taunts him with a song and expatiates on the idiocy of people like Belmonte. Belmonte encounters Pedrillo, who tells him that they are all alive, and that Constanze is the favourite of the Pasha, which is not good news. Pedrillo announces a plan to introduce

Belmonte into the palace as an expert in architecture and gardening – two of the Pasha's passions – so that together the lovers can escape with their ladies. Belmonte's heart beats wildly with the thought of seeing Constanze again. The Pasha's entrance in a sailboat, with Constanze, is celebrated with a chorus, and when he and Constanze are left alone, she explains that she cannot love him: she loved before and the loss of that love has devastated her. The Pasha continues to believe that she will come around and finds her steadfast attachment to her previous love quite stimulating. Belmonte is introduced to the Pasha as a possible architectural consultant, but when he and Pedrillo try to enter the inner sanctum of the house, Osmin once more prevents them.

Act II begins in a garden of the Pasha's palace next to Osmin's dwelling. Osmin and Blonde, who has been made his personal slave, have an extended scene. Its burden is that despite Osmin's antediluvian ideas about the relationships between men and women (he master, she slave), Blonde is completely in control of the situation. Constanze laments her fate alone; the Pasha enters, and she assures him in the longest and most vocally elaborate aria in Mozart's mature operas that she would rather endure tortures of all sorts ("Martern aller Arten") than love him. The Pasha is astonished at her steadfastness. In the next scene Pedrillo tells Blonde that Belmonte is in the vicinity; she's delighted; he girds himself to attempt the escape, repeating the mantra that only cowards would be frightened of such a task. The plan starts with the old expedient of getting the Muslim blind drunk. Constanze and Belmonte finally see each other for the first time and the act ends with a finale-like quartet in which both Constanze and Blonde have to defend their honour to their menfolk.

Back in front of the palace at midnight, the two couples begin Act III by making an attempt to escape, but Osmin's tolerance for alcohol seems to be better than Pedrillo had predicted, and the lovers are recaptured once a mute spy for the palace has mimed an alert to Osmin. Osmin raises the alarm and gloats about the nasty end to which the Westerners will come. In a room within the palace, confronted with the Pasha, Constanze offers to die in Belmonte's place. The Pasha determines that Belmonte is in fact the son of his most hated enemy, the man who banished him from his homeland, deprived him of his beloved, and ruined his life. Reminding Belmonte of the kind of punishment his father would mete out if the tables were turned the Pasha leaves Belmonte and Constanze to imagine dying together. When the Pasha returns, however, he announces that he has decided to assert his moral superiority over his old enemy and set the lovers free, asking only that Belmonte tell his father of this act of magnanimity.

COMMENTARY

Origins

Joseph II's National-Singspiel enterprise (1778–83) was in more or less perpetual search of German operas that were not simply French or Italian works in translation. Mozart's arrival in Vienna in 1781 offered the company the opportunity to have a new work from a local composer other than the resident Kapellmeister Ignaz Umlauf, who had already provided the company with four of the five works he would produce for them, or the Italian Antonio Salieri, whose one Singspiel was essentially a German-language opera buffa. Mozart would certainly have been eager to write for the Burgtheater, partly because it was the most prestigious theater in Vienna, but partly because he had only weeks earlier been literally kicked out of his post with the Archbishop of Salzburg, in whose retinue he had traveled to Vienna. He was thus extremely anxious for work. In addition, he was of course particularly interested in operatic composition.

Mozart first mentions the commission in a letter of 16 June 1781; the great actor Friedrich Ludwig Schröder had been asked to find a suitable libretto for him, and the eventual result of the search was that Gottlieb Stephanie the Younger presented him with a copy of *Belmont und Konstanze* by Christoph Friedrich Bretzner, a libretto that had already been set by Johann André in Berlin in 1780 but whose music Mozart evidently did not know. As director of the National-Singspiel, Stephanie had adapted or translated a large number of the works shown on the Burgtheater stage, so he understood the company, knew the audience, and was well-versed in various dramatic traditions. Mozart's first mention of the actual libretto is on 1 August 1781, along with the information that the work was to appear in mid-September to mark the visit to Vienna of the Russian Grand Duke Paul Petrovich and his wife. With that schedule in mind, it seems likely that neither Stephanie nor Mozart imagined very significant changes to the libretto. Nor is it surprising that within two days of receiving the text, Mozart had composed Constanze's "Ach ich liebte" ("Ah, I was in love"), Belmonte's "O wie ängstlich" ("Oh how anxiously"), and the trio "Marsch, marsch, marsch" ("March, march, march") at the end of Act I. He had also planned the overture, the Act I chorus, and the closing chorus in "Turkish" style, which is to say with conspicuous "Turkish" percussion – cymbals, bass drum and triangle. In contrast to his seria operas for Milan, where the star singers arrived from other engagements shortly before the production, and where composition proper of their arias could not begin until they were present, Mozart wrote all his Viennese operas for a relatively stable resident company, so the singers were mostly on hand to try things out throughout the process. Thus only a week after reporting that he had written the first act arias for Constanze and Belmonte, Mozart could tell his father that Caterina Cavalieri (Constanze), Valentin Adamberger (Belmonte) and Ludwig Fischer (Osmin) were "exceedingly pleased with their arias," presumably having tried them through with the keyboard.[23]

In the event the work did not premiere until July of 1782; first of all, the Grand Ducal visit was postponed until December 1781 and then celebrated with two serious operas by Gluck, which were thought more adequate to the magnificence of the occasion. This delay allowed Mozart time to think more deeply about the libretto. On 26 September he wrote to his father that he had asked Stephanie to alter the story to allow for a finale-like ensemble at the end of Act II and a new beginning to Act III. (Bretzner and Andre had set the attempted escape at the beginning of Act III as an ensemble.) After the initial delay the record does not tell us why there was a further seven months wait; after that, rehearsals began on 3 June but five days later were held up for a week because of a flu epidemic. Nevertheless, the delays, for whatever reason, allowed Mozart and Stephanie to depart considerably from the source text.[24]

Among the most important changes that Stephanie made to Bretzner's libretto – prompted by Mozart's interest in writing for Johann Ignaz Ludwig Fischer, one of the most celebrated bass singers of his day – was to expand the role of Osmin, the excitable and proudly Muslim overseer of the Pasha's estate. Whereas Bretzner had given him only the opening song "Wer ein Liebchen hat gefunden" ("He who has found a sweetheart") and participation in three ensembles, Mozart and Stephanie had him sing two big arias in addition to the opening song, and participate in five ensembles.[25] And perhaps further stimulated by the participation of another first-rate singer, the very young and very accomplished Caterina Cavalieri, Mozart also added the second act aria-complex for Constanze: the sorrowful "Traurigkeit," ("Sadness") and the astonishing "Martern aller Arten." Mozart and Stephanie also devised a new reason for the Pasha's ultimate change of heart; whereas Bretzner had used the purely sentimental device of having the Pasha recognize Belmonte as his long-lost son, Stephanie and Mozart constructed a more politically-charged dénouement whereby the Pasha wants to demonstrate generosity superior to that of his old enemy, Belmonte's father.

Mozart documented his initial progress on the opera in letters to his father, but soon that correspondence was given over to Mozart's defense of his good name against Leopold's apparent accusations that he was living too wild a life, and then to a protracted justification of his decision to marry Constanze Weber, of whom Leopold heartily disapproved. (They married on 4 August 1782, without Leopold's blessing.) But before the correspondence got devoted to family matters, Mozart provided his father, and posterity, with the most pointed remarks on operatic aesthetics he ever committed to paper. These aesthetic principles, however, are mixed in with his infectious enthusiasm about the effect that the "Turkish" music will have on his audience, the way the orchestra enacts Belmonte's anxiously-beating heart in "O wie ängstlich," and his "sacrifice" of the aria "Traurigkeit" to "Cavalieri's flexible throat."

Unlike the correspondence over *Idomeneo*, which primarily documents a compositional process, the correspondence regarding *Die Entführung* primarily concerns general operatic principles, though of course it also suggests the chronology of composition. The two most significant of these principles are musical and theatrical decorum and the proper relation between music and poetry. With respect to decorum, the moment Mozart discusses is the *envoi* (tacked-on end section) to Osmin's first aria:

> Osmin's rage is rendered comical by the use of the Turkish music. In working out the aria I have . . . allowed Fischer's beautiful deep notes to glow. The passage "Drum beim Barte des Propheten" is indeed in the same time, but with quick notes, but as Osmin's rage gradually increases, there comes (just when the aria seems to be at an end) the allegro assai, which is in a totally different tempo and in a different key; this is bound to be very effective. For just as a man in such a towering rage oversteps all the bounds of order, moderation and propriety and completely forgets himself, so must the music too forget itself. But since passions, whether violent or not, must never be expressed to the point of exciting disgust, and as music, even in the most terrible situations, must never offend the ear, but must please the listener, or in other words must never cease to be *music*, so I have not chosen a key remote from F (in which the aria is written) but one related to it – not the nearest, D minor, but the more remote A minor.[26]

A minor is also the key of the famous Rondo *alla turca* from the piano sonata K 331 (1781–3) (and of the "Turkish" episode in the last movement of the A major violin concerto [1775]), so the choice of key may also have been influenced by a more general sense that "Turkishness" was best communicated in A minor, regardless of the key of the surrounding music. The text of this part of the aria is both barbaric and nonsensical. Osmin prescribes the following exquisitely impossible series of punishments to the fools who arrive in the Pasha's realm uninvited: beheading, then hanging, then impaling with hot spikes, then burning, then tying up and drowning and finally flaying alive. The music, as Mozart himself notes, refers to the "alla turca" style in the swirling ornaments in the oboes and in the use of cymbals and the bass drum. The apparent poverty of melodic and harmonic invention also goes along with this picture of Oriental barbarity. But the section is also quite symmetrically structured and has some variety of melody, thus preserving the decorum of "real" music. This balance between dramatic or psychological and purely musical demands was to remain at the heart of Mozart's mature operas.

The other principle Mozart expressed in this series of letters was the subservience of the words to the music: he writes, "the poetry must be altogether the obedient daughter of the music."[27] Indeed, in the case of Osmin's first aria this was literally true, since Mozart wrote that the substance of the aria was done and the basic outlines of the text specified (presumably to work with the music) before he told Stephanie about it.[28] But the broader principle he articulates is that the words should not draw attention to themselves *as poetry* – that is, the text should be essentially transparent to its meaning rather than being conspicuously clever. Mozart makes this very clear with respect to rhyme; he writes "Verses are indeed the most indispensable element for music – but rhymes – solely for the sake of rhyming – the most detrimental." What he valued in a poet far more than purely verbal skills was an appreciation of what would work on stage, and a willingness to take a composer's advice(!): "The best thing of all is when a good composer, who understands the stage and is talented enough to make sound suggestions, meets an able poet, that true phoenix; in that case no fears need to be entertained as to the applause even of the ignorant."[29] Stephanie was exactly a man who understood the stage and who did not insist on his own creative prerogative: his experience translating and adapting French and Italian as well as other German works for the National Singspiel surely made him an exceptionally versatile collaborator.

Except for the July 1782 letter describing the first and second performances of *Die Entführung*, Mozart's correspondence about the composition of the opera ends with this discussion of poetry and music. We do not know what factors led to the insertion of Constanze's massive aria "Martern aller Arten," other than the obvious attraction of Caterina Cavalieri's extraordinary technique. Nor do we know how the reason for the Pasha's change of heart at the end of the opera came to be altered from the Bretzner libretto. Nevertheless, the stimulation of writing an opera in a genre that was currently under construction in Vienna and of great importance to the Emperor, at a moment when Mozart was desperately looking for employment and approval, resulted not only in a masterwork of a scale and complexity quite distinct from the surrounding repertory, but also in a precious articulation of ideas seminal to his mature operas.

Dissemination and reputation

The initial reception of this opera as described by Mozart himself after the second performance, was somewhat mixed:

The whole first act was accompanied by hissing. But indeed they could not prevent the loud shouts of 'bravo' during the arias. I was relying on the closing trio [in the first act], but as ill-luck would have it Fischer [the Osmin] went wrong, which made Dauer (Pedrillo) go wrong too; and Adamberger [Belmonte] alone could not sustain the trio, with the result that the whole effect was lost and that this time *it was not repeated*. I was in such a rage (and so was Adamberger) that I was simply beside myself and said that I would not let the opera be given again without having a short rehearsal for the singers. In the second act both duets [Osmin/Blonde and Osmin/Pedrillo] were repeated as on the first night, and in addition [Belmonte's Rondò] "Wenn der Freude Tränen fliessen" ["If tears of joy flow"]. The theater was almost more crowded than on the first night and on the preceding day no reserved seats were to be had, either in the stalls [orchestra] or in the third circle, and not a single box. My opera had brought in 1200 gulden in the two days. . . . Well I am up to the eyes in work, for by Sunday week I have to arrange my opera for wind instruments. If I don't, someone will anticipate me and secure the profits."[30]

A week later Mozart wrote, "I may say that people are absolutely infatuated with this opera."[31]

Even taking into account Mozart's intense desire to prove to his father that he was a success in Vienna, these excerpts show that the all-but-inevitable nay-sayers at the opera were defeated or at least driven into the background, that the success of the work was such that people wanted to buy a version that could be performed by more modest resources, and that the reputation of the opera grew as the audience got to know it. And in fact, *Die Entführung* was the biggest operatic success in Mozart's lifetime. It spread rapidly through the German-speaking lands, receiving forty premieres in these countries before the end of 1791 and one in Polish, in Warsaw in 1783, six months after the German-language premiere there.[32] Mozart himself noted productions in Berlin and Munich; Leopold Mozart also proudly recounted to Nannerl (Mozart's sister) the enormous success of the opera in Salzburg in 1785. The opera was revived in Vienna as early as 1784 (produced by Emanuel Schikaneder) and then again in 1785 as competition for the Italian opera that had won back the imperial stage in 1783.

One of the features of favorite operas at this time was that more or less domesticated versions of them were published, unlike the full scores, which tended to remain in manuscript and circulate from person to person rather than through publication. *Die Entführung* spawned an unusual number of arrangements: Mozart himself mentions a wind-band arrangement, which may or may not have come into existence. He also worked on a piano arrangement, which seems not to have been published. In addition, many other solo piano, and piano and voice arrangements were made in the eighteenth century, both of the entire opera and of individual numbers. Selections for two flutes or two violins, string quartet, piano and violin, piano duet, flute and strings, voice and guitar, were also popular. The opera remained beloved in Germany, though nineteenth-century reviews suggest that the parts of Osmin and Constanze in particular were too difficult for many singers. It was also well known outside the German-speaking countries, though during the nineteenth century it did not hold the same place in public affection or admiration as did *Don Giovanni* or *The Marriage of Figaro*. An 1881 review in the London-based *Musical Times*, for example, describes a production in Italian, with recitatives replacing the spoken dialogue, and an Osmin who had to omit the lowest notes in "Ha! wie will ich triumphieren" ("Aha! How I shall triumph!").[33] Today, the Turkish setting and theme of (sexual) slavery have allowed directors to work currently relevant social and political messages into their productions: an explosive production by Calixto Bieito at the Berlin Komische Oper in 2004, for example, was set in a brothel (not in itself particularly remarkable), and featured newly-written dialogue (again, not uniquely) and constant and explicit sexual violence, including Osmin's bloody murder of a prostitute after oral sex. And productions like François Abou Salem's at the 1997 Salzburg Festival play on the modern version of the eighteenth-century fascination with the Muslim world, dressing Osmin and his henchmen in skullcaps and fatigues, and spreading barbed wire around the stage.[34]

Turkey and the figure of the magnanimous tyrant

Turkey was a place of enormous fascination for Westerners in the seventeenth and eighteenth centuries, and for none more than the Viennese, whose city was besieged more than once by the Ottoman Empire. Indeed, as late as the 1960s it was thought worthwhile to embed and label a cannonball from the Second Turkish Siege of 1683 in the wall of a modern apartment building, the excavation for the building having unearthed this piece of history. The Treaty of Passarowitz in 1718 effectively ended the immediate threat from the Ottoman Empire, and Turkish culture began to make its way into Europe. Among the loudest examples of Turkish culture found in Europe was the janissary (Sultan's bodyguard) band – which, prefiguring the modern marching band – featured a large contingent of percussion. Bass drum, cymbals and triangle are particular markers of Janissary style. By the mid-eighteenth century various European courts – including that of the Habsburgs in Vienna – had their own janissary bands.[35] The so-called "Turkish" music in

Die Entführung refers to janissary music, and not to the more delicate tradition of Ottoman court music, of which we can reasonably infer that Mozart knew nothing. This janissary splendor is most evident in the overture, the choruses praising the Pasha in the first act and at the end of the opera, in the drunken duet between Pedrillo and Osmin, "Vivat Bacchus" (which also uses a piccolo), and in the above-mentioned ending to Osmin's first aria, "Solche hergelaufene Laffen" ("Such vagabonds"). But Osmin's arias in particular also betray other "Turkish" characteristics – hopping melodies, crudely rudimentary harmonies and extremely repetitive duple meter rhythms that mark him as less sophisticated and less psychologically rich than some of the other characters, just as the janissary music marks its moments as connected to the "Other."[36] Osmin's susceptibility to wine despite his faith's prohibition against it, and his attitude to women are also both part of a stereotype of the Oriental Other. The extraordinary low notes that Mozart writes for the character – even if they were a showcase for Fischer's beautiful bass voice – also add to the grotesqueness of this character. In both Osmin's second aria and his duet with Blonde these notes are set apart rhythmically and melodically in such a way as to focus attention simply on the physical feat of achieving them; this attention to the physical body rather than to the message it conveys was very much part of the idea of the grotesque.

The Pasha, on the other hand, does not sing at all, and turns out to be the most noble character in the opera. That is, he is both the only character who actually sacrifices anything, and the only one in the end motivated by an abstract principle rather than by desire. This kind of nobility seems quite at odds with the dismissive Orientalism of the portrayal of Osmin, but in fact it is as much a part of the Enlightenment view of the Muslim world as is Osmin, in that it turns the mirror back towards Europe and asks in what nobility and generosity really consist. Montesquieu's *Lettres Persanes* of 1721, in which two Persians visit Paris and write home about it while also receiving news from their own culture, are a famous example of using exotic protagonists to refract truths about the author's own culture and circumstances, but closer to Mozart and Stephanie was the well-known motif of the Generous Turk, a theme found in a ballet-pantomime performed in Vienna in 1759 and immortalized in an engraving by Canaletto (ill. 2). This tells a similar story of an enslaved young woman given her freedom by the Pasha when he realizes her love for her European betrothed. *La rencontre imprévue*, an *opéra comique* by Gluck, written in 1764 and still being performed at the Burgtheater in the early 1780s, would have provided a direct comparison.[36] Joseph Haydn's 1774 opera buffa, *L'incontro improvviso*, based on the same source as Gluck's opera, but probably unknown to Mozart, is also part of the cultural milieu of *Die Entführung*. In both these earlier works the Pasha is truly Turkish. In

Bretzner's libretto, however, he is a "renegade," a European living as a Turk. Mozart and Stephanie do not specify his ethnicity. Mozart always thrived in competition with well-established composers.[37] Joseph Haydn's 1774 opera buffa *L'incontro improvviso*, based on the same original French opéra comique as Gluck's opera, but which Mozart probably did not know, also belongs to the cultural milieu of *Die Entführung*.

Part of the message of the theme of the Generous Turk is the notion that if "barbarians" can behave so nobly, there is even more obligation on putatively "civilized" people to do likewise. And this holds whether the motivation for the Pasha's generosity is simple sympathy with a loving couple, the discovery of a long-lost son (as in the Bretzner libretto) or something more like a political principle, as in Mozart's opera. But part of the Pasha's nobility also has to do with the way characters in comic opera relate to each other. Just as Papageno's too-human hungers and desires balance Tamino's noble ethos in *The Magic Flute*, or Leporello's cowardice and venality foil Don Ottavio's noble self-control in *Don Giovanni*, so the Pasha's eventual generosity of spirit balances Osmin's vindictiveness. His speaking-only role may well have been an "operatic" choice, based on the absence of a suitable singer in the company: the singer who sang the corresponding role in the Gluck opera was dismissed as Mozart was starting work on the opera, and he was in any case a tenor, of which Mozart may well have not wanted a third example.[38] It may also have been simple adherence to the Bretzner libretto, in which the Pasha did not sing. But it could equally well have been a political or cultural choice to make the Pasha a more mysterious and thus at least potentially more powerful figure, and thus to enhance the fantastic effect of this orientalist opera.

Der Schauspieldirektor (*The Impresario*) Singspiel. Libretto by Gottlieb Stephanie the Younger. Orangerie, Schönbrunn Castle, Vienna, 7 February 1786.

CHARACTERS

Frank, an impresario	Speaking role
Eiler, a banker	Speaking role
Buff, an actor	Bass
Herz, an actor	Speaking role
Madame Pfeil, an actress	Speaking role
Madame Krone, an actress	Speaking role
Madame Vogelsang, an actress	Speaking role
Monsieur Vogelsang, a singer	Tenor

Madame Herz, a singer   Soprano
Madame Silberklang, a singer   Soprano

Translations of names: Eiler = in a hurry; Pfeil = arrow; Krone = crown; Vogelsang = birdsong; Herz = heart; Silberklang = silvery sound.

SYNOPSIS

Frank is thinking of putting together a new theatrical company. He and Buff spar about theatrical aesthetics, Buff being cynical about audience taste and about the frauds it is possible to perpetrate on an ill-educated and inattentive audience. The banker Eiler enters, willing to pay Frank (or at least give him an interest-free loan) to take Madame Pfeil, who has made Eiler practice her scenes with her until he is desperate. Madame Pfeil enters, lauding her own accomplishments to the skies and demanding twelve Thalers per week in addition to all the principal roles. She and Eiler play a quarrel-and-reconciliation scene together, from a pastiche play in Restoration style[39] and Frank sarcastically praises Madame's teaching. Madame Krone, a serious actress, appears, also wanting a part in the company. She and Monsieur Herz play a shortened scene from F. J. Junger's adaptation of August Gottlieb Meissner's *Bianca Capella*, a serious play.[40] Frank is enraptured by this and offers her fourteen Thalers per week, but Buff thinks the audience will find it ridiculous. Madame Vogelsang then arrives, touting her own accomplishments, and plays a *galant* scene with Buff, in the style of a recent Rautenstrauch play.[41] This produces a request for eighteen Thalers a week if she joins the company. The actors decide that singers are needed: conveniently Herz and Madame Voglesang have singing spouses, who arrive and sing scenes in different styles: Madame Herz sings a sentimental but also virtuosic two-part aria about fidelity, after which Frank offers the couple sixteen and fourteen Thalers a week each, to Buff's consternation. Madame Silberklang arrives and sings a more *galant* aria with more virtuosic passage work, which Frank also likes. The two singers compete with each other in "Ich bin die erste Sängerin" ("I am the prima donna"), a trio in which Mr. Vogelsang also joins, more as a referee than as a competitor. This features competitive affects (sentimental vs. virtuosic), competitive coloratura, and competitive high notes (up to the F an octave above the treble clef). Madame Pfeil arrives, having heard that these singers have been offered more than the twelve Thalers she seems to be going to receive. Frank decides at this point to give up on the company completely, but in the finale singers offer to sing for free, agreeing that competition between them diminishes both the art and the artist.

COMMENTARY

This is a very short work, and Mozart's contribution includes only an over-ture, the two arias, the competitive trio and the finale. It was commissioned by Joseph II for a double bill in the Orangerie in Schönbrunn, the Habsburg summer palace. Fortunately, since the performance took place in February, the venue was heated. The occasion was a feast for the Governor-General of the Netherlands (a Habsburg territory), and the idea for the work was evidently Joseph II's own.[42] The other work on the double bill was another short work about theatrical life: Salieri's *Prima la musica e poi le parole* ("First the Music, Then the Words") involving the problem of how to write an opera in four days – the answer being for the librettist to write new words to a pre-existing operatic score. And just as the Stephanie libretto for Mozart includes quotations and imitations of other dramas, the Salieri score included refer-ences to some numbers from *Giulio Sabino*, Giuseppe Sarti's successful opera seria, in which the castrato Luigi Marchesi had appeared in Vienna the previous year. The two operas were given at opposite ends of the Orangerie, on two separate stages; Mozart's was first; the audience then turned their chairs around and watched the Salieri.

Mozart's cast included Caterina Cavalieri, for whose "flexible throat" he had created the role of Konstanze in *Die Entführung aus dem Serail,* and Aloysia Lange, née Weber, his sister-in-law and his first real love. (They had met in Mannheim on Mozart's journey there in 1777–78, but when he saw her again after the continuation of that journey to Paris, she had lost interest.) Cavalieri was Madame Vogelsang, as befitted her throat, and Lange was Madame Herz.

If the two operas were in as much competition as the two singers, Salieri would probably have won. Count Zinzendorf found the Mozart "fort mediocre" but enjoyed the way Nancy Storace (Mozart's first Susanna) imitated Marchesi's singing in the Salieri. It may be that Zinzendorf's comment was directed as much at Stephanie's libretto as at the music, but if he represented the audience's opinion, they seem to have enjoyed the gossipy pleasure of Storace's imitation more than the more abstract fun of Mozart's dueling heroines.

Despite the highly Italianate character of Mozart's soprano arias in this work, and the fact that "metatheatrical" drama (plays or libretti about theatrical life) was a long-established subgenre of Italian comic opera, Mozart's work is still more Germanic than Salieri's, partly in the obvious fact that it is in German, but partly in its inclusion of so many references to German-language spoken drama. Unlike the Singspiel, which had, by 1783 turned out to be unsustainable in the court theaters in Vienna, spoken drama in German had taken fast hold in the Burgtheater in 1776, and continued to provide about half the total entertainment in that theater throughout Mozart's stay in Vienna (and, indeed, beyond). Although aristocrats attended the spoken theater, its ethos and pricing structure were aimed at a bourgeois audience and sensibility. Thus for the first audience, the competition between Mozart and Salieri in the Orangerie may have put more at stake than operatic style. Indeed, perhaps, given the historical lack of enthusiasm for Singspiel among the aristocratic audience in attendance, as well as their political discomforts with Joseph II, the embedded references to German spoken drama were an unwelcome reminder of the increasingly unpopular ruler's program of bourgeoisification, which the virtuosic efforts of the singers did little to mitigate.

Die Zauberflöte (The Magic Flute). Singspiel. Libretto by Emanuel Schikaneder. Vienna, Theater auf der Wieden, 30 September 1791.

CHARACTERS

Sarastro	Bass
Tamino	Tenor
Speaker	Bass
First Priest	Tenor
Second Priest	Bass
Third Priest	Speaking part
Queen of the Night	Soprano
Pamina, her daughter	Soprano
First Lady	Soprano
Second Lady	Soprano
Third Lady	Soprano
First Boy	Soprano
Second Boy	Soprano
Third Boy	Soprano
Old Woman (Papagena)	Soprano
Papageno	Bass
Monostatos, a Moor	Tenor
First armed man	Tenor
Second armed man	Bass
First slave	Speaking role
Second slave	Speaking role
Third slave	Speaking role

Chorus of priests, slaves, attendants

SUMMARY

The opera starts as a rescue opera, with Tamino recruited by the Queen of the Night and her three ladies to rescue the Queen's daughter Pamina, who has been kidnapped by the "evil" Sarastro. It turns out, however, that Sarastro, who was a close friend of Pamina's late father, abducted her in order to save her from the clutches of her evil mother. Tamino learns this as he enters Sarastro's realm, and thenceforth the opera concerns Tamino's quest to join Sarastro's Enlightened brotherhood as a means of partnering Pamina and defeating the forces of darkness.

SYNOPSIS

Act I begins in a hilly place strewn with rocks and trees, and containing a small temple, Tamino is pursued by a serpent until he faints. The three ladies armed with spears emerge from the temple and slay the monster. They bicker about who will remain with the lovely youth but all leave him. Tamino wakes, astonished to find the monster already dead. Papageno introduces himself as a bird-catcher for the Queen of the Night; he has never been out of this little valley and has no idea that there is any other world beyond it. He is, however, canny enough to take the credit for killing the serpent. The three ladies, re-entering, put that lie to rights by locking Papageno's mouth shut and telling Tamino the truth. They also hand him a picture of Pamina, the Queen of the Night's daughter. Tamino takes one look at the picture and is smitten. The ladies tell him that she has been abducted by a very wicked man, and that the Queen of the Night has charged Tamino with her rescue.

The scene changes to an apartment with a starry throne, on which is the Queen of the Night. She tells Tamino the dreadful story of her daughter's abduction, and repeats her expectation that he will rescue Pamina. The scene changes back to the original setting, and Papageno arrives humming desperately, since he can't talk with the lock on his mouth. The ladies unlock him with the admonition that he should tell no more lies. They give Tamino a magic flute as a talisman for his journey to rescue Pamina from Sarastro, and they send Papageno – against his will – with him, equipping the latter with a magic glockenspiel, and telling both men that a trio of boys will be their guides into this realm.

In a magnificent Egyptian room in Sarastro's kingdom, the slaves celebrate Pamina's escape and the punishment Monostatos, their overseer, will be in for, having let her go. But Monostatos brings Pamina in and wants to tie her up; he also lusts after her. Papageno has found his way to this part of the land, and watches the events, figuring out that the young girl in captivity is Pamina.

He and Monostatos encounter each other, and each one thinks the other is the devil, Monostatos being black, and Papageno being dressed like a bird. Monostatos runs away. Papageno convinces Pamina that he is there to help rescue her, and that there is a young prince who loves her. They extol the heavenliness of love, and head out on their escape.

The Act I finale takes place in a grove with three temples, dedicated, respectively, to Wisdom, Reason, and Nature. Three boys tell Tamino that he is on the right path, but that he will need to exercise constancy, patience and restraint. He tries to enter each temple in turn, but is repulsed by a voice. He meets a priest who discredits Tamino's understanding of Sarastro's nature, in part because it was instigated by a woman. Tamino is discouraged by the priest's words, but the boys tell him that Pamina is alive, and he plays his flute in gratitude, which, as if he were Orpheus, makes the local animals dance. He and Papageno meet up again by hearing each others' instruments, and since Papageno has Pamina with him, the would be lovers meet for the first time. Monostatos appears, ready to re-imprison Pamina, but Papageno enchants him and his slaves, making them dance just as Tamino enchanted the animals. Sarastro arrives with much pomp, forgives Pamina for her escape attempt, but refuses to free her until she is attached to a man who can lead her through life, as is necessary for any woman. Sarastro orders that Monostatos undergo a beating on the soles of his feet, and the finale ends with general praise of the ruler.

Act II begins in a gold and silver palm forest, with palm-covered seats and pyramids marking the places of the members of Sarastro's brotherhood. Sarastro ceremoniously announces to the brotherhood that Tamino is the young man who will protect their realm from the Queen of the Night's attempts to destroy it; he will marry Pamina and join their company in a fully enlightened state. In order to reach this state, however, Tamino will have to undergo severe tests to prove his strength and virtue. Tamino and Papageno find themselves in a horrid place of ruins. A priest ensures that Tamino is willing to undergo the trials to achieve enlightenment and Pamina. Papageno is also promised a wife, though his willingness to undergo the trials does not match Tamino's. The first trial is that Tamino can see Pamina but not speak to her, or, indeed, to any woman. The three Ladies try to tempt them: Papageno chatters away despite Tamino's warnings. When a clap of thunder disperses the ladies, Papageno faints.

The scene changes to a lovely moonlit garden. Pamina sleeps, and Monostatos watches her salaciously, regretting that his dark skin makes him unavailable to her. The Queen of the Night appears, to give Pamina a dagger with which to kill Sarastro; she learns that Pamina has fallen for Tamino, and is outraged. Monostatos tries to use possession of the dagger to blackmail her into submitting to him. Sarastro appears just in time, and Pamina pleads with him not to kill the Queen. Sarastro assures her that Tamino will pass the tests, marry her, and that this will drive the Queen back to her own realm.

In a new setting, with a rose-bedecked flying machine, Papageno meets a very ugly old woman who swears that her beloved is called Papageno. She disappears in a clap of thunder, and Papageno is so terrified that he promises to remain silent for the duration of the trial. Three boys arrive in the flying machine, encourage Tamino, and tell Papageno to keep quiet. They also bring food; Tamino, in his manly way, forgoes it, but Papageno tucks in enthusiastically. Pamina appears but Tamino will not speak to her. She is devastated. Trombones indicate that Tamino and Papageno need to continue, but Papageno won't leave the food.

In a vault with pyramids, the priests sing that Tamino is nearly through with the trials. Sarastro brings Pamina in to wish him a last farewell before his final trial, which he must undergo alone. Her still cannot talk to her. Papageno is left to imagine a comfy little wife for himself. The old woman appears again, makes him promise himself to her on the threat of a life of starvation, and promptly turns into a young and beautiful bird-woman who disappears as soon as she is revealed

The second act finale begins in a garden, with the boys announcing that enlightenment is on the way. Pamina appears with the dagger, ready to kill herself. The boys explain that Tamino's silence was part of his trial, and they rush off to find him. The scene changes to a fantastic outlook with two mountains, one with a waterfall and the other with fire inside it. Tamino is led in by the armed men, who warn him of the dangers of the final trial. Pamina arrives as well, and they go through the fire and water together. Meanwhile, back in the garden, Papageno decides that if Papagena doesn't appear on the count of three (or perhaps three and a half) he will hang himself. The boys stop him, as they stopped Pamina, and bring him his magic glockenspiel, whose silvery tones conjure Papagena. They imagine a long life together with many little Papageni.

The Queen of the Night and Monostatos make a final assault on Sarastro's kingdom, but are driven back, after which the stage turns into a vast sun, and the opera ends with general rejoicing about the power of enlightenment.

Commentary

Origins

Less is known about the origin of this work than about Mozart's earlier Singspiel, *Die Entführung aus dem Serail*. It was probably written in the spring and summer of 1791, largely before *La clemenza di Tito*, though the latter was premiered first, on 6 September, in Prague. *The Magic Flute* was clearly an enormous undertaking, as Mozart's letters to his wife during this period describe constant work – it is not, however, clear, to what extent he worked on *The Magic Flute* and *Tito* simultaneously, and to what extent he felt pressed over the former in order to leave time for the latter. It is clear, however, that he did not quite finish *The Magic Flute* before the visit to Prague for the premiere of *Tito*, since he marked the overture and the Priests' chorus in Act II with the date of 28 September, a mere two days before the premiere. *The Magic Flute* came about at the request of Emanuel Schikaneder, the author of the libretto, impresario of the suburban Theater auf der Wieden, and the first Papageno (ill. 3). The opening cast included not only Schikaneder himself as Papageno, but Mozart's sister-in-law Josefa (Weber) Hofer as the Queen of the Night. The young Anna Gottlieb, his first Barbarina in *The Marriage of Figaro*, aged only twelve at its 1786 premiere, and now a fully grown-up seventeen, was Pamina, Benedikt Schack played Tamino and Franz Gerl Sarastro; these two men also composed for Schikaneder's company. The remaining parts were played by other members of the company, including the wives of Schack and Gerl. Mozart directed the first couple of performances, and then attended later ones as an audience member. On 8 October he wrote to Constanze that he had tricked Schikaneder by sneaking into the wings and playing the glockenspiel part – wrong – himself, which allowed Schikaneder to get a laugh from the audience by telling the instrument to shut up, and which taught the audience that Schikaneder was in fact only miming the playing of this instrument.[43]

Mozart had become acquainted with Schikaneder, his senior by only five years, in 1780, when the latter's touring theatrical troupe made an extended visit to Salzburg. Schikaneder was present in Vienna, performing at the Kärntnertor theater and eventually at his own Theater auf der Wieden, for most of Mozart's time in that city. (He did, however, work in Regensburg from 1787 until 1789.)[44] He acted both serious and comic roles, playing, for example, Hamlet as well as developing his now better-known comic characters; these were directly descended from the beloved Viennese clown Hanswurst (Jack Sausage). Papageno is an obvious example of such a character.

Schikaneder based his libretto on the story "Lulu, oder Die Zauberflöte," by August Jacob Liebeskind, from Christoph Martin Wieland's fairy tale collection, *Dschinnistan*, which appeared in three volumes between 1787 and 1789. That story tells of Prince Lulu, who finds himself in the realm of the "radiant fairy," who sends him off on a mission to rescue a maiden captured by an evil sorcerer, and gives him a magic flute to help him in the mission. The maiden turns out to be her daughter, the mission is accomplished, and the couple marry.[45] One obvious difference between this source and the opera, however, is that the fairy queen is a force for good throughout the story. However, in Jean Terasson's faux-Egyptian story *Sethos* (ca. 1777), from which Schikaneder closely imitated some text (see below), the hero has to undergo a series of trials, including by fire and water, and emerges through a passage crowned with statues of Isis, Osiris, and Horus to the awaiting high priest.[46] It seems fairly clear that Schikaneder grafted these two sources together, making a somewhat awkward transition from one to the other. The part of Papageno is in neither source; on the one hand this type of character is, as noted above, a continuation of the Viennese Hanswurst tradition; on the other, it has been suggested that a more specific source for the name and possibly for some of the dialogue might have been Goethe's translation of Aristophanes' *The Birds*, to which he added a servant character, Papagey. (*Papagei* is the German for parrot.)[47]

Dissemination/reputation

The Magic Flute was an instant success in Vienna. In every relevant letter Mozart wrote to his wife, who was taking a cure in the nearby spa town of Baden, he described a full theater and praise for the work, even from Salieri (who may have been relieved that Mozart was turning his attention to German opera). Arrangements and excerpts began to be published in November, and by 1800 Schikaneder had given over 200 performances.[48] Like *Die Entführung*, it spread rapidly throughout Germany and then through Europe, in a variety of versions more or less close to the original (an 1801 French version entitled *Les Mystères d'Isis*, for example, bore remarkably little relation to the original). However, unlike *Die Entführung*, *The Magic Flute* remained a central part of the mainstream operatic repertory throughout the nineteenth century, becoming one of the pillars of pre-Wagnerian German opera. Shortly after the premiere, in 1795, Goethe was so taken with it that he started a sequel but did not finish it. Schikaneder did write *Das Labyrinth* (1798) as a sequel, which was set to music by Peter Winter.

The early success of *The Magic Flute* in Vienna was surely due in part to the elaborate sets and costumes, and also to Schikaneder's ability to please the Viennese. A report in a Berlin newspaper in December, for example, describes the enormous cost and splendour of the sets and machines, but says the opera "did not please" because "the content and the dialogue (Sprache) of the work were just too terrible."[49] The ever-present Viennese diarist Count Zinzendorf felt similarly: "The music and the decorations are pretty; the rest an unbeliev- able farce."[50] Indeed, the notion that the libretto was not up to the standards of Mozart's music was common throughout the nineteenth and well into the twentieth century. *The Magic Flute* is by no means alone in this criticism, however; *Die Entführung* suffered a similar judgment; *Così fan tutte* received equally vitriolic accusations about the triviality (or immorality) of its text, and that kind of accusation is even an undercurrent in *Don Giovanni* criticism, especially with respect to the episodic nature of the second act.

The physical setup of *The Magic Flute* has always been of particular importance – perhaps more than in any other Mozart opera. It is the only opera for which any real pictorial record of its earliest sets survive: the engravings of Johann Schinkel's 1815 sets for Berlin are well known. And Joseph and Peter Schaffer's six miniatures from as early as 1795, showing Sarastro's lions, among other things, suggest the active visual imaginary that attended the work from its earliest days. One instance of this is a review from 1820, which praised the splendid new sets as no more than this opera deserved, and as a signal of its value in contrast to the "frivolous" taste of the day.[51] Pictures from an early twentieth-century Metropolitan Opera production make it look like the grandest of grand operas, complete with mechanical elephant and Biblical era costumes and sets (ill. 4). And today, stellar artists like David Hockney make this opera a centerpiece of their stage design careers.

Nineteenth-century reviews also praise the fullness of characterization: Pamina is an obvious example in such writings, but all the principal characters were obviously part of European sensibility from very early in the century, and the reviews often read as though the writers knew them as individuals. As a corollary to this, but also as part of the rhetoric about this opera as a "model" German music drama, its "Innigkeit" (interiority) and the "Seelenvoll" (soul-ful) character of the music were often emphasized. A Viennese music journal in 1842, for example, described it as "the only one of Mozart's operas that thoroughly represents the German character."[52] This same review praises the "psychological truth" of Mozart's portrayal of the Queen of the Night – not the character we might now choose for that distinction. Sarastro is often, however, described as the archetype of transcendent or passionless goodness, and singers who added too many ornaments to his hymn-like music, especially those, who, like Herr Siebert in an 1820 Viennese production, added ornaments in falsetto voice, were roundly criticized for diminishing the dignity and spiritual significance of the role.[53]

What does The Magic Flute *mean?*

This is not a question one asks so readily of any other Mozart opera. More than any other Mozart opera, *The Magic Flute* has been subject to elaborate speculation about its "true" meaning. It combines fairy tale elements – Tamino's coming-of-age and seeking-the-princess quests, the monster, the magic instruments, the opposed forces of good and evil – and references to a variety of higher questions and truths including the nature of enlightenment and wisdom and the value of truth. The elaborate stage effects – sets, lighting, and machinery – contribute to the fairy tale atmosphere, while the obvious use of symbolism and a crude numerology have fueled speculation about the value system underlying it. It is set in an unspecified place, but the engraving at the beginning of the libretto and many of the stage sets described in the libretto (as well as those preserved in images from productions during the first few years after the premiere) suggest an ancient Egyptian milieu, with pyramids and many-columned halls and façades.

One longstanding reading of this opera is that it was a Masonic allegory, with Tamino's absorption into Sarastro's brotherhood a public playing-out of the Freeemasons' initiation rites. The evidence for this reading is partly biographical. Mozart had become a Freemason in 1784, following his father into that secret order. Schikaneder also belonged, though more briefly and less successfully (he was suspended after a personal scandal), and many of Mozart's other friends, patrons, and associates, were also Masons.[54] Freemasonry was regarded with mixed feelings in Josephinian Vienna; its "dangers" included anti-Catholic theistic thinking and potentially dangerous sentiments about the universal brotherhood of mankind and the power of reason. Joseph II permitted unlimited numbers of Masonic lodges in Vienna until December 1785, when he "reorganized" the lodges, allowing only three in place of the earlier eight and demanding that their proceedings be reported to the police. Mozart remained a Mason, relying on his lodge brothers for financial help in his later years in Vienna, and including in his letters moral and spiritual statements that could well be Masonic in origin. He was, thus in a position to understand, support, and convey any Masonic message that Schikaneder wanted to include in the text.

Supporters of the Masonic reading have also pointed to similarities between parts of the librettos and some explicitly Masonic texts. One of these was an essay, "On the Mysteries of the Egyptians" (1784), by Ignaz von Born, a distinguished mineralogist, leader of a Masonic lodge in Vienna (not the one with which Mozart was associated), and a Masonic sponsor of both Mozart and his father. The sentiments expressed in Tamino's first encounter with the brotherhood, in the finale to Act I, are the strongest link to von Born's essay.[55] The other supposed Masonic source for Schikaneder was the novel *Sethos*, on an Egyptian plot, by Jean Terasson. "O Isis und Osiris," Sarastro's prayer with chorus, as well as the hymn of the two armed men in the finale to Act II, describing the final trials of the protagonist, both bear some resemblance to passages in Terasson's book.

But in addition to the literary, biographical and historical circumstances that make a Masonic subtext possible, the opera itself has stimulated critics almost since the inception of the opera, to want to find the single "key" to its meaning, and Freemasonry has offered a spiritually and politically capacious enough narrative to accommodate the issues in the story. The analogies between elements of the opera and Masonic symbols and rituals were noticed as early as 1794,[56] and in the 1828 biography of Mozart by Georg Nikolaus Nissen, Constanze Mozart's second husband, the author noted that many interpretations of the opera were "on offer," including the one whereby the opera became an "apotheosis of Freemasonry" (see below).[57] Among the most extreme modern purveyors of this reading is French musicologist Jacques Chailley, who, in addition to finding close similarities between Tamino's trials and the Masonic initiation ritual, also "unveiled" a system of symbolic oppositions in the opera that matched the symbolism in the Masonic rite. In this system masculinity, gold, day, the sun, continence, bravery, virtue are opposed to women, silver, night, the moon, lack of self-control, cowardice and wickedness.[58] Chailley also includes in his Masonic reading the opera's prominent use of the number three (three Ladies, three Boys, three wind-band calls in the first act finale, three flats in the opening and concluding key of the work, etc.).

The argument against an exclusively, or even primarily, Masonic reading of the opera is twofold. The first element of this argument is that many of the symbols and devices adduced as evidence of the Masonic subtext are by no means exclusively Masonic, but, rather, perfectly common in fairy tales,[59] in ancient folklore[60] and, connected with both of these, in the human subconscious.[61] Elemental oppositions between light and dark and male and female, for example, are the stuff of innumerable fables, from the story of Persephone (and before) to Star Wars (and after). The young man's quest and initiation into adulthood had been a basic narrative framework since before the *Odyssey*; and the significance of the number three, which is often taken to represent the elemental family of mother father and child, was by no means confined to the Masonic rite. The point here is not that these symbols are not part of Masonic ritual, nor that they could not point in various ways to the practices of Freemasonry during the 1780s and '90s, but simply that they were by no means exclusive to that context. The other argument against an exclusively Masonic reading of the opera is that neither Mozart nor Schikaneder was likely to embed an arcane message into a work whose most urgent need was to succeed at the box office, with an audience most of whom would not have understood the coded references.[62] Again, this argument does not preclude the possibility of Masonic meaning – even of cleverly coded messages aimed at the initiated – but it does insist that the opera also be meaningful to non-Masons.

Another way of looking at the opera is as a fairy tale. *Dschinnistan,* Christoph Martin Wieland's collection of tales (mostly not by him) on which Schikaneder's libretto is largely based, was enormously popular, and participated in a characteristically Enlightened paradox whereby the ascendancy of Reason and the banishment of "superstition" in public rhetoric went hand in hand with an increasing fascination with the irrational, the exotic, and the magic. The brothers Grimm were to start publishing their still-fundamental collection of fairy tales only two decades after the premiere of *The Magic Flute,* and this collection was only the most comprehensive of many such sets published in German-speaking countries in the Enlightenment and early Romantic era. Many of these were based on the famous stories collected and adapted by Charles Perrault in the late seventeenth century, and republished and translated for generations thereafter. *The Magic Flute* as fairy tale was evidently the favoured interpretation of Georg Nissen (see p. 105) who wrote:

> What was, then, the intention of the poet? A parody, an apotheosis of the Masonic order. Symbolically: the battle of wisdom against foolishness, virtue against vice, light against darkness ... Remember childhood if you want to understand *The Magic Flute* ... the child's soul is enchantedly moved only by the inexplicable ... the fairy tale alone and the belief in it will justify the story. Therefore, believe for two short hours, or deny [yourself] the pleasure of this lovely illusion.
>
> Mozart surely intended nothing different from this. He was not looking for the deep [meaning] in foolish wisdom.... Just listen to the overture, how serious it was to him, how to the lovely child his belief in a magic world awakens the first hint of the divine in such a solemn and sweetly innocent manner![63]

Just as the insistence on a purely Masonic reading of the opera proceeds from an understanding of Mozart as a genius concerned primarily with the promulgation of abstract principles and arcane formulas, so Nissen's reading relies on the well-tried trope of Mozart as the eternal child. But Nissen's reading (like other interpretations relying primarily on the fairy tale element in the story) does have the advantage, as Nissen himself hints, of allowing for the apparent reversal in the middle of the story, whereby the Queen suddenly turns out to be wicked and Sarastro virtuous, without requiring elaborate historical justifications.[64] Fairy tales are full of transformations and false self-presentations, perhaps especially of mother figures; Tamino's transformation from a callow knight in shining armor to a humble seeker after wisdom is clumsy, to be sure, but the underlying structure that supports it is unproblematically part of the fairy tale genre.

The fairy tale reading of this opera also connects the opera with the repertory that surrounded and contextualized it in Vienna. One of the most popular operas on the Viennese stage was a German translation of Grétry's *Zémire et Azore*, a version of Beauty and the Beast, complete with magic mirror and communication across time and space. Another opera performed at the Theater auf der Wieden during these years was the pasticcio *Der Stein der Weisen* ("The Philosopher's Stone"), written by Schikaneder with music pasted together (hence the term *pasticcio*) by a various members of his company, probably also including Mozart.[65] This is also loosely based on a story (one of the two actually by Wieland himself) from *Dschinnistan*, and also involves trials and magic spells. And preceding this at the Theater auf der Wieden were an opera based on Wieland's long fairy tale *Oberon: König der Elfen* ("Oberon, King of the Elves") and Schikaneder's own *Die schöne Islanderin oder Der Mufti von Samarkand* ("The Beautiful Island-Dweller, or the Mufti of Samarkand").[66]

If fairy tales and folklore are in fact repositories of basic human desires and terrors, then it is not surprising that *The Magic Flute* has also been subject to archetypal interpretations that rely on its fairy tale character but go beyond simply labeling it as that literary subgenre. One such reading is a Jungian interpretation of the opera as a narrative about the formation of a complete human soul, whose feminine (Pamina, anima) and masculine (Tamino, animus) sides find and complete one another. In this reading, the Queen of the Night is the "devouring mother," Monostatos the carnal underbelly of masculinity, and Sarastro the Self who has transcended the flesh – the state of being towards which initiated beings frequently aspire.[67] (The movie *Amadeus* makes this interpretation of the Queen of the Night quite literal, as it morphs Madame Weber [Constanze's difficult mother] into this character at the height of her second aria.)

These readings do not need to be mutually exclusive: a Masonic reading can acknowledge that Freemasonry taps into fundamental symbols and rituals as well as having specific cultural and political meanings connected with the Viennese Enlightenment. A reading of the opera as a fairy tale can acknowledge both that fairy tales play out psychological and spiritual archetypes and that in given circumstances such tales will be appropriately understandable as allegories for particular groups intent on the higher understanding towards which many fairy tales point. And a reading of the opera as more grandly symbolic must acknowledge that symbols have to take material and comprehensible forms connected to the lives and circumstances of real people in order to be effective.

Neither Schikaneder nor Mozart left any unambiguous indication of his own intentions regarding this opera. It is condescending (in particular with respect to Mozart) to assume that he was exclusively concerned with making a hit, though this was clearly of immediate and perhaps even primary importance, and he would not have written a work that was likely to displease an audience. Schikaneder was financially responsible for the theater in a way that Mozart was not, and so his concern with immediate success had to be even more urgent than Mozart's. In addition, his productions without Mozart are generally considered to be geared for immediate box office profit, so there is no reason to deny even here that his first motivation, at least, was to bring in the crowds. However, Mozart's often-quoted remark in a letter to his wife that he was most touched by the silent appreciation of the audience suggests that he wanted the work to appeal to the audience's capacity for reflection.[68] And his equally-often-quoted comment to his father in 1787, shortly before the latter's death, that he himself had quite come to terms with Death as the goal of life, and that he was glad to have had the opportunity (presumably through Freemasonry) to have achieved this understanding, suggests that he took the spiritual side of his Masonic life quite seriously.[69]

Whether Mozart in particular would have written a work with subtextual meanings intentionally inserted is a more difficult question. He regularly referred to other operas on the Viennese stage in his own works, and quite shamelessly one-upped his contemporaries – the most explicit example of this being in the finale to *Don Giovanni* where the wind band plays excerpts from two contemporary operas and then one from *Figaro*. He also used the implicitly referential language of *topoi* (musical topics) like marches, minuets, learned style, and pastoral music to clarify or deepen the meaning of many moments in his operas. And his early work *Ascanio in Alba* was an explicit allegory for the wedding of the Archduke Ferdinand and Beatrice d'Este (see pp. 38–42). None of this really clarifies his sense of the deeper meaning of *The Magic Flute*, for which, as we have seen, much more cosmic and comprehensive interpretations have been advanced. It is hard to believe that Mozart was unaware of the archetypal nature of Tamino's quest for enlightenment, membership in a band of brothers, and personal fulfilment, or of the "cosmic" struggle between darkness and light represented by Sarastro and the Queen of the Night. It is equally hard to believe that he would not also have related these and other such themes to his Masonic experiences. On the other hand, in his mature buffa operas he evoked a world of human experience by deploying entirely conventional character types and situations both more and less literally, and in more and less complex layers, to create apparently three-dimensional characters; similarly in *The Magic Flute* he plays with archetypes from the worlds of fable and ritual to construct an opera rich in meanings, not limitable to a single "code". The extent to which any particular meaning or archetype was intentional is neither recoverable nor important beyond the confines of psychobiography.

The Magic Flute contains attitudes to women and people of African descent that do not accord with modern liberal thought. Some authors have attributed these to Schikaneder and asserted that Mozart subverted them in this music,[70] but Mozart was a man of his time, and there is no reason to believe that he was politically far in advance of it. Modern productions sometimes omit the most frankly sexist sentences in the dialogue, and often cast Monostatos as something other than African; it is, however, impossible to do the opera without the fundamental opposition between good and evil, the latter represented by a hysterical woman, allied with a black slave. And whatever colour Monostatos may be painted in a given production, his status as a slave, his lust for Pamina, and his enchantment by Papageno's music, which equates him with the animals enchanted by Tamino's flute playing, ineluctably raises the stereotype of the (African) "savage." These attitudes have been protected by the canonic status of the opera, and the idea that the beauty of the music erases the difficulty of these sentiments. With respect to gender, one could argue that the overall message of enlightenment and of equal partnership between husband and wife (whether that is meant literally, or in a more Jungian sense as two halves of an individual) outweigh the negative stereotypes embodied especially in the Queen of the Night. One could also argue that, just as in fairy tales, the characters embody principles rather than representing actual humans, and thus that female and black audience members should not take the portrayals personally. There is, of course, something to both arguments, but because opera, unlike collections of fairy tales, is enacted on stage by real men and women, and because a performance of a classic often seems like an endorsement of everything in a work, the argument about "mere" principles is harder to sustain. Some productions seem more aware of these issues than others; the most playful and fantastic have the best chance of making the work a drama of ideas and archetypes rather than plausible people, whereas those that hew more closely to historical "authenticity" might succeed in presenting the problematic social views as a product of their time, but this is a difficult position to communicate. In either case, Mozart's music complicates the issue by speaking remarkably directly and effectively of love, longing, innocence, and high ideals; as an audience member, it is hard to be both seduced by the music and wary of the attitudes it supports (and why go to the opera if not to be seduced by the music?). It is not the purpose of a short commentary like this to make an argument that productions should follow a particular line of thinking on the subject, but it is up to audiences not to fall into the complacent assumption that because this is a great work it is socially and morally comfortable.

CHAPTER 5

Mozart and opera buffa

Terminology and definition

The most defining characteristics of opera buffa in the second half of the eighteenth century are Italian-language text, the use of recitative rather than spoken dialogue between the full musical numbers, a (more or less) contemporary setting, characters from the middle and lower ranks of society, though there may also be some nobles, and a *lieto fine* (happy end).

"Opera buffa" was a term used in the eighteenth century, usually in discussions of the genre as a whole. However, many of the individual works in this genre were designated "dramma giocoso" (comic play) or "commedia per musica."[1] The other designation used at this time was "intermezzo," which earlier in the century indicated a small-scale, usually two-act, work interpolated between the three acts of an opera seria. By the later part of the century, the intermezzo was largely freed from its attachment to the higher genre, and the title was not uniformly meaningful, though the implication of two acts remained.

Origins

Opera buffa as a separate genre was in part a result of the purging of opera seria of its "impurities". That is to say, once the more mixed genres of the seventeenth century had their comic, bawdy, or lower-class elements excised, those elements did not disappear from opera, but rather were gathered together in various ways, or attached to a variety of previously-existing kinds of comic musical drama to form their own subgenres. As mentioned above, the intermezzo was one of these.[2] Often featuring the servant characters now banned from opera seria, they were played between the acts of opera seria, but also between the acts of plays (whether comic or serious), and eventually on their own, especially in the second half of the century once ballet had become the favored inter-act entertainment for opera seria.[3] A development parallel to the early eighteenth-century intermezzo was the contemporaneous Neapolitan *commedia per musica*; a genre that was always "self-standing", so to speak, and that became enormously popular in the smaller theaters of Naples in the 1720s and beyond.[4] This kind of comic opera was typically in three acts rather than the intermezzo's two; it had more characters than the intermezzo's two or three, and it always had a range of social classes represented. It was also conspicuously local, both in its settings and in its use of language: many early Neapolitan comic operas were entirely in Neapolitan dialect. Later on, and as the genre began to spread across Europe, the lower-class characters would speak in dialect, while the aristocrats and other high-ranked characters would speak in Tuscan, the high class literary language of the whole Italian peninsula.[5]

Both the intermezzo and the Neapolitan *commedia per musica* derived significant features from the much older Italian dramatic tradition of commedia dell'arte. This was a pan-Italian (and by the sixteenth and seventeenth centuries, pan-European), largely improvised, comic tradition featuring a set of stock characters in easily recognizeable masks and costumes, and a series of highly conventional plot skeletons, around which the actors would invent dialogue and *lazzi* – essentially comic riffs, often with a slapstick or other visual element.[6] The characters included Harlequin the wily servant, Pulcinella the deformed lecher, Pantalone the miserly merchant, his friend the pompous Doctor, Scaramouche the braggart, a pair of *innamorati* (lovers), and Columbine the clever maidservant of the female lover. These characters found their way into innumerable buffa operas throughout the eighteenth century, including Mozart's mature works. For example, Figaro and Susanna in *The Marriage of Figaro* are descendants of Harlequin and Columbine; Don Alfonso in *Così fan tutte* is related to the Doctor; and Donna Anna and Don Ottavio in *Don Giovanni* are the *innamorati*.

GOLDONI AND THE SENTIMENTAL

Although the librettos of late eighteenth-century opera buffa owe their fundamental principles to the intermezzo, the Neapolitan *commedia per musica* and the commedia dell'arte, the more immediate influence on the particular form of this genre at this time was the eminent Venetian playwright and librettist, Carlo Goldoni (1707–93). Goldoni wanted his contribution to Italian drama (including opera) to be the eradication (or at least serious diminishment) of the "abuses" of the commedia, which included both improbability and crudity, and the establishment of a kind of comedy that used some commedia characters, conventions and even riffs, but that was more based in human "truth," and that served as a more effective school of manners than the commedia. Indeed, in his preface to a printed edition of his play *Il servitore di due padroni* (The Servant of Two Masters), which was in fact written for a celebrated commedia dell'arte actor and was most likely based on a previous Harlequin play, Goldoni was at pains to stress his expurgation of the "coarsenesses" of the genre. At the same time he argued that the servant's remaining improprieties were both necessary to the play and common not only in many comedies but also even in tragedies.[7]

The central issue for Goldoni – at least as it appears in the prefaces to his plays and librettos – was the morality of showing vice on stage. His basic position was that he showed only minor vices, and then only to hold them up to ridicule, so that audience members would not be seduced by them. Comedy, of course, had always engaged in ridicule (and still does, for that matter). What was new with Goldoni (and in this he was in line with literary and dramatic developments in England and France) was his interest in the sentimental, with its concomitant expectation that the audience would identify with the feelings of the characters who deserved sympathy. His dramas thus had to make clear the desired audience attitudes to a variety of characters and to do so in a way that seemed "natural." Both the clarification of the characters' "sympathy quotients" and the need for the appearance of some degree of plausibility were intensified by the fact that Goldoni's dramas and libretti, like those of the Neapolitan *commedia per musica*, were set in the present day, in places that were often entirely familiar to the audience. The "safety net" of a mythological or allegorical setting was thus unavailable.

One of Goldoni's most influential librettos, *La buona figliuola* (The Good Girl), was based on his play *Pamela,* which in turn was based on the 1740 novel of the same name by the English author Samuel Richardson.[8] The novel, written in epistolary form, concerns the steadfastness of the eponymous heroine, a young woman of relatively lowly birth, in the face of increasingly importunate approaches by a nobleman. Eventually, Pamela's defense of her chastity and lack of interest in the riches offered her by the nobleman win his heart, and they marry. Many parodies arose, in no small part because Pamela's letters describe the nobleman's advances and her own responses in such detail that the novel's appeal consisted as least as much of prurient interest in the ways she attracted the nobleman's desires as of admiration for her virtue. Parodies notwithstanding, Pamela was spectacularly successful, taking Europe by storm. Goldoni's adaptations make the heroine, now called Cecchina, a noblewoman in disguise, because the Italian norms about marriage between the classes were different from the British ones. As Goldoni himself notes in his preface to the play: "The reward of virtue is the aim of the English author; such a purpose would please me greatly, but I would not want the propriety of the family to be sacrificed to the merit of virtue." The libretto also includes stock figures: a pair of noble lovers as concerned with social standing as with the true conditions of their hearts, a jealous farm girl, an honest bumpkin, and a braggart (but sympathetic) German soldier who is actually the source of the truth about Cecchina's birth.

As set by Niccolo Piccinni in 1760, *La buona figliuola* had a place in the 1760s and '70s similar to that of Gennaro Federico's *La serva padrona*, set by Giovanni Battista Pergolesi in 1733. This work detailed the way a clever and manipulative serving girl essentially tricked her master into marrying her, and functioned as the paradigm of opera buffa for decades thereafter. The distance between Pergolesi's ambitious minx and Goldoni's and Piccinni's importuned innocent is precisely the distance between comic ridicule and sentimental identification, and it is the distance between the opera buffa of the early middle of the eighteenth century and that of Mozart's time.

THE DRAMATIC AND MUSICAL AESTHETICS OF GOLDONIAN OPERA BUFFA

The point here is not that in works like *La buona figliuola* every character was sentimentalized, or even sympathetic. Rather, there was a range of characters from the utterly ridiculous to the positively saccharine, and a range of conventional stories, situations, and musical devices that would clarify and articulate the types within the overall range. For example, whereas Cecchina opens Piccinni's opera singing a short, simple, pastoral song about the flowers she is tending, the snobbish Marchioness Lucinda's first aria is an opera seria-like exercise in militaristic melodies and vocal acrobatics, and the German soldier Tagliaferro has the typically comic combination of a bass voice, and arias with short-breathed melodies and patter singing.

The librettos of opera buffa – and Goldoni refined this trend – encouraged this musical variety in part by structuring the texts for arias in many more ways than had the librettists of serious opera, and in part by building in situations that called for a wider variety of kinds of expression. The two-stanza ABA da capo structure so beloved in opera seria was still used, but it was typically reserved for the seria *innamorati*. Sentimental characters and moments were often given short texts with no contrasting sections. Comic characters, especially old men and bumpkins (who were usually played by basses) often had remarkably long texts which traced a path from pride or anger to confusion or babbling idiocy. Bits of the text were always repeated in such arias, but overall, the words were sung from beginning to end, and the end of the text marked the end of the aria (unlike in da capo form where the end of the first verse was the end of the aria).[9] And in general, the opera buffa convention in all kinds of arias was increasingly to set the text all the way through, ending at the end, even if there were returns and repetitions along the way. The overall effect of this practice was to allow arias to progress, either psychologically or dramatically, or both. The da capo arias of opera seria certainly deepened and nuanced the audience's sense of the character singing, and intensified or complicated the audience's sympathy for, or admiration of, him or her, but their overall effect was more a temporary crystallization of the plot than a way to move it forward.

With the support of the Goldonian libretto, mid-century opera buffa also deployed ensembles (musical numbers in which several characters sing) much more often than did opera seria. Some ensembles, like the last-act love duet, or the trio or quartet of final celebration, had long been used in opera seria to cement a resolution of some sort, but opera buffa increasingly used ensembles to express disagreements and differences between characters, or simply dramatic complication (see Chapter 2). One of the first places ensembles were found to be effective in opera buffa was the finale – the scene or collection of scenes at the end of an act in which the imbroglio is tightened or speeded up, and characters confront themselves and each other with the (often unintended) consequences of their actions. Ensembles have little or no recitative; rather they typically consist of speech-like statements and sections of dialogue wrapped in a blanket of orchestral music that sustains the mood or the pace of the action; at the end of each section of dialogue there is usually a moment (or longer) where the characters sing together and sum up the current state of the drama – often in collective statements like "What is to become of us?" or "What a terrible mess!"; but also sometimes with words reflecting the simultaneous but incompatible individual dilemmas at that moment. Finales allowed both librettists and composers the flexibility to present both fast-paced dramatic action and continuous music; as a result these segments often seem the most "natural" of these works, though in fact they require the greatest art to write.

Goldoni's librettos also made frequent and influential use of the *introduzione*, an introductory ensemble which often lays out both the collective arena in which the drama will take place and the dissatisfactions or tensions that will animate the plot. Goldoni's *introduzioni* are rarely as dynamic as his finales, partly because they often end with a chorus which may be a musical repeat of the opening statement, thus closing off the *introduzione* from the rest of the opera. But they do emphasize the collective, socially-oriented nature of opera buffa; this contrasts with opera seria, whose overwhelming preponderance of solo numbers emphasizes by analogy the power of the individual ruler/patron, and the powers of oratory or rhetoric (necessarily a solo undertaking) rather than the collective energy of dramatic action.

Ensembles in opera buffa are also an extension of the notion that musical numbers are addressed as much or as frequently to the other characters onstage as to the audience. Whereas in opera seria, the majority of arias are more or less abstract statements of an emotional or philosophical position, even if they are sung in direct response to something another character has said or done, in opera buffa, many arias (particularly those for the most comic or least noble characters) are addressed directly to onstage interlocutors and demand some kind of gestural response from them. For example, comic old men in Goldonian librettos often address more than one person at once (sometimes with contradictory information), usually tying themselves into hopeless knots in the process. The ensemble acting necessary for such arias connects naturally to ensemble singing; and increasingly through the latter half of the eighteenth century, duets, trios, quartets, quintets, and even larger ensembles would erupt or coalesce in various places throughout the acts of the opera.

One important characteristic of opera buffa in the Goldoni tradition, then, was an increased "naturalness" arising from the genre's everyday characters and situations, a wider variety of dramatic rhythm, and more immediate inter-character responses. This apparent naturalness, however, co-existed with, and was even dependent upon, a highly conventionalized language of types: character types, situation types, plot types, and musical types at a variety of levels. Just as in opera seria, predictability was an integral part of the aesthetic, and it was the variations on the predictable elements that provided the entertainment. As noted above (p. 111), commedia dell'arte provided the basic character types – servants from pert and wily to terminally dumb, sentimental lovers, pompous or lecherous old men, and so on. The commedia also provided many of the plot archetypes. The most common plots in opera buffa included the gulling of an old man – often a father or guardian figure – to engineer a marriage between true lovers; mistaken or switched identities almost leading to the wrong liaisons; identities unknown to their owners; class tensions resulting from inappropriate amorous desires, and experiments in human behaviour. Favourite comic riffs in opera buffa involved disguise, partly-heard and consequently misunderstood conversations, advice on affairs of the heart by characters unequipped to deliver it, unwarranted and much-touted self-confidence on the part of those with no right to it, and asides to the audience explaining whatever trickery is taking place.

Musical types used frequently in opera buffa throughout the latter part of the century included the mock-seria aria in a march-like tempo; the parodistic lament, the buffo aria for bass (described above, p. 13); the two-tempo aria, beginning slowly and ending fast, where the fast section could represent either a decision or a way of undercutting the first section; and the graceful short aria (usually for maidservants) with minimal but effective vocal passagework. The orchestral accompaniments in opera buffa – especially in comic arias – were somewhat more gestural and interactive with the voice than were opera seria accompaniments, and orchestral introductions to arias were considerably abbreviated in order to allow for more plausible stage action. This abbreviation also happened in opera seria during the second half of the century.

SINGERS

The singers of opera buffa in Mozart's time overlapped to some extent with those of opera seria. Female sopranos sang both, though some, like Mozart's Nancy Storace, who premiered the role of Susanna in *The Marriage of Figaro*, specialized in the kind of acting more characteristic of opera buffa, and others, like Adriana Ferrarese, the first Fiordiligi in *Così fan tutte*, as well as the second Susanna when *Figaro* was revived in 1789, were more famous for their seria vocal abilities. But basses sang almost exclusively in opera buffa, there being no bass roles to speak of in the higher genre. And there were relatively few castrati in opera buffa, particularly as the century wore on. Occasionally a castrato would sing the part of the noble lover in an opera buffa, but this usually happened only if a famous singer was passing through. The exception with respect to castrati was Rome, where women were banned from appearing on stage, and so castrati took all the female roles in both seria and buffa operas. But the overlapping of singers in the two genres had not only to do with the singers' versatility but also with the increasing similarity in the economic and distribution systems for the two genres. In the first couple of decades of the century, it was more usual for comic operas to be produced by peripatetic troupes traveling from one city to another with engagements for some months in each. The singers in these troupes were not normally "free agents", and so could not be engaged individually, whereas for opera seria one of the main jobs of the theater impresario was to put together a company, singer by singer, for each carnival season. Even once repertory theaters for comic opera had been established in Venice, Naples and Florence, which had happened by the 1740s, peripatetic troupes were still not unusual.[10] Nevertheless, by Mozart's time, there was a free market in the best opera buffa singers, just as there was in seria singers, and increasingly, impresarios and patrons were simply looking for the best singers *tout court*.

Fer. Quando volete.

D. Al. Intanto

     Silenzio, e ubbidienza,

     Fino a doman mattina.

Guil. Siamo foldati, e amiam la difciplina.

D. Al. Or bene: andate un poco

     Ad attendermi entrambi in giardinetto,

     Colà vi manderò gli ordini miei.

Guil. Ed oggi non si mangia?

Fer. Cofa ferve.

     A battaglia finita

     Fia la cena per noi più faporita.

     Un'aura amorofa

         Del noftro teforo

         Un dolce riftoro

         Al cor porgerà.

     Al cor che nudrito

         Da fpeme, da Amore

         Di un'efca migliore

         Bifogno non ha.   (*Partono.*)

S C E N A XIII.

D. Alf. folo poi Defpina.

Oh la faria da ridere: sì poche

Son le donne coftanti in quefto mondo,

E quì ve ne fon due .. non farà nulla ..

Vieni vieni fanciulla, e dimmi un poco

Dove fono, e che fan le tue padrone.

                    Defp.

1 A page from the 1790 printed libretto to *Così fan tutte,* showing the typographical distinction between recitative and the aria "Un'aura amorosa."

Le Turc Génereux.

Ballet Pantomime executé à Vienne sur le Teatre près de la Cour, le 26 Avril, 1758.
Presenté à S.Exc. Mons. le Comte de Durazzo Conseiller intime actuel de L.M.M.I.I. et R.R. et Surintendant
general des Plaisirs et Spectacles &c. &c.   par Ber. Belotti dit Canaletto Peintre de S.M. le Roy de Pol. Elec. de Saxe &c. &c. 1759

2 Bernardo Bellotto (Canaletto). A performance of the ballet-pantomime *Le Turc généreux* in the Burgtheater, Vienna, 1758.

3 Papageno's costume from the original libretto of *The Magic Flute*, Vienna, 1791.

4 *The Magic Flute*, Act I finale. Metropolitan Opera, 1912. Director: Anton Schertel. Set designer: Hans Kautsky.

5 "A Scene from Don Giovanni as performed at the King's Theatre, London", 1820.

6 View of the stage and wings of the Burgtheater, 1785. Engraving by Mansfeld.

7 Engraving of Act II Scene 10 of Giuseppe Sarti, *Giulio Sabino*.

8 "Street Scene" from the Drottningholm Castle Theatre.

9 *The Marriage of Figaro.* Metropolitan Opera, 1917. Frieda Hempel as Susanna, Geraldine Farrar as Cherubino, Giuseppe Di Luca as Figaro.

10 Peter Schaffer, illustration for Act II Scene 18 of *The Magic Flute* (1795).

Opera buffa in society

Whereas opera seria was most strongly associated with a particular season, namely carnival (the pre-Lent period); opera buffa was everywhere a more year-round genre. In cities with several theaters, like Venice, Naples and Rome, the largest and most prestigious one was dedicated to opera seria, and one or more smaller ones would mount opera buffa throughout the year with the frequent exception of the summer. In places with only one theater, like Milan, that theater would divide the year between seria and buffa productions, often interspersed with spoken drama and ballet. By Mozart's time, opera buffa was a pan-European phenomenon, and scores and librettos circulated (often by means of singers) from one place to the next. Unlike seria operas, whose music was typically composed for a single occasion and not repeated, though the texts were repeatedly re-set, buffa operas were transported whole from one place to another, with the "original" work doctored to various degrees to fit the new circumstances, but not completely re-composed. This contributed to the cheapness of opera buffa compared to opera seria. Some buffa singers were cheaper than some seria ones, comic operas were almost never explicit vehicles for one or two superstars, the sets and costumes were less elaborate, and the time spent learning roles was reduced when singers essentially repeated them in one city after another.

The social status of opera buffa was, by Mozart's time, very comparable to that of opera seria. Although earlier in the century some theaters, like the San Cassiano in Venice, specialized in a repertory not likely to appeal to the most respectable classes, the Goldonian sentimentalization of the genre and its subsequent dissemination across the entirety of Europe had made it as likely to be frequented by aristocrats as by lower-ranked people. The system of long-term rental or purchase of boxes by the aristocracy was as prevalent in buffa theaters as in seria ones, and the degree of attention the audience paid to any given performance was comparable. The highly conventionalized language of character, plot, and musical types certainly assisted audience members in making sense of works to which they were paying intermittent attention. Nevertheless, for certain ceremonial occasions, royal or aristocratic, opera seria remained the preferred genre, and during the 1790s in some places (that is, after the French Revolution) serious opera – now tinged with elements of Gluckian reform and French lyric tragedy – began a resurgence. However, the end-of-century works were played for a less conspicuously stratified audience, with moral content (like praise of marital fidelity) that would appeal to the upper middle classes, and with a dramatic variety and naturalness deriving from opera buffa.

Mozart and opera buffa

About a third of Mozart's operas are buffa operas, and three of these, *The Marriage of Figaro*, *Don Giovanni*, and *Così fan tutte*, are among his most celebrated masterpieces. Two of these three – *Figaro* and *Così* – were written for the court theater in Vienna, while *Don Giovanni* was written originally for the Nostitz (National) Theater in Prague, and then performed the next year at the court theater in Vienna. When Mozart moved to the imperial capital in 1781, German opera was the genre sponsored by the court, but by 1783 the German troupe was disbanded, and opera buffa was reinstated as the reigning operatic genre. Mozart's works in this genre were profoundly influenced by the Viennese context. The orchestra there was sizeable and had a remarkably talented and stable group of wind players, including clarinets;[11] this clearly allowed Mozart to write richly orchestrated music with some confidence that it would come across effectively. The principal singers were recruited from Italy, and were international stars, scouted, to begin with, even by the Emperor Joseph himself.[12]

Perhaps even more important than these resources was the context provided by the Viennese repertory, which included works by the best opera buffa composers of the day, played on the same stage and in the same seasons as Mozart's. To win the audience's comprehension and approval, Mozart had to work within the general idiom provided by these works. For his own satisfaction, he seems to have needed to exceed them in quality and complexity, and also to make the comparisons evident, at least to the initiated. *The Marriage of Figaro*, for example, is based on the scandalous French play *Le marriage de Figaro* by Beaumarchais; but more saliently in this context, it serves as a sequel to Giovanni Paisiello's *Il barbiere di Siviglia*. That opera, written in 1782, was based on *Le barbier de Séville*, Beaumarchais's "prequel" to *Le marriage de Figaro*, in which the Count woos and wins Rosina despite the objections of her lustful guardian Bartolo, and Figaro is the wily servant who makes it happen. The not-so-happy later state of that marriage is one of the central issues in *The Marriage of Figaro*. Paisiello's opera was vastly popular in Vienna, and played in the same season as the premiere of *The Marriage of Figaro*. It is thus not surprising that Mozart embedded a number of references to that opera in his own.[13] *Così fan tutte* also includes references to other works recently seen on the Viennese stage.[14]

Despite his evident investment in the Viennese opera buffa "scene" and the unprecedented brilliance of his Viennese works in this genre, some credit for which has to go to his librettist, Lorenzo Da Ponte, Mozart wrote opera buffa much as he wrote opera seria and Singspiel; that is, in response to specific commissions and opportunities. The two incomplete buffa operas (*Lo sposo deluso* and *L'oca del Cairo*) are incomplete because no opportunity arose to stage them, not because Mozart thought better of them. There is no evidence in the family correspondence that he had a strong preference for this genre.

Mozart's two early buffa works (*La finta semplice* of 1768–9 and *La finta giardiniera* of 1775) are quite conventional in their plots, dramatic rhythms, and means of characterization. In contrast, the mature trio of buffa works on texts by Lorenzo Da Ponte use the deeply ingrained habits of the genre in dazzling and profoundly affecting ways to evoke complex worlds of social pressures and individual responses. Those Mozartean worlds could never have happened without the background of Goldoni's libretti and their predecessors and imitators; at the same time, Mozart's marriage of a characteristically Italianate combination of wit and sweetness to a more Germanic richness of harmony and orchestration resulted in works which have remained meaningful for over two hundred years.

La finta semplice (*The Feigned Simpleton*) Dramma giocoso per musica. Libretto by Carlo Goldoni, adapted by Marco Coltellini. Written for Vienna but not performed there. First performance in Salzburg, Archbishop's palace, ca. 1 May 1769.

CHARACTERS

Fracasso, Hungarian captain	Tenor
Rosina, baroness, sister of Fracasso; the one who pretends to be simple	Soprano
Giacinta, sister of Don Cassandro and Don Polidoro	Mezzo Soprano
Ninetta, chamber maid	Soprano
Don Polidoro, crazy gentleman, brother of Cassandro	Tenor
Don Cassandro, crazy gentleman and a miser, brother of Polidoro	Bass
Simone, the captain's lieutenant	Bass

The opera takes place in and around the little country house of Don Cassandro and Don Polidoro.

SUMMARY

As with many buffa operas, this one focuses on the gulling of an apparently obdurate man of some status by his "inferiors": women and servants, and the achievement of desired and socially appropriate weddings. In this case, Don

Cassandro is tricked into allowing the weddings of his sister and his servant by being tricked into his own by the wily Baroness Rosina.

SYNOPSIS

Act I begins in a garden. It emerges that Fracasso and Giacinta want to marry, as do Ninetta and Simone. The ladies need to get permission from Don Cassandro, Giacinta's oldest brother and Ninetta's employer. He, however, has no patience for women or marriage. Ninetta promises that she will make Don Cassandro fall in love, which should grease the wheels for everyone else's plans. Fracasso's sister Rosina is shortly to arrive, and she is chosen as the object of Don Cassandro's affections. A series of arias elaborates on the characters' positions: Giacinta wants a malleable man, Fracasso is perfectly happy to marry her, but is not smitten, and Cassandro, as predicted, would rather have nothing to do with women. When Fracasso announces Rosina's arrival, Cassandro is not pleased, but is willing to impress Rosina with his classical learning and oratorical skills.

In a little room in Cassandro's house, Rosina announces her philosophy of love (to make everyone fall in love with her but to love only one in return). Ninetta gives her her task, and warns her about Don Polidoro, the ugly and unkempt but highly amorous younger brother. True to form, Polidoro proposes as soon as he sees Rosina, but she says he has to court her in the French manner, with gifts and letters – the latter a problem because Polidoro cannot write. The first interview between Rosina and Cassandro is quite successful from her point of view. She pretends to be quite stupid, which he takes as charming innocence, though he's suspicious enough not to give her his expensive ring. He then compares himself to a dog caught between the meat and his master's stick – naturally he'll choose the meat, despite the consequences. Rosina reveals herself, unsurprisingly, as a manipulative minx. Meanwhile, Ninetta has written a letter for Polidoro to give to Rosina; in the finale, Fracasso and Giacinta pretend to take offense both at the letter and at Polidoro's gift of money. Rosina, in the meantime, flatters Cassandro by giving him a letter she has written, and persuades him to give her his ring, just temporarily.

Act II opens on a terrace in Cassandro's house, with Ninetta asserting her need to manipulate men, and Simone his desire for a wife who can keep him fed. Cassandro and Polidoro have evidently come to blows over Rosina, and Cassandro has gotten drunk to boot. Giacinta helps Polidoro plot how to catch Rosina, and Rosina reveals privately that she is really in love with Cassandro, though she maintains publicly until the very end that she loves them equally.

In an illuminated room at night, Polidoro presses his suit again, and Rosina says he still has to woo her by singing in the French manner. At Cassandro's pretend-drunk arrival she says she wants enough *sposi* to have back-ups if necessary, which goads Cassandro into threatening her. She then tests him by having him communicate to her only in signs, which sends him to sleep. While he's asleep she puts the ring back on his finger, which he fails to notice. He and Fracasso almost come to a duel after Cassandro confronts Fracasso about the stolen ring, but Cassandro knows he's no match for Fracasso's pugilistic expertise, and tries to wriggle out of fighting. Luckily Rosina interrupts them. Fracasso and Giacinta, and Simone and Ninetta start to hatch a plan to escape together so that Giacinta can avoid the wrath of her brothers, but this plan is shelved for the second-act finale, where Rosina continues to be coy about which brother she'll choose.

Act III ties up the loose ends: Rosina confronts Polidoro with his impecunious situation (as a younger brother he has no estate and no income), as a baroness she would find this insupportable. In the finale, however, she continues to tease Polidoro by pretending to offer him her hand, even as she actually extends it to Cassandro. The remaining couples unite and sing the praises of female trickery and spirit.

COMMENTARY

Probably the most striking fact about *La finta semplice* is that it is a full-length, full-cast opera buffa written by a twelve-year-old. One must ask first, then, how it came about; how even the miraculous Wolfgang was asked to write a work which would occupy so much time, involve so many performers, and be in the public eye for at least several performances. In fact the details of the commission, which occurred on the Mozarts' second family trip to Vienna in 1767–9, are not completely clear, but Leopold Mozart wrote a very excited letter in January 1768 to his Salzburg landlord Lorenz Hagenauer, which described Joseph II asking Mozart whether he would like to write an opera to be performed sometime after Easter. Leopold noted the constraints on what Joseph could promise, since the person in charge of the theaters was not the emperor himself, but the theater administrator, Giuseppe Afflisio (also known as d'Affligio). Nevertheless Leopold reported in a later letter that 100 ducats had changed hands when Joseph announced the commission to Afflisio, so it was clearly not a simply a casual suggestion; in addition, Marco Coltellini, one of the court poets, was engaged to adapt Goldoni's libretto, written for Venice in 1764 and first set to music by Salvatore Perillo. In his initial excitement over the conversation with the emperor, Leopold could not restrain himself from noting that it would be a full-length (two- to three-hour) work, that it would be a comic opera because opera seria was out of style in Vienna, and because there were no seria singers to hand, though the buffa singers were important artists, and finally that Wolfgang's fame would grow exponentially if he had a Viennese opera on what we would now call his resumé. In any event, the opera was started by March, and in a later letter to Hagenauer, Leopold surmised that the opera could be done by June, to celebrate Joseph II's return from a diplomatic trip east.

Unfortunately the opera was never performed in Vienna. Leopold's letters home and his letter of complaint to Joseph II – the best sources we have – claim that the operatic establishment in Vienna had spread rumors that the work was incompetent or unsingable, and/or that it was not Wolfgang's own work. The first claim is absurd, but the second was understandable given Mozart's youth and Leopold's musical expertise; indeed, the autograph shows that Leopold offered corrections in the setting of the Italian, and also in musical matters. The singers also evidently demanded changes to their own parts.[15]

The difficulties evidently started right away with Coltellini being slow in making his adaptations, but continued with Afflisio as the chief villain, arranging the schedule so there was no rehearsal of a finale until the orchestra was present, at which point the singers could not sing it, and insulting Leopold and Wolfgang by repeatedly scheduling other operas ahead of *La finta semplice*. The musicians claimed to Leopold's face that they admired the music, and that administrative decisions were Afflisio's alone; at the same time, Afflisio repeatedly reported to the Mozarts that the musicians had described the opera as unperformable. Leopold also describes the opposition of the most important composer in Vienna at the time: Christoph Willibald Gluck. However the famous librettist Metastasio (the imperial court poet) and his close associate the composer Johann Adolf Hasse evidently supported Mozart. Leopold was also at pains to demonstrate Wolfgang's compositional independence by having him set, in public and at sight, a randomly-selected text of Metastasio.[16] Afflisio strung the Mozarts along for months, perhaps hoping that Leopold would get the message, but finally told them that he could not mount the opera, after which Wolfgang composed a mass for the dedication of the foundling-house church on the Rennweg.

The family returned to Salzburg in January 1769, and the opera seems to have been performed there around the beginning of May. The principal evidence for such a performance is a printed libretto, whose title page describes the opera as having been performed by order of the Archbishop of Salzburg, in whose court Leopold was employed. The singers also came from the Archbishop's court, and if the Viennese plans and Leopold's situation in

Salzburg are any guide, Wolfgang might have directed the performance, probably from the keyboard, and Leopold could have played violin in the orchestra. The Salzburg production was the only one in Mozart's lifetime; like Mozart's other early operas *La finta semplice* was out of the repertory in the nineteenth and early twentieth centuries, although it was a subject of scholarly interest as early as the 1840s,[17] and certainly by the early twentieth century. It has, however, enjoyed relatively regular production since 1956, the centenary of Mozart's birth, when a doctored version was given at the Salzburg birthday celebrations.[18]

La finta semplice is not a transcendentally great work. For modern tastes the plot is too inconsequential, the arias and recitatives follow each other in too regular a rhythm, the absence of ensembles makes the drama less engaging, and the range of expression in the arias is, on the whole, rather narrow. Nevertheless, it is a remarkable mirror of the prevailing norms in 1760s opera buffa. This is not altogether surprising: Carlo Goldoni, the original librettist, essentially laid the groundwork for the late eighteenth-century florescence of this genre; and Mozart's capacity to absorb musical styles and to grasp the musical conventions associated with a variety of operatic texts was evident from his earliest childhood. The most striking evidence of this comes from Dr. Daines Barrington's description of his "examination" of the nine-year old Mozart in London, in 1765. Barrington relates:

> I said to the boy, that I should be glad to hear an extemporary *Love Song*, such as his friend Manzoli [Italian castrato Giovanni Manzuoli, visiting London for the 1764–5 season] might choose in an opera.
>
> The boy on this (who continued to sit at his harpsichord) looked back with much archness, and immediately began five or six lines of a jargon recitative proper to introduce a love song.
>
> He then played a symphony which might correspond with an air composed to the single word, *Affetto.*
>
> It had a first and second part, which, together with the symphonies, was of the length that opera songs generally last: if this extemporary composition was not amazingly capital, yet it was really above mediocrity, and showed extraordinary readiness of invention.
>
> Finding that he was in humour, and as it were inspired, I then desired him to compose a *Song of Rage*, such as might be proper for the opera stage.
>
> The boy again looked back with much archness and began five or six lines of a jargon recitative proper to precede a *Song of Anger.*
>
> This lasted also about the same time with the *Song of Love*, and in the middle of it, he had worked himself up to such a pitch, that he beat his harpsichord like a person possessed, rising sometimes in his chair.[19]

This story informs us about Mozart's astonishing imitative powers, but also about the highly conventional musical language of opera in that period. The love and rage aria types that Barrington requested were more likely in seria than buffa style, but the two genres shared many stylistic features, and the story retains its pertinence for the composition of *La finta semplice*. Just as in opera seria, where arias typically expounded on a single *Affekt*, or emotion, sometimes introducing a contrasting sentiment in a middle section, opera buffa arias of this period also typically set up a single dramatic or emotional situation and elaborated on it throughout. Thus the lieutenant Simone's second-act aria "Con certe persone vuol esser bastone," ("One needs a stick with certain people") keeps a steady triple rhythm throughout, and alternates patter (speedily-declaimed words, often on the same note) with a slower, more pompous mode of declaration over triplets in the accompaniment. This particular aria is an extremely coherent expression of masculine bombast. It is also an entirely typical example of a comic bass aria of the time. Mozart's audience would have grasped instantly what kind of aria it was, and would not have looked for subtleties of meaning or nuances of expression in it.

Most of the arias in *La finta semplice* are of this one-*Affekt* type, though some have a bit more variety in the way the *Affekt* is enacted. Nevertheless, this opera is notable for the number of arias which alternate between slower and faster music, the fast second and fourth sections often undercutting or explaining the sentiment of the slow first and third ones. Thus Rosina's first-act aria "Senti l'eco" ("You hear the echo") begins with a gorgeously illustrative pastoral section in which she describes the lover listening for an echo, and then switches to a cutely comic section in which she tells Fracasso (and the audience) that this is the way to speak to men in order to get your way, and that in love one should, like the echo, never give more than one receives. These two-tempo arias mostly express a static relation between the content of the slow sections and that of the fast, but they contain the seeds of arias which progress dramatically and psychologically, such as we find in Mozart's later operas. Mozart's finales in *La finta semplice*, though somewhat pedestrian in comparison to those in the great works of the 1780s and 90s, are smoothly composed, with a good sense of both continuity and contrast. The moment in the third-act finale where Giacinta explains to the still-simmering Cassandro that she helped instigate the imbroglio because of love, and thus should be forgiven – a moment where the tempo suddenly slows down and the vocal part changes from patter to cantabile – is, again, common in operas of this sort, but Mozart's pre-adolescent ability to make something of it foreshadows the astonishing moment of forgiveness at the end of *The Marriage of Figaro*.

One should not expect the characters in this opera to tell us deep truths about the human condition, or to seem psychologically complex or interesting. Even in the greatest buffa operas of the mid-eighteenth century it is the interactions between the characters and the situations in which they find themselves that animate the operas, rather than the inner motivations or struggles of the individuals themselves. On the other hand, the characters in *La finta semplice*, like those in Goldoni's other comic libretti, do exemplify some of the most salient social issues of their time. The right of women to marry for love rather than family politics, the financial situation of younger brothers, and the relations between the sexes in marriage, were all pertinent questions in a Europe moving from the rural, basically feudal arrangements that form the backdrop to this opera, to a more entrepreneurial, bourgeois world. The fact that *La finta semplice* – like so many works of its ilk – mocks the attempts of women to exert more control and offers no solutions for impoverished younger brothers does not mean that the comedy did not help keep those issues alive.

La finta giardiniera (*The False Gardener Girl*) Dramma giocoso. Libretto anonymous: Giuseppe Petrosellini is a possible author. First performance Munich, Salvatortheater, 13 January 1775.

CHARACTERS

Don Anchise, Mayor of Lagonero, in love with Sandrina	Tenor
The Marchioness Violante, lover of the Contino Belfiore, believed dead, going under the name of Sandrina and disguised as a gardener	Soprano
The Contino Belfiore, originally the lover of Violante and now of Arminda	Tenor
Arminda, Milanese gentlewoman, originally the beloved of the Cavalier Ramiro, now betrothed to the Contino Belfiore	Soprano
The Cavalier Ramiro, lover of Arminda, and abandoned by her	Soprano
Serpetta, the mayor's chambermaid, in love with him	Soprano
Roberto, Violante's servant, pretending to be Nardo, her cousin, dressed as a gardener; unrequited lover of Serpetta	Bass

SUMMARY

Before the plot begins, the Contino has stabbed Violante in a fit of jealousy and left her for dead. They still love one another, however; thus when he arrives at the Mayor's estate to be betrothed to the Mayor's niece Arminda, he recognizes and wants to reunite with Violante/Sandrina despite her attempts to remain incognito. The opera is spent unraveling this knot and pointing the other characters in the opera towards their rightful mates,

SYNOPSIS

Act I begins in a pretty garden with a staircase leading into it from the Mayor's house. The Mayor, Ramiro, Serpetta, "Sandrina" and Nardo rejoice in the lovely day, expose the fault lines in their relationships with each other and return to praising the day. Ramiro regrets the loss of Arminda. Serpetta and Nardo are sent, unwillingly, to prepare for the separate arrivals of the Contino and Arminda. Left alone, the Mayor presses his suit with Sandrina, who demurs on the grounds of their difference in rank. The Mayor tells her how much he loves her by comparing his heart to an orchestra. Sandrina admits to Nardo that she still loves the Contino and cannot play along with the Mayor. Ramiro interrupts them and he and Sandrina discuss whether men or women are more to blame for amorous unhappiness. She sings an aria about the miseries of womanhood. Ramiro wishes Arminda dead, and Nardo, left alone, complains about Serpetta's hardheartedness, generalizing that to all women.

In a portico the Mayor greets his niece Arminda, who rapidly proves to be arrogant and demanding. The Contino arrives, offering extravagant compliments to Arminda almost before he has laid eyes on her. Although the Mayor is enthusiastic to conclude the match, Arminda is less taken with the Contino, and announces that she will be calling the shots in this relationship. The Contino takes this all in stride and in an aria attributes his high-minded temperament to his improbably long and noble lineage. The noble characters leave, and Serpetta arrives, complaining about her work; she decides to play a trick on Nardo by singing a love song, by which he is of course taken in. She ends the scene with an aria describing the way she handles men.

In a hanging garden, Sandrina sings an aria about the turtle dove far from home who arouses sympathy in others. Arminda comes in and announces that she is about to be betrothed to the Contino Belfiore. Sandrina faints at the news. The Contino arrives to help and the first act Finale begins as the former lovers recognize one another. Ramiro arrives and he and Arminda also recognize one another. They all remark on their astonishment. The Mayor does not understand why the four former lovers are so thunderstruck, and when the two original pairs leave together, he is quite unhappy. Sandrina denies to the Contino that she is Violante as the other characters watch their dialogue and respond from their own situations. The act ends in confusion.

Act II begins in an atrium of the Mayor's palace, where Ramiro and Arminda quarrel about her abandonment of him. The Contino arrives, in a state after having recognized Sandrina, which Arminda takes as a personal insult. Serpetta advises the Contino about the proper behaviour with a raging woman; he is not interested. Nardo pines for Serpetta; she is mean and then pretends she's interested, telling him to woo her with a foreign aria. Nardo obliges, in the Italian and the French styles, and Serpetta begins to be interested. Sandrina and the Contino meet, and she accuses him of heartlessness, but then claims she is quoting a text rather than speaking for herself. The Contino sings a love song to her, observed by the Mayor, who inches closer as the song goes on. At the end, as the Contino reaches out to Sandrina's hand, the one he actually touches is the Mayor's. The Mayor is furious at the Contino's infidelity to his niece (and also at his interest in the Mayor's own object of affection). The Mayor attempts to offer Sandrina his own hand, but she refuses him, hoping that he will continue to feel affection and pity for her when he understands how unhappy she is. The Mayor and Arminda commiserate; she urges her uncle to proceed with the wedding, when Ramiro comes in with a letter from relatives in Milan describing the Contino as a murderer. The Mayor is thoroughly confused about the proper course of action. Ramiro tries again to recover Arminda but she will have none of it, and he sings about the temptations of hope.

In a grand room, the Mayor asks the Contino about this reputed crime. Despite Arminda's promptings, the Contino almost admits to it when Sandrina bursts in to defend him. She identifies herself as the Marchioness he is supposed to have killed, and points out that she is alive. Once the Mayor has left and the Contino tries to kiss her hand, she once again denies that she is Violante, saying that she only pretended in order to save him. The Contino left alone, is miserable and confused until he thinks he sees the Elysian fields. The other characters discover that Sandrina has fled, and react variously. Serpetta still feels two ways about Nardo, and once again pronounces her philosophy about the need to manipulate men with deceit.

In a deserted and mountainous place, with ruined aqueducts and a practicable grotto, Sandrina is discovered bewailing her fate. The Act II finale begins as the other characters, now in the darkness, arrive separately to find her. There is confusion and deceit about their identities, but when these are sorted out, Armida berates the Contino, the Mayor berates Sandrina, Serpetta and Nardo quarrel; in the midst of this, the Contino and Sandrina become insane, believing they are in a pastoral drama and that they are the mythological characters Thyrsis and Clori. While everyone else laments their situation, the two lovers are blissfully, if deludedly, happy.

Act III begins in a courtyard, where, as Serpetta continues to play with Nardo's affections, the Contino wanders in, still orating like a mythological character.

Sandrina joins him, also still hallucinating, and offering the Contino her hand. Nardo tries to jog them out of this mode by pointing out a "duel" between the sun and the moon. They depart, terrified. The Mayor tells Serpetta that the way to solve this is for Arminda to be left spouse-less and for him to marry Sandrina. Serpetta tries unsuccessfully to remind him of her interest in him, but he rejects her. Arminda and Ramiro arrive to remind the Mayor of his duty: Ramiro wants him to force Arminda to marry him; Arminda wants to marry the Contino, or so it seems. The Mayor is confused and disgusted. Arminda tells Ramiro she will never love him.

In a garden, Sandrina and the Contino are discovered asleep. When they wake, they go through the usual deceit but in the course of a duet agree that they love each other as the birds do. In the last scene, Nardo tells the Mayor that the lovers have been reconciled; neither he nor Arminda is pleased at the news. When the happy couple enter, the other couples fall into place: Arminda takes Ramiro, and Serpetta gets Nardo. The opera ends with praise of the "gardener-girl's" fidelity.

COMMENTARY

It is not entirely clear who commissioned *La finta giardiniera*. It seems likely that Count Seeau, the theater intendant for the Elector of Bavaria, was the proximate source of the commission, but it is also possible that Seeau was encouraged to ask Mozart by Count Ferdinand Christoph Waldburg-Zeil, Bishop of Chiemsee, and a longstanding patron of Mozart.[20] The libretto for the Munich performance is no longer extant, but the text of the version set by Pasquale Anfossi for Rome in 1774 exists, and it was quite clearly the source for this work. Mozart's setting differs remarkably little from that text, which is surprising given his later habits of extensive interference in the construction of the text.

As usual, Mozart traveled a couple of months in advance to the city where the opera was to be mounted, in order to fit it to the particular singers and to be on hand for the rehearsals and the initial performances. The performances in early 1775 were an enormous success, according to both Wolfgang and his father, who had accompanied him on this visit. Unfortunately, although Mozart was away from home, his letters to his mother and sister say very little about his compositional process or ideas about the work, other than that the postponement of the opera was in the end a good thing, since it allowed more time for rehearsal. The performances took place during the carnival season, and so they were attended by high and mighty and dignitaries from many different places. Mozart's employer, Archbishop Collorcdo of Salzburg, attended with his retinue, as did the members of the Saxon ruling family.

Members of the Mozart family's circle in Salzburg also made the day-long freezing journey from Salzburg to Munich.[21]

The opera was translated into German as *Die verstellte Gärtnerin* and performed in Augsburg in 1780; the German version enjoyed a modest success, being played in Frankfurt in 1782 and 1789, and in Mainz in 1789. The Italian version was less popular, appearing, as far as we know, only in Prague in 1796.[22] The opera largely disappeared from the stage in the nineteenth century, and was the subject of very little commentary. The first modern revival was in German, in Vienna in 1891; thereafter the German version was performed, with spoken dialogue rather than the recitatives, until the sources for the Italian version were discovered in the 1970s.

La finta giardiniera belongs to a type of comic opera quite popular in the second third of the eighteenth century. Such operas center on a sentimental heroine, often a noblewoman in disguise, who is importuned by inappropriate suitors and persecuted by other characters until a dénouement which usually clarifies her social station, proves her virtue or constancy, and allows her to marry the man she loves. This plot type originated in the literary world: Samuel Richardson's novel *Pamela* (1740) is perhaps the signal example. Here the saucy but unimpeachably virtuous heroine is relentlessly importuned by the lustful Mr. B_____. Her stolid refusal to submit despite the wickedest of schemes turns Mr. B____'s heart, and he eventually marries her. The novel includes no question of mistaken identity, but when the Italian dramatist Carlo Goldoni adapted the novel as a play (also entitled *Pamela*), the heroine was turned into a noblewoman abandoned at birth so she did not know her proper status. That way, once the heroine's origins were revealed, the nobleman could marry someone of his own station, which was, as Goldoni noted, necessary on the Italian stage at that time. Goldoni adapted his play as a libretto, *La buona figliuola*, and the 1760 setting by Niccolò Piccinni was a runaway success all over Europe, chiefly because of the touching figure of the heroine, now a gardener girl called Cecchina. In this version the Marquis della Conchiglia is in love with the heroine, but his class-conscious sister and her snobbish lover threaten all kinds of havoc if he marries her; two spiteful female servants and a variety of misunderstandings that force her to flee and fall asleep, exhausted, away from the imbroglio. Fortunately a German soldier discovers a document proving that she is a German baroness, and the wedding takes place.

The similarity of *La buona figliuola* to *La finta giardiniera* is obvious; however, the device of having the gardener girl conscious of her own noble origins and fleeing the violence of her lover is a novel twist on the theme, and the contrivance of having the lovers go mythologically mad and reconcile through alternate personae is also new to this libretto; it reinforces the pastoral tone of the whole as well as introducing new opportunities for comedy. However, the flight of the heroine into a gloomy place where she despairs is classic for the genre. The other characters in this kind of opera all in one way or another show up the innocence and virtue of the heroine. Within her gender, her difference from both the spiteful serving girl and the arrogant noblewoman shows that she is above the norm of her apparent class and at the same time too virtuous to pull rank in her proper social circle. And the fact that all the men are either in love with, or at least sympathetic to her suggests her outer beauty, which complements her inner sweetness.

Mozart responded to these character types with his customary alacrity and vividness. The libretto assisted him to the extent that it provides numerous opportunities for the characters to strike a pose or assume a metaphor and perform it at some length. The Mayor's first aria, for example, in which he compares his bestirred heart to an orchestra, is an invitation to the composer to illustrate the text literally, and Mozart does this, with divided violas, solo moments for the oboes and flute, and in the end an entire brass section with timpani. Although both *La finta giardiniera* and *Idomeneo* (1781) were written for Munich, only the latter opera could use the famous Mannheim orchestra, which had decamped to Munich with the Elector of Bavaria by 1778. Thus the wind writing in *La finta giardiniera* is not as prominent overall as it is in the later opera; nevertheless, the young composer showed off the band when invited by the text. The Contino's ridiculous exposition of his lineage in "Da Scirocco a Tramontana" ("From the south winds to the north winds") builds on the normal practice in comic male arias of having the orchestra illustrate or respond to the text. Moreover, the way Mozart differentiates the diction in the endless and repeated lists of ancestors not only allows the character to seem vacuous but also retains the listener's interest. Arminda's aria "Vorrei punirti, indegno" ("I want to punish you, wretch"), sung to the Contino once she has discovered him with Sandrina, is an obvious precursor to Elettra's incandescent rage arias in *Idomeneo*, with its use of the minor mode, its sudden stabs of loudness, its short vocal phrases with largely syllabic declamation, and its occasional striking harmonies. The moment most critics find to be the finest in the opera is Sandrina's second-act scena (a linked succession of numbers) "Crudeli" ("Cruel ones"), where she flees the other characters. This starts out with a panicked aria over an obsessive orchestral accompaniment (Don Alfonso parodies this kind of aria in *Così fan tutte* when he tells the young ladies that their lovers are going to war). Sandrina's panicked aria moves seamlessly into a accompanied recitative vividly expressing her exhaustion; this in turn slides into a description of her inability to breathe, with short phrases in the voice and a kind of heartbeat accompaniment; another accompanied recitative follows as she finds a place to hide, and this moves seamlessly into the Act II finale. Mozart would exploit this kind of fluid scene construction to greater effect in *Idomeneo*, partly because the scene complexes there include choruses and allow a dramatically effective interaction between private and public. But this scena in *La finta giardiniera* is an extraordinarily vivid portrait of desperation.

With the exception of this striking exercise in structure, the beauties in *La finta giardiniera* tend to be in the details – especially in Mozart's wonderfully inventive use of the orchestra, and his often surprising and complex harmonies. As a whole this opera does not have the variety of dramatic rhythm that we find even in *Idomeneo* and certainly in the Viennese operas of his last decade. With the exceptions of the finales and the two duets in the third act, it consists, like opera seria, of a rather rigid alternation between aria and recitative without the dignity of the high style to make sense of that rigidity. Even the finales, with their much greater potential for fluidity, work more by juxtaposition and repetition than by development and accumulation. This is in large part attributable to the libretto, whose mechanics in these sections are quite contrived; but the fact that Mozart did not (or felt he could not) insist on significant changes in the libretto as handed to him means that the dramatic genius of the later comic operas is here latent only.

Le nozze di Figaro (*The Marriage of Figaro*) Commedia per musica. Libretto by Lorenzo Da Ponte, based on the play *Le marriage de Figaro* by Augustin Caron de Beaumarchais. Vienna, Burgtheater, 1 May 1786

CHARACTERS

Count Almaviva	Bass
Countess Almaviva	Soprano
Susanna [the Countess's chambermaid], betrothed to	Soprano
Figaro [the Count's valet]	Bass
Cherubino, the Count's page	Soprano
Marcellina [an older woman]	Soprano
Bartolo, doctor from Seville	Bass
Basilio, music teacher	Tenor
Don Curzio, judge	Tenor
Barbarina, daughter of	Soprano
Antonio, the Count's gardener and Susanna's uncle	Bass

SUMMARY

This is perhaps the most complex plot among Mozart's operas. The basic energy of the story, however, is quite simple. The Count is inappropriately interested in Susanna, which angers both Figaro and the Countess, who unite with Susanna to help her avoid the Count and exact revenge. The Count gains some leverage against his valet by way of Figaro's longstanding debt to Marcellina and by Dr. Bartolo's desire to take revenge on Figaro for his part, years ago, in helping the Count win the Countess against Bartolo's wishes. Everyone's plans are confounded by the gossiping of Basilio and the hormone-driven exploits of the adolescent page Cherubino.

SYNOPSIS

The opera opens in an unfurnished room, with Figaro measuring the space for a bed, and Susanna admiring her hat. It turns out that she is not happy with the location of their room, right next to the noble couple's quarters, and after some hesitation she tells Figaro that her unhappiness stems from the Count's desire to re-establish his previously-abolished feudal right to sleep with the women in his household before they marry, starting with her. Figaro is determined to prevent this and to make the Count dance to his tune. Marcellina and Bartolo discuss Marcellina's plans to marry Figaro; she's determined to prevent his wedding to Susanna; her back-up is that Figaro is financially obliged to her, and that when Susanna refuses the Count's advances, the Count will be so annoyed that he will force Figaro into marrying Marcellina as compensation for not repaying her money. Bartolo is only too eager to help, since he has a bone to pick with Figaro for helping the Countess (formerly Rosina, his ward) escape from his lustful clutches. (This was the plot of *The Barber of Seville*, the previous play in Beaumarchais' Figaro trilogy.) He leaves, and Susanna and Marcellina insult each other. Marcellina leaves in a huff, and Cherubino rushes in; the Count has told him to leave the household because of his antics with Barbarina, and he is distraught to be parted from the Countess, on whom he has a serious crush. Susanna is mockingly sympathetic, and Cherubino describes his adolescent romantic confusion. The Count is heard, and Susanna hides Cherubino in a chair under a dress. The Count makes advances to Susanna, asking whether she would like to accompany him to London, but Basilio approaches, looking for the Count. The Count hides behind the chair in which Cherubino is hidden. Basilio carries out his job of reporting the Count's interest in Susanna – surely she would prefer such a fine man to a mere page. The Count leaps up at the insinuation about Cherubino; Susanna is terrified, and Basilio tries to smooth things over. In the course of a trio the Count re-enacts a story about finding Cherubino under a tablecloth, and re-finds the trembling page under the dress. Figaro enters with a chorus of peasants dressed in white and scattering flowers; this is his first stratagem to flatter and shame the Count into re-abolishing the *droit du seigneur* and marrying him and Susanna immediately. The Count asks for enough time "to organize a more elaborate wedding" and orders Cherubino into the military. The first act ends with Figaro's famous "Non più andrai," ("No more will you go") in which he describes the grand military life that the page will enjoy.

Act II opens in a richly-appointed room, with an alcove and three doors. The Countess is alone, lamenting her situation. Susanna arrives and the two women commiserate about the Count. Figaro brings in his next idea, which is to have Basilio give the Count a letter arranging an assignation in the garden with a young woman, who will actually be Cherubino (whom Figaro has kept in the household) dressed as a girl; the Countess will discover the Count in flagrante delicto, and shame him into behaving with propriety. The ladies like the idea, and plan to disguise the page. Cherubino enters, covered in embarrassment to find the Countess, but is persuaded to sing the amorous song he has just written ("Voi che sapete") before being undressed by the women. Cherubino is fitted out with girls' clothing, Susanna leaves to get a ribbon, and the Countess affectionately comforts the not-completely-dressed Cherubino. The Count, who was thought to be out hunting, approaches. Cherubino is stuffed into the closet. The Count is suspicious of the Countess's agitation, the more so when he hears a noise in the closet. She will not open it for him, and he drags her off to find the key. Susanna comes in through a different door and makes Cherubino leave the closet; he escapes through the window and she replaces him in the closet. The finale begins as the Count and Countess return, he with a hammer and a great deal of anger, and she forced into explaining that he'll find Cherubino in the closet and that his half-dressed state means nothing. This does nothing to appease the Count, but Susanna's exit from the closet confounds them both. The Countess claims to have been teasing the Count, and he is compelled to make the first of his apologies to his wife. Figaro enters, once again asking the Count to perform the wedding right away. The Count confronts him with the note that Basilio gave him about the assignation with Cherubino which has already been revealed as a trick. Susanna, the Countess, and Figaro ask the Count to get beyond the failed trick and agree to the marriage, but he holds out, hoping that Marcellina will arrive with her unfulfilled contract. Things get more complicated when the gardener Antonio comes in complaining that something or someone jumped onto his flowers. Figaro claims it was him, but that is patently unconvincing. Antonio also has Cherubino's commission, which fell out of his pocket as he jumped out of the window. This identifies him, but the document's lack of a seal means that the Count cannot simply send him away. The finale ends as Marcellina, Bartolo and Don Curzio come in demanding a judgment from the Count that will make Figaro marry Marcellina.

Act III begins in a room with two thrones and preparations for a wedding feast. The Count angrily cogitates about the confusions of the situation. The Countess and Susanna, unseen by the Count, plan for Susanna to pretend to accede to the Count's desires by meeting him in the garden in the evening; the trick will be that it will be the Countess, dressed as Susanna, who will actually make the rendezvous. Susanna approaches the Count on the pretext of needing to get smelling salts for the Countess, and makes known that his wish will be her command; a duet seals the arrangement. Figaro enters briefly, and the Count overhears Susanna telling Figaro on their way out that she's won her case, which sends the Count into a paroxysm of rage. Marcellina, Bartolo, Don Curzio and Figaro enter, with Don Curzio pronouncing that Marcellina's case is good: Figaro should pay her or marry her. Figaro explains that he can't possibly marry Marcellina without the consent of his parents; in the course of describing his origins it turns out that he is actually Raffaello, the long-lost son of Marcellina and Bartolo, abducted by gypsies as an infant. Parents and son embrace; Susanna enters and misinterprets this until she learns the truth. Marcellina and Bartolo decide finally to marry. Everyone is delighted, and leaves. Cherubino and Barbarina briefly enter, announcing that Cherubino is still around, and about to be disguised as a girl once more, to be able to consort with the other pretty girls in the castle. They run off, and the Countess arrives to lament her situation and then to decide that her fidelity should give her the hope of reigniting the Count's love. She and Susanna confirm their plans and write the note to the Count that will tell him the time and place of the assignation they have planned. The castle girls arrive, singing the Countess's praises; she recognizes Cherubino. The Count arrives, also recognizes Cherubino and is about to send him away when Barbarina asks for him as a spouse, since the Count had promised her anything she wanted in the course of fondling her. Finally, the wedding march begins, and the two couples (Susanna and Figaro, Marcellina and Bartolo) kneel in front of the Count and Countess to receive their blessings. Susanna sneaks the Count a note sealed with a pin, on which he pricks his finger. Figaro sees this, but does not know that the assignation will be with Susanna.

Act IV begins in a little room, with Barbarina looking for the pin, which the Count gave her to return to Susanna as a sign that he accepted the assignation.

Figaro, who has helped her look for it, worms out of her that it is from Susanna, and about an assignation under the pines. Marcellina arrives, and Figaro seeks her motherly comfort. She wonders why men and women cannot get along like male and female animal pairs.

In a dark garden with two practicable niches, Barbarina rushes through, and Figaro, Bartolo and Basilio arrive in preparation for accosting the Count as he approaches Susanna. Basilio describes the perils of confronting those in power by telling a fable about a donkey-skin cape. Figaro vents his fury at the female sex; Susanna realizes that Figaro has heard about the assignation and has misinterpreted it; she decides to tease him by singing a serenade, ostensibly to the Count, but actually to him. Cherubino arrives, mistakes the Countess for Susanna and flirts with her. The Count arrives to meet Susanna, and just as Cherubino is about to give the disguised Countess a kiss, the Count interposes himself, and (once again) sends Cherubino away. The Count starts to woo "Susanna", with Figaro and the real Susanna commenting separately from the sidelines until the Count takes "Susanna" into a private garden house. Figaro starts to tell the "Countess" (actually Susanna) about the Count's misdeeds, but recognizes Susanna's voice, and starts to woo her as if she were really the Countess. Susanna cannot bear this, reveals herself and slaps Figaro. They are blissfully reunited. The Count arrives, looking for "Susanna", who has evidently slipped away. The real Susanna and Figaro continue the pretence that Figaro is wooing the Countess. The commotion brings everyone out, last of all the real Countess, who nobly accepts the Count's humble apology and the "crazy day" of the opera ends in rejoicing.

COMMENTARY

Origins

The exact story about the commission of *Figaro* is not knowable. The Beaumarchais play *Le marriage de Figaro*, on which this opera was based, premiered in Paris in 1784 after many royal attempts at censoring it, and after Beaumarchais's masterful manipulation of that censorship into a *cause célèbre*. It was a monstrous success, and was instantly known throughout Europe. Its notoriety was due in part to the overtly political content: Figaro, for example, has a long diatribe in which he asserts his social equality to the Count. It was also notorious for its indecency; in addition to the Count's improprieties the Countess dallies with Cherubino, and there are implications that Susanna is not as innocent as she might seem. But it was also scandalous because the minor characters included barely disguised caricatures of current officials, and the trial scene (essentially cut in Da Ponte's adaptation) was a replay of a famous judicial affair in Paris. With his famous tolerance, Joseph II (older brother of Marie-Antoinette) allowed at least one German translation to be published, uncut, in Vienna, but at the last moment he banned its perform-ance. Lorenzo Da Ponte's memoirs describe a process whereby he and Mozart wrote the opera together, and then he personally persuaded the emperor to allow it to be performed. However Da Ponte's memoirs are often self-congrat-ulatory beyond the bounds of strict truthfulness, his chronology does not fit with other evidence about the creation of the opera,[23] and there is evidence suggesting that Joseph was willing, or even eager, to have a less inflammatory version of the work performed, in part to shore up his reputation for supporting freedom of expression, and in part as a lesson to the nobility under his jurisdiction.

Regardless of who instigated this particular work, Mozart had been looking for a good Italian libretto since the demise of the Singspiel troupe in 1783. He had started but not completed a couple of buffa operas, and must have been delighted to find in Da Ponte, who had been hired as the poet to the court theater in 1783, a willing and gifted collaborator. He seems to have started work on *Figaro* in February 1785, with Count Rosenberg, the superintendent of the court opera, pushing him to finish in the autumn. However, due to the absence of Luisa Laschi, scheduled to play the Countess, and the schedule of other operas on the Burgtheater stage, it actually did not premiere until May 1786. It was certainly well along by the late autumn however, and the project was well-known across Europe before it came to fruition.[24]

In addition to the Beaumarchais play as a source, Mozart and Da Ponte had to deal with the great success of Giovanni Paisiello's setting of *The Barber of Seville*, which had played in Vienna since the re-establishment of opera buffa in 1783, and which was performed only three months before the premiere of *Figaro*. *The Barber of Seville* is closely based on the Beaumarchais play which is the "prequel" to *The Marriage of Figaro*; in this work, Bartolo is the guardian of Rosina, with whom the young Count Almaviva is desperately in love. Bartolo has his own designs upon Rosina and keeps her locked up in the house. But the barber Figaro, who happens to re-encounter his friend and former employer the Count after many years, is successfully enlisted to engi-neer Rosina's liberation into the Count's arms. Mozart recognized the affec-tion of the Viennese public for this opera, and built in a number of references to it: the Countess's "Porgi amor" resembles in style, key and orchestration Rosina's lament "Giusto ciel" ("Just heavens") when she thinks her amorous ambitions are in vain. And the second section of Figaro's "Se vuol ballare" quotes a moment in Paisiello's great introductory aria for Figaro, "Scorsi già molto paesi" ("I have traveled in many countries").[25] This kind of reference cements the narrative relation between the two works, but it also serves to mark Mozart as a kind of heir to Paisiello – or as a competitor, depending how one reads the evidence.

Reception and reputation

The opera had nine performances in its first run in Vienna; an average-length run. A reporter for the Vienna *Realzeitung* noted that the first performance was not as good as it could have been due to the unusual difficulty of the music, that the less-musically-educated majority of the audience was a bit puzzled by the work, and that there was a certain amount of hissing from the hired cabal (a group dedicated to heckling the works of some composers in order to aggrandize those of others) in the gallery. But by the third performance, according to this reporter, one would have had to be without taste or a member of a cabal not to comprehend that Mozart's music was a masterwork.[26] According to the memoirs of Mozart's friend Michael Kelly, a tenor who sang the part of Don Curzio, the audience encored everything, leading the emperor to place a blanket ban on repeating ensembles. The opera was performed in Prague in December of 1786, and there it was an unalloyed success. Mozart proudly reported to his friend Baron Gottfried von Jacquin that "here they talk about nothing but 'Figaro'. Nothing is played, sung or whistled but 'Figaro'. Nothing is drawing like 'Figaro'. Nothing, nothing but 'Figaro'."[27] And indeed, Prague did seem particularly favorable towards Mozart's music: Pasquale Bondini, the impresario who put on *Figaro* in Prague commissioned *Don Giovanni* for the next year, and *La clemenza di Tito* was also written for that city.

As was the custom at the time, domestically performable arrangements from the opera began to appear quite soon after its premiere, and performances abroad began with a much adapted version for Monza in Lombardy in 1787, a Paris production in 1793, and the first performance in London in 1812, though some of the music was already known there from being interpolated into other operas.[28] In Vienna, the work was revived in 1789, with a different cast, and notably with Adriana Ferrarese del Bene (the first Fiordiligi) as Susanna, which necessitated Mozart replacing the original "Venite inginocchiatevi" and "Deh vieni non tardar" with music better suited to Ferrarese's virtuosic singing, if not to our sense of the drama. This revival ran for 29 performances until February 1791, and overlapped with the premiere production of *Così fan tutte*. Viennese diarist Count Zinzendorf reported twice that he enjoyed the letter duet, sung by Ferrarese and Caterina Cavalieri, and that he enjoyed Madame Ferrarese's Rondò ("Al desio di chi t'adora" ["To the desire of the one who adores you"] the virtuosic aria that replaced "Deh vieni, non tardar").[29] This suggests that his pleasure (like that of opera goers through the ages) was as much in the singing as in what we might think of as the integrity or consistency of the drama.

Although the opera was performed steadily throughout the nineteenth century, it was not nearly as popular as *Don Giovanni*, whose dramatic music and supernatural content appealed to Romantic sensibilities.[30] Not only was it not performed as often as *Don Giovanni*, but (unsurprisingly) it also excited less intellectual interest and fewer parodies and spin-offs. Nevertheless, alterations and additions were rife. Some English reviews from the early nineteenth century tell us, for example, that Cherubino's "Voi che sapete," was routinely sung by Susanna,[31] while Henry Bishop's version for London in 1819 gave that aria to the Countess, made the Count a speaking part, added a character from Rossini's *Barber of Seville*, and radically diminished the amount of ensemble music in the opera.[32] One of the interesting aspects of nineteenth-century reception was a gradual change from thinking of Susanna as the main role to emphasizing the Countess. In an 1823 issue of *The Harmonicon*, for example, the response to the first appearance of Miss Louisa Dance on the London stage as Susanna was: "To appear in this character was ... to announce her intention of occupying the first vocal place in the theater."[33] And a Viennese magazine in 1818 simply called this role "the main part."[34] As a corollary to this, a review in an 1826 issue of a music journal in Berlin praised the "lightness" of the Countess's role as sung by Madame Finke.[35] Later in the nineteenth century and certainly well into the twentieth, and in many quarters all the way up to the present day, the focus shifted to the trials and character of the Countess. For example, Henry C. Lunn, reviewing the 1866 opera season in London, wrote of a Mlle. Tietens, who played the Countess, "Who could more exquisitely deliver the quiet and melodious music of Mozart; who could more eloquently reveal the patient suffering of the jealous but resigned wife of the libertine Count?"[36]

The nineteenth- and early twentieth-century reviews of the *The Marriage of Figaro* are not nearly as interesting as those of *Don Giovanni* or of the few performances of *Così*: in the latter case there was moral indignation to be vented, and in the former the Don Juan myth was always at hand to elaborate the commentary. *Figaro* has no interpretations as influential as those of E. T. A. Hoffmann and Søren Kierkegaard for *Don Giovanni*. Rather, it was typically described as a masterpiece of musical and sometimes of dramatic construction, and reviews then typically describe the performers without much commentary about the meaning or quality of the characters. The issue that has periodically rattled at this opera's cage concerns its political implications. The first commentator, for the Vienna *Realzeitung* in 1786, referred to Joseph II's banning performances of the spoken play by noting that "what may not be said can yet be sung," suggesting that the political content of the play was still quite present in the opera.[37] After the immediate period of the opera's origin, however, the political context seems to have died away, and the work was played simply as a comedy. The renowned composer and conductor Gustav Mahler conducted (and apparently directed) the work at the Vienna Opera in 1906, and this performance was evidently not only stellar with respect to its musical qualities, but also, as a reviewer later noted, newly political. "With Mahler *The Marriage of Figaro* was a social drama, a foreboding of the French Revolution in the combat of the humble servants against their aristocratic lords; and besides, he made it a drama of strong human passions."[38] This kind of political engagement with the content did not really become normal again until the 1960s.[39] Since then the broader context of the relations between the characters has been quite routinely examined or suggested in performance. Other recent interpretations include Nicholas Till's religiously-tinged reading, and Wye Allanbrook's thoroughgoing interpretation of the work as a pastoral, neither of which seem to have found their way into mainstream productions despite their intellectual and historical appeal.[40]

Men, women, class and power in Figaro

Despite the original reviewer's comments about singing and speaking, and *pace* Mahler's reading, The *Marriage of Figaro* is not in the narrow sense a political opera – that is, it is not a work that suggests the "revolution in action," as Beaumarchais's play has been described. Comparison with other comic operas on the Viennese stage suggests no greater class tension between the characters, and no greater boldness on Figaro's part than can be found in most comic operas involving masters and servants. (Figaro's most incendiary speech in the Beaumarchais play was omitted in the opera.) Nevertheless, it most certainly is a work about the exercise of power, and is in that sense profoundly political. Even in Da Ponte's adaptation the opera cannot avoid being about the power of privilege based both on rank and on gender. However, it is also about the power of suffering and the powers of friendship and love. It is obviously about power "within" the plot, as it were – that is, the capacity of some characters to compel the attention and even the behavior of the others – but it is also about the kinds of power that a work and its characters can have over the audience.

The most obviously powerful character is the Count. He is a king-like figure, the absolute ruler of his little domain, which is configured in many ways like the highly stratified larger society of which it is a part. His inferiors seem to be economically dependent upon him; he has connections to royalty, as his proposed ambassadorial trip to London suggests; he has connections to the military, as his speedy production of a commission for Cherubino shows;

he has some judicial authority, as shown by his capacity to legalize marriages; and he even has sexual power over the women in his manor. All but the last kind of power accurately reflect the kinds of authority exercised by landed aristocrats in a feudal society; it is not clear that the sexual *droit du seigneur* ever existed, and even if it had been in existence in the Middle Ages, it was not an official part of eighteenth-century feudalism. Nevertheless, it was no doubt the case that lords of the manor could and did exercise sexual privilege over the women in their domain, because, at least in rural jurisdictions, those women had no recourse other than the very person who had abused them. For Beaumarchais, however, this device was a compelling metaphor for the kinds of untrammeled and intrusive power characteristic of the aristocracy. The animating energy of the play also comes from the circumstance that Figaro himself feels that he has the right to resist the Count's advances on his beloved without fear of debilitating punishment. As the audience knows from *The Barber of Seville*, before he started to work for the Count, Figaro had managed to earn a living as a barber after running away from a variety of debts, including those accruing from a failed opera. He has lived successfully by his wits and could do so again if necessary. The extremity of the Count's incursion on Figaro's rights, then, can be seen as a reaction to Figaro's potential independence, and this anxiety about the self-determination and increasing authority of those above serfdom but below the aristocracy certainly reflects the political situation in much of Europe towards the end of the eighteenth century.

The Count, then, is a figure whose power is felt by weight of tradition to be enormous and whose primary goal in the opera is a real threat to propriety and to the autonomy of others under his authority – not only to Figaro and Susanna, but also to his wife. At the same time, however, he also occupies a position in the plot comparable to that which Dr. Bartolo held in *The Barber of Seville*, namely, the paternal figure who blocks the way to the fulfillment of young love, and who is undone both by the scheming of the lovers and by his own pride, lust, or simple stupidity. This plot type is essentially as old as comedy itself, and as soon as the basic character configuration of two lovers and one bumbling father/ward/uncle is announced, the audience knows that young love will triumph and the father-figure will, graciously or ungraciously, accede to their wishes at the end. The Count's major humiliation is, of course, having to ask, first in the second-act finale, and then, most famously at the very end of the opera, for his wife's (and implicitly for Susanna's and Figaro's) forgiveness. But he is also thwarted by Susanna's cleverness, by the happy accident that Figaro cannot marry Marcellina, and most persistently by Cherubino, who manages to be with Barbarina when the Count has designs upon her, with "Susanna" (actually the Countess) when the Count finally gets his rendezvous with her, with the Countess, whom the Count suspects of infidelity, and generally underfoot when the Count feels the need for space. The Count's major aria, "Vedrò mentr'io sospiro" ("Shall I see, while I languish") is of course a rage aria, but because the Count is a bass (a voice type employed primarily in comic opera) and because the aria ends with his delight in the idea of revenge, just like a basso buffo aria would (and Bartolo's has), it reinforces the idea that he is a character who can in fact be defeated.

Within the drama, it is the Count's action – his philandering – that sets the plot in motion: without him there would be no story. Within the world of the plot once it has been set in motion, he exercises power until the end, but in the auditorium, beyond the fourth wall, the audience knows early on that he has less command over the other characters' fates than they themselves may feel.

It is precisely the opposite with the Countess. She exercises a largely reactive role in the second act (the first in which she appears), and it is not until she decides to rely on her knowledge of her own unimpeachable fidelity that she can act on her own behalf; within the drama, her trajectory rises just as the Count's begins to fall. Within the world of the plot she exercises very little power; she has little temporal authority over the other members of the household, and to the extent that the other characters act with her in mind, they act out of sympathy rather than fear. But in the auditorium, to the audience (at least in modern times), the Countess's power is unparalleled; she is the one who literally stops the show with "Porgi amor," and who provides the literal coup de grace at the end by agreeing to pardon the Count for his transgressions.

It is obvious that the Count's power is rooted in his rank and gender: he rules his domain, and exercises kinds of power unavailable to women during this period. It is equally obvious that the Countess's power is deeply connected to her rank and gender; what may be less intuitively clear is that her kind of power was the result of changes in the conception of the aristocratic wife. *The Marriage of Figaro* is relatively unusual among buffa operas in including an already-married aristocratic couple; it is also relatively unusual in this genre in setting up the expectation that that married couple will, several years into the marriage, be united primarily by bonds of affection rather than by convenience, dynastic obligation, or class solidarity. Unlike many aristocratic women in opera buffa, the Countess expresses almost no pride or overweening jealousy. Her comment before her second aria "Dove sono i bei momenti," that she is ashamed and annoyed to have to pretend to be a servant in order to win back her husband, is as close to the usual aristocratic *amour propre* as she gets. The underlying assumption with respect to the normal opera buffa aristocratic couple is that although their rhetoric concerns affection and fidelity, it would in fact be usual for both members of an aristocratic partnership contracted for reasons of state, money, or rank, to stray; the

Viennese social commentator Johann Pezzl, for example, noted that a *cicisbeo* or gallant was a normal accoutrement for an aristocratic woman.[41]

The Countess, however, seems to believe in (or expects the Count to believe in) the emerging bourgeois notion of fidelity regardless of rank. This is not altogether surprising, since her origins as Rosina in *The Barber of Seville* are less elevated than those of Count Almaviva, who pursues and wins her in that play. This bourgeois sensibility encourages the particular kind of power she exercises in the auditorium. She is a quintessential "sentimental heroine;" a type of character quite familiar in opera buffa. Such characters very often believe themselves to be shepherdesses, gardener-girls, or of comparably pretty pastoral origins; in fact they usually turn out, after many trials and tribulations, including being importuned, threatened and abandoned by men of higher rank, to be of a station appropriate for marriage to that man, and everything turns out happily. In the meantime, however, they have presented themselves to the audience as both "unpretentious" and possessed of an unusual capacity for feeling. They very often sing cantabile arias alone on stage, and like the Countess's "Porgi Amor," those arias are quite often not introduced by recitative. The character does not explain or act before she sings; rather, musical introspection seems to be her "default" mode. Such arias often give the audience the sense that they are "overhearing" a thought process rather than being addressed directly (indeed, the Countess in "Porgi Amor" is quite explicitly addressing Cupid), and just as the averted gaze of many painted or photographed nudes allows the spectators to look at the bodies on display without inhibition, so the unmediated interiority of these arias encourages the audience freely to eavesdrop on the plight of these heroines. The power here might seem to be with the audience, but in performance, the singer artfully and completely compels and controls their attention, and the singer/character turns her vulnerability into power unique in the opera.

The power of observed vulnerability or suffering has strong resonances in Christian culture, the crucifix being the obvious symbol. The Countess is in many ways a Christian figure, particularly in her dispensation of forgiveness at the end. But in the world of opera buffa this kind of power was also peculiarly female, and, importantly, a marker of rank. Servant girls were not accorded the sensibility of their betters: it is no accident that when Susanna sings her ravishing love song to Figaro, "Deh vieni non tardar," at the end of *Figaro*, for example, it is couched as a trick, is overheard by other characters, and is part and parcel of the imbroglio. The Countess's arias are of course relevant to the plot, but her particular power lies in her inner characteristics rather than in her actions, and it is through her arias – both, significantly, soliloquies – that we are made to feel that power.

Susanna's power is more contained within the world of the plot than is the Countess's. Although it is the Count's initial action in pursuing Susanna that gets the plot started, and the forgiveness of the Countess that finishes the action up, in between, it is Susanna who provides the short-term wit and energy to grease the hinges of the action. She disguises Cherubino, she steps out of the closet to confound the Count and exonerate the Countess, she agrees to meet the Count in the garden, and in the end she tests and proves Figaro's love by seeming to serenade the Count. Everything she does in the plot works; she is the heir of generations of sly serving girls who trick and flatter their way to success. It is entirely normal in opera buffa for serving girls to act while their "betters" reflect; what is different (though not unique) about Susanna is that she is not interested in outwitting her antagonists to marry a rich man or gain social status. She simply wants to marry her beloved, but needs to use the resources of her kind to do so. It is, however, entirely typical of the genre that her actions can only take place within the framework set up by her social superiors.

Figaro's power within the drama is more like Susanna's than like the Count's; he acts and reacts within the framework set up by his social superiors. But unlike Susanna, he is relatively ineffectual within the plot. He is full of ideas and quick on his feet, but not one of his suggestions is actually acted upon. In some respects he is more like the Countess than like Susanna or the Count, in that his power is largely exercised in the act of performance. For example, in "Se vuol ballare" ("If you want to dance") he enacts both an aristocratic minuet and a lower-class contredanse; these dance rhythms suggest first his assumption of the Count's demeanour in order to address him on his own level, and then the more comfortable range of action that will allow Figaro to scheme and trick to bring the Count down. And in "Non più andrai" he performs a dizzying list of changes that Cherubino will have to undergo to be in the military. But unlike the Countess's arias, these arias of Figaro's are addressed to other characters, whether present or absent and the music extrovertedly illustrates objects in the text (dances, feathers, military music) rather than providing a more abstract atmospheric accompaniment. His final aria, "Aprite un po' quegli occhi," is addressed to the men in the audience, using the time-honoured comic ploy of "breaking the fourth wall" of the stage to expose the artifice of the occasion.

Cherubino's power is different from that of any other character, and quite unusual for opera buffa. His name means "little cherub," and he is clearly a kind of Cupid figure, representing, if not the power to make people fall in and out of love, at least the disruptive power of Eros. This is clear from his own behavior: infatuated with the Countess, he also plays with Barbarina and flirts shamelessly with "Susanna" in the last finale. Indeed, the only woman in the plot with whom he does not dally is Marcellina. But he is also the Count's "advance shadow," so to speak, already there whenever the Count is about to indulge in his own interests. Other than being in the way, Cherubino does not have very much effect on the progress of the narrative, particularly since Da Ponte cut from the Beaumarchais play the Countess's explicit attraction to him. But he does have a kind of mythological power on a more abstract level within the plot, and in the auditorium he is a perpetual indication that the best laid plans are subject to disruption.

Don Giovanni o sia Il dissoluto punito (*Don Giovanni, or the Rake Punished*) Dramma giocoso. Libretto by Lorenzo Da Ponte, based on *Don Giovanni* by Giovanni Bertati. Prague, National Theater, 29 October 1787: Vienna, Burgtheater, 7 May 1788.

CHARACTERS

Don Giovanni, young cavalier, extremely licentious	Bass
Donna Anna, lady, promised to	Soprano
Don Ottavio	Tenor
The Commendatore [Donna Anna's father]	Bass
Donna Elvira, lady from Burgos, abandoned by Don Giovanni	Soprano
Leporello, Don Giovanni's servant	Bass
Masetto, lover of	Bass
Zerlina, peasant girl	Soprano

SUMMARY

The plot turns on the exploits of Don Giovanni, who assaults Donna Anna at the beginning of the opera, kills her father in the aftermath, and tries to rape Zerlina in the first act. Vengeance comes in the form of Donna Elvira, an earlier conquest now determined to reform Don Giovanni and to prevent his further abuse of women, of Donna Anna and her fiancé Don Ottavio, determined to bring him to justice, and eventually, of Donna Anna's father, the Commendatore, who appears as a ghost at the end of the opera and drags Giovanni to Hell.

Synopsis

The opera begins in a garden, at night, where Leporello complains about his lot as a servant. Donna Anna and Don Giovanni appear in some tumult, with Anna trying to prevent Giovanni from escaping and Don Giovanni keeping his face hidden. The noise brings out the Commendatore, who challenges his daughter's attacker to a duel. After initially refusing to fight an old man, Don Giovanni takes the challenge and kills him. Don Giovanni and Leporello escape after the servant berates the master for the murder and Don Giovanni threatens his servant with further violence. Don Ottavio, for whom Anna had mistaken Giovanni, arrives, hears the horror story and promises his support and love to his fiancée in her grief.

On a street at dawn, Leporello plucks up the courage to tell Don Giovanni that he's a scoundrel, which is not taken kindly. Just then, Don Giovanni senses a woman and hides to watch her arrival. It is Donna Elvira, raging against Don Giovanni's abandonment of her. Not realizing her identity, Don Giovanni steps out to offer her assistance, but they are both thunderstruck as they recognize each other. Don Giovanni makes his escape by leaving Leporello to smooth things over, which he tries to do by telling Donna Elvira the truth about Don Giovanni's literally thousands of conquests, made all over the globe and recorded in a book that Leporello carries everywhere with him.

The next scene shows a chorus of peasants celebrating the wedding of Zerlina and Masetto. Don Giovanni and Leporello come upon them: Don Giovanni's interest is instantly piqued: Zerlina in particular catches his attention. He tells Leporello to offer all kinds of goodies to the peasants, especially Masetto, so that he (Giovanni) can manage a little time with Zerlina. She is at first suspicious of the nobleman's interest in her, and Masetto is particularly aggressive about his own suspicions. The separation of the peasant couple is effected, and Don Giovanni seduces Zerlina into agreeing to a betrothal in his "little cottage." Just as they are about to depart, Donna Elvira rushes in to tell Zerlina to run away. Giovanni tries to pass Elvira off as insane, but Elvira prevails and leads Zerlina away. Don Ottavio and Donna Anna arrive to ask Don Giovanni's help, as a nobleman, in identifying and punishing the murderer of her father. Once again, Donna Elvira arrives and starts to berate Don Giovanni while the noble couple comment in astonishment. At the end of the quartet expressing this contretemps, Don Giovanni again tries to brush Donna Elvira off as insane: this time Donna Anna recognizes his voice from the night before, and for the first time tells Don Ottavio about the attack she endured; she demands that Don Ottavio exact revenge. Don Ottavio states that duty compels him to avenge her. [Vienna 1788: Don Ottavio adds that his peace of mind depends on hers.] Leporello and Don Giovanni reappear, the former describing his attempts at distracting Masetto and Zerlina's subsequent arrival with Donna Elvira disastrous, and the latter insisting that things are going fine: he will organize a celebration, get the peasants drunk and dancing, and take Zerlina during the confusion.

In a garden with two locked doors, Zerlina mollifies Masetto by saying that nothing happened between her and Don Giovanni, and pretending to be willing to be punished for her straying. Don Giovanni arrives after the finale has begun, and starts to organize the party by once again trying to separate Zerlina from Masetto. Don Ottavio, Donna Anna and Donna Elvira have decided to gatecrash the party disguised in masks, and to confront Don Giovanni with his sins. Leporello invites them in, and after a prayer for Heaven's protection, they enter.

The scene changes to a large illuminated ballroom with multiple dances playing at once: a minuet for the nobles, a contredanse for the middle ranks, and a "Teitsch" or German dance, for the peasants. In this melée, Don Giovanni manages to drag Zerlina away, and her screams are heard as he assaults her. As the door is knocked down by Don Ottavio, Don Giovanni produces Leporello as the criminal, even though the guests continue to believe that Don Giovanni is the guilty one, and the finale ends in both inner and outer storminess.

Act II begins on a street; Don Giovanni and Leporello engage in their usual recriminations and bluster. Don Giovanni has been attracted to Donna Elvira's serving girl; in order to seem more plausible to her he insists upon changing clothes with Leporello. Donna Elvira comes to her window, trying to persuade herself not to love Don Giovanni any more. Don Giovanni takes the opportunity, hidden behind Leporello, who is disguised as his master, to pretend to woo her ardently and to call her down – that way the serving girl will be more easily available, and Donna Elvira can think she is reconciled with Don Giovanni through Leporello's disguise. Leporello goes along unwillingly, indeed, at gunpoint, with the scheme. Don Giovanni then (dressed as Leporello) pretends to kill someone in a fight, to scare off the real Leporello (disguised as Giovanni) and Elvira. He serenades the lovely maid. Masetto and colleagues arrive looking to beat Don Giovanni up: Govanni (still disguised as Leporello) offers to help but beats Masetto up instead. Zerlina find the bruised Masetto and comforts him with the promise of a special antidote stored close to her heart.

In a dark ground floor room, Donna Elvira and Leporello enter, with Leporello escaping from Donna Elvira's clutches as soon as they arrive on stage. Don Ottavio and Donna Anna enter: she is still demanding the ultimate revenge. Zerlina and Masetto join the others, and finding "Don Giovanni," start to attack him. They are astonished and not pleased to discover Leporello's true identity. He begs for mercy, and [Prague 1787 only: leaves with Donna Anna]. [Vienna 1788 only: the remaining characters berate Leporello until he escapes. Don Ottavio announces that it is now certain that Don Giovanni is the killer and attacker, and that it is time for vengeance.] [Prague 1787 only: he asks the assembled company to go and tell Anna that he is about to avenge her.] [Vienna 1788 only: Zerlina continues to abuse Leporello, this time by shaving him with no soap. Masetto and Donna Elvira arrive: he has been fruitlessly chasing someone he thought was Don Giovanni (or Leporello). Donna Elvira is left alone to contemplate her anguished feelings.]

In a cemetery at night again, Leporello and Don Giovanni meet and catch up; the Don describes the latest conquest. Leporello is beginning to see it from another perspective: what if one of Don Giovanni's women was his own wife? This makes Don Giovanni laugh until the statue of the Commendatore (very quickly erected, and with a vengeful phrase engraved on the pedestal) promises him that by dawn he will be laughing no more. Leporello is terrified, but Don Giovanni brashly invites the statue to dinner.

In a dark room, Donna Anna asks Don Ottavio again to delay their marriage for a year to allow her properly to mourn her father. He agrees to share her grief in order to lighten it for her.

The finale opens in a great hall, with Don Giovanni eating a splendid meal, accompanied by a wind-band playing the latest hits (including "Non più andrai" from *Figaro*), and enlivened by Leporello's attempt to steal some of the food. Donna Elvira rushes in to ask Don Giovanni one last time to give up his wicked ways as a sign of his love for her. He is not interested, and as she leaves, she screams. Leporello follows suit, and their terror is explained by the arrival of the Commendatore's statue making good on his promise to come to dinner. He demands that Don Giovanni repent; Don Giovanni boldly refuses; he gives the statue his hand and is dragged screaming to Hell. In the Prague libretto only, the other characters return to the stage. Leporello explains what happened, Donna Elvira says she will enter a convent, Donna Anna continues to ask for a delay in her wedding, Zerlina and Masetto expect to go home to a good meal, and Leporello will find a new master at a tavern. They all join in an "old song" which declares that the wicked man has got his come-uppance.

COMMENTARY

Origins

As with the other two operas with libretti by Da Ponte, relatively little is known about the compositional process of this opera. The commission came early in 1787 from Pasquale Bondini, the impresario of the Prague National Theater, in the wake of the magnificent success of *Figaro* in that city. It seems as if the choice of topic was left up to Da Ponte; at least that is how he describes it in his memoirs. He was engaged on three operas at the same time: the grandiose *Axur, re di Ormus* for Salieri, the comic pastoral *L'arbore di Diana* for Martín y Soler, and *Don Giovanni* for Mozart. Given the speed at which librettos had to be written, this was quite an enterprise. His description of his plan for getting the work done was as follows: "I will write at night for Mozart and imagine I'm reading Dante's *Inferno*. I'll write in the morning for Martini and imagine I'm studying Petrarch. The evening is for Salieri, and I will imagine him to be my Tasso." The enterprise as a whole was assisted by bottles of Tokay wine and the stimulating presence of a young woman. *Don Giovanni* was supposed to be premiered on 14 October, to celebrate the Prague visit of the newly-wedded Archduchess Maria Theresia and Prince Anton Clemens of Saxony. Both Mozart and Da Ponte traveled to Prague in early October to supervise rehearsals but quickly discovered that due to the small size of the troupe, the sickness of at least one singer, and the relative inexperience of the cast, it could not be put up in the time available. It was thus postponed until 29 October, the noble couple being feted with a performance of *Figaro,* directed by Mozart. Once up, *Don Giovanni* was a terrific success, but also generally acknowledged to be unusually difficult for both the orchestra and the singers.

According to Da Ponte, it was the emperor who encouraged Mozart to bring the work to the Viennese stage, and various alterations were made to adapt the work to the new venue. Don Ottavio's only aria, "Il mio tesoro intanto" ("Meanwhile, [tell] my darling") was cut, and the plainer "Dalla sua pace" ("On her peace of mind") substituted for it, but at a much earlier point in the opera (right after Donna Anna has narrated the story of the assault and sung "Or sai chi l'onore" ("Now you know that honour [demands]"). The traditional explanation for this is that the Viennese tenor, Francesco Morella, could not manage the coloratura in "Il mio tesoro," written for Antonio Baglioni, also the first Tito in *La clemenza di Tito*. A comic scene between Leporello and Zerlina was also inserted toward the end of the opera, after Leporello has been discovered masquerading as Don Giovanni. And Mozart and Da Ponte also added a scene for Donna Elvira in which she continues to contemplate her divided feelings for her seducer. In Da Ponte's view, the first performances in Vienna were not very successful: he reports the emperor himself as saying that although the music was "perhaps, perhaps better than that of *Figaro*" it was "no meat for the teeth of my Viennese." Da Ponte reports Mozart's response as "let them chew on it longer," and also notes that the opera grew on the Viennese public over the course of its fourteen performances there.[42]

Although we do not know much about Mozart's own compositional process with this work, the deeper origins of the libretto in literary and cultural history are quite well known. Da Ponte based his work most immediately on a recent libretto by Giovanni Bertati: *Don Giovanni o sia Il convitato di pietra* ("Don Giovanni, or The Stone Guest"), which was set by Giuseppe Gazzaniga and played in Venice early in 1787. Da Ponte adapted its one-act format to two acts by adding a series of comic episodes in the second act, and fleshing out and making grander the role of Donna Elvira (partly by combining two of Bertati's female roles into one).[43] However, the story of the libertine and the stone guest goes back to Spanish folk tradition, and the earliest literary version dates from the early seventeenth century and the playwright Tirso da Molina; his *El burlador de Sevilla* appeared in 1630. Spoken plays on this theme prior to the Mozart opera include Molière's *Le festin de Pierre* (1665) and Goldoni's *Don Giovanni Tenorio* (1736), the latter of which Da Ponte could easily have known (it was published in 1754); operas on this subject prior to Mozart's include works by Eustachio Bambini, Vincenzo Righini and Gazzaniga; there was also a much-performed ballet, written for Vienna in 1761 with music by Gluck.

Common (but not universally present) elements in these versions include the assault of a noble lady and the murder of her father, the presence of one or more other seducees with varying degrees of attraction to the Don, the servant (sometimes in the guise of Harlequin or another commedia dell'arte character) who acts as foil and mirror to the Don himself, and the stone guest's arrival at dinner and subsequent consignment of Don Juan to Hell.[44] The operatic treatments before Mozart are all comic; the plays are a more mixed bag of comic and serious. Mozart's and Da Ponte's opera mixes the two modes to an unusual, but not then incomprehensible degree. The opera's generic designation "dramma giocoso" (jolly drama), found in the libretto, has sometimes been taken as a sign of the authors' intention to mix comic and serious more thoroughly, or more jarringly, than usual. However, *dramma giocoso* was the normal designation for comic operas, and *Così fan tutte* – certifiably without the grandiosity of *Don Giovanni* – is also designated in this way in the libretto. (*Figaro* is called "Commedia per musica," perhaps acknowledging the spoken-play origin of the libretto.) In his own catalogue of his works Mozart called all three comic operas written with Da Ponte "opera buffa."

It is not clear why the Don Juan myth had such resonance in seventeenth- and eighteenth-century Europe. What is clear is that Mozart's and Da Ponte's audiences would have been entirely familiar with the outlines of the story, and would have recognized the striking ways this version mixed the risible and the terrifying.

Reputation

Despite the first Burgtheater audience's difficulties with mastication, *Don Giovanni* quickly established itself in Europe: German versions with spoken dialogue (often different from Da Ponte's text) were played in the suburban theaters and, indeed, all throughout Germany beginning as early as 1789.[45] The nineteenth century received it as the opera of all operas: not only Mozart's best essay in the genre, but also, and more importantly, the model for the genre as a whole. *Don Giovanni, The Marriage of Figaro* and *The Magic Flute* are the first operas to hold the stage continuously since their inception.

The nineteenth century's adoration of the work, however, did not translate to performances that stuck close to either the libretto or the score (in either version). A famous 1834 French-language production in Paris, for example, divided the work into five acts, split the Act I finale into two so that the producers could add a ballet based on a medley of other Mozart themes, and had Donna Anna fall in love with Don Giovanni and then kill herself out of guilt. (Her funeral featured music from Mozart's Requiem.) In addition, Don Giovanni himself was both sung by a tenor and turned into a self-reflective, tortured character.[46] The interesting thing about this production is that it protested a kind of fidelity to Mozart that seems almost incredible from a modern perspective. As musicologist Katharine Ellis points out, this production was strongly influenced by E. T. A. Hoffmann's reading of the work (see below), and also by French literary trends, particularly the writings of Alfred de Musset.[47] It was, like Hoffmann's story described below, a recreation of the Don Juan folk tale using Mozart's and Da Ponte's own reworking of that story as a vehicle. This production occasioned considerable criticism at the time, in part because of the liberties it took with Mozart's music. At the same time, however, this kind of reworking/updating was indubitably intended as homage to Mozart (if not to Da Ponte). Katharine Ellis notes that it "naturalized" the work in French culture by bringing it closer to the norms of French grand opera;[48] in addition it was, like much Romantic performance practice, supposed to reflect what the interpreters considered the essence of Mozart's intentions.

One of this Paris production's features – namely, casting a tenor in the title role – was quite normal in the nineteenth century. Indeed, it seems that bass (or more properly, baritone) singers did not monopolize the role until the end of the nineteenth century.[49] Changing the voice range of this character, whose original voice range is identical to that of Leporello and the Commendatore, distinguishes him from the pack, and makes it clear that he is the hero that writers like Hoffmann and de Musset wanted him to be.

In addition to productions that in various ways aggrandized the work or brought it into line with Romantic notions of the Don Juan myth or the nature of operatic heroism, the nineteenth century saw reworkings – as operas, plays, and stories – that parodied it, turning it into a ridiculous comedy. Such parodies started almost immediately in the German-language suburban theaters of Vienna, and spread quickly elsewhere. Among the more striking of these was William Thomas Moncrieff's *Don Giovanni in London*, which enjoyed a successful run in London between 1817 and the 1820s, and which featured a woman as the title character.[50] Also in London during the same period appeared a political cartoon "starring" George IV as the Don, interrupted in his conquests by his wife (ill. 5). London was particularly attuned to *Don Giovanni* during this period because of Henry Bishop's popular arrangement of it as *The Libertine*, which premiered in London in 1817.

The enduring power of the Don Juan myth was surely part of the reason for the multitudes of nineteenth-century performances and reworkings of this opera whether grandiose or ridiculous, whether announced as truly Mozartean or frankly distant from the composer.[51] The modern era has been equally unable to avoid the conflation of the myth with the opera. Literary critic Brigid Brophy's famous idea that Don Giovanni is a repressed homosexual, for example, is based on nothing particular to the Mozart and Da Ponte telling of the story, but rather takes the power of the music as emblematic of the reach of the myth.[52] And recent concern about how the work might function today in a society that is both highly sexualized and more conscious of the toll taken by violence against women, relies and comments upon the conflation of a pervasive myth with the particulars of this work.[53]

Who or what is Don Giovanni? How should his opera end?

Although *The Magic Flute* has been subjected to more symbolic "decodings" than any other Mozart opera, *Don Giovanni* has enjoyed (or suffered from) the largest amount of psychological and cultural interpretation. The most persistent question across time has concerned the nature of Don Giovanni himself, and in particular the extent to which he is an individual human being or a symbol of something greater. The Danish philosopher Søren Kierkegaard posed this question trenchantly in *Either/Or* (1843). He wrote: "Don Juan constantly hovers between being an idea, that is to say, energy, life – and being an individual."[54] Kierkegaard's notion that the figure of Don Giovanni stands for a primal life-energy was enormously influential, as was its corollary, that this kind of life-energy was realizable only through music. Somewhat less abstract but comparably grand was E. T. A. Hoffmann's reading of the opera, in his novella-cum-review *Don Juan* (1813, pub. 1819), in which Don Giovanni is the daemonic personification of the ever-seeking spirit, the soul never satisfied with whatever pleasure has just passed, a fundamentally noble being aware of the Highest, but seduced into a Fall of Biblical proportions, and thus a symbol of the battle between Heaven and Hell. Hoffmann writes: "A strong, noble body, a carriage [Bildung] emitting sparks of light, igniting the intimations of higher things, possessing a deep spirit and a quick understanding, struck my heart. But it is the horrifying consequence of a Fall, that the enemy possesses the power to waylay Man with wicked traps just as he is striving towards the Highest, in which activity he expresses his holy nature. This conflict of the Heavenly and demonic forces, like the hard-fought victory of the concept of life beyond, produces the idea of the earthly." [55] Here Hoffmann suggests that Don Giovanni was an individual to the extent of needing an appropriate human frame, but that his role in the opera and in culture more generally was to represent moral and spiritual contradiction.

These Romantic interpretations were probably not inspired by the music that Don Giovanni himself sings, and especially not by his arias, which are famously brief and un-revealing of his self;[56] rather, they were a response to the opera as a whole, and in particular to the magnificently terrifying music of the Commendatore's appearance and pronouncement of Don Giovanni's sentence. The fact that the whole opera begins with this climactic music allows it to set the tone for the whole work, but having done so, its very magnificence can seem in many ways out of proportion to Don Giovanni's sordid history of rape and seduction, even of murder, and perhaps especially of his banal pursuit of Zerlina, who is, for reasons both social and personal, the easiest of prey. Seen in this light, E. T. A. Hoffmann's repeated explicit insistence that the opera was about far more important issues than the progress of a rake (and, that he as an artist was uniquely qualified to perceive the work's deeper meanings) makes sense; it is a response to a problem that Mozart and Da Ponte pose but do not resolve.[57]

This problem – namely, the gap between the rather ordinary criminal quality of Don Giovanni's actual behavior and the aesthetic and spiritual enormity of the supernatural reaction it causes, combined with the grandiose Romantic interpretations of that gap – have laid the groundwork for a plethora of readings of Don Giovanni's character. Where Kierkegaard made him a manifestation of the life-force and the inner essence of music, and Hoffmann presented him as the embodiment of the interface between Heaven and Hell, or the epitome of the ever-yearning human soul, later critics have noted his "blankness": his musical and textual refusal to reveal his inner self, since he is always speaking the musical language needed to effect the next conquest or avoid the consequences of the previous ones. Many modern readings take this blankness as a consciously-crafted invitation to project the audience's own desires and fears onto this character. Charles Russell, for example, writes – as much about Don Juan the legend as about Don Giovanni the character: "Don Juan lives in us all . . . our daydream of adventure, our nighttime dream of escape . . . the sexual act of conquest or submission that we have all longed for . . . the act of daring we have never attempted . . . he is our ego asserting itself in its most elemental and selfish fashion."[58] The grandiloquence of the Commendatore's music, then, is justified by the "universality" of the guilty passions Don Giovanni excites, and perhaps by the extent of the social disruption that would occur if we all felt as free as Don Giovanni to act upon them. In the same vein but within the frame of the drama, critics have also noted that Don Giovanni's infinitely interpretable qualities combined with his undeniable power force the other characters in the drama to define themselves primarily in relation to him; he is the screen on which they project their desires.[59]

Twentieth- and twenty-first century readings of Don Giovanni's character have certainly continued the trends started by Hoffmann and Kierkegaard, but there is also a more socially-grounded set of readings, in which he transgresses against the social order rather than against nature (as Hoffmann would have it), or against the divine, as the supernatural come-uppance has suggested to many. As a nobleman, for example, it might be expected that he would attempt to seduce Zerlina, but to assault Donna Anna, a woman his equal or possibly even his superior would be a crime worthy of the most extreme social censure. Those inclined to read the opera in a more socially and historically grounded way have also seen in this figure a sign of the historical period in which the opera was created. "Viva la libertà," Don Giovanni's toast in the first-act finale, for example, has been mapped on to the moment of the opera's origin – during the American, and just before the French, revolutions. Joseph Losey's celebrated film of the opera (1979) took a related tack by showing Don Giovanni as a figure at the intersection of the feudal era and the industrial revolution. Peter Hall's celebrated 1977 Glyndebourne production set the opera in the early nineteenth century; the historically consistent and careful just-post-revolutionary setting in some ways intensifies the wickedness of Don Giovanni's behaviour because even the lame excuse of feudal privilege over Zerlina has been stripped away.

These readings of Don Giovanni's character, especially the more grandiose ones, have typically taken a male point of view, and have often, it must be said, exhibited a remarkable level of identification with Don Giovanni. For example, E. T. A. Hoffmann's narrator, who is a stand in for Hoffmann himself, feels his lips burning with an un-offered kiss as he listens to Donna Anna's "Non mi dir" ("Do not tell me"). Later in the story we learn that during

Don Giovanni's assault Donna Anna was overwhelmed by a superhuman sensuality, and "she was not rescued." The narrator's burning lips are clearly both his own and Don Giovanni's; this is emphasized in the story by having the spirit of Donna Anna visit the narrator in his box and declare a special affinity with him. Hoffmann also describes the narrator's virtual kiss as being transformed into an infinitely yearning musical note: an intimation that Hoffmann has become Mozart as well as Don Giovanni. Kierkegaard's ideas are less personal than Hoffmann's, but he moves with remarkable smoothness from the notion that Don Giovanni is sensuous desire incarnate – that is, a natural and essential aspect of human nature in the abstract – to the idea that he is the "exuberant joy of life," which suggests some identification between the philosopher and the character.[60] Kierkegaard does not explicitly describe this exuberance as possessed only by men, but its object is all of womankind, and there is no room in his argument for womankind to feel this kind of sensuality.

To many who insist on the essential nobility or universality of Don Giovanni's character, Donna Anna is Don Giovanni's true antagonist, in part because she is of – or above – his class and thus an apparently worthy opponent, and in part because her motive for putting off Don Ottavio is opaque and thus subject to multiple interpretations. Hoffmann imagines her as the basically incorruptible virgin, the depth of whose fall is a testament to Don Giovanni's superhuman powers: "Only he, only Don Juan, could ignite in her the voluptuous madness with which she clung to him, which possessed her spirit with the overpowering, destructive fury of hellish demons." Her fury is both high-tragic and titillating: "Eyes, out of which love, fury, hate, confusion were thrown, as if from the crater of a volcano, as if her soul was burning as inextinguishably as a Greek (Olympic) flame. Loosened strands of her dark hair curled in ringlets around her neck. Her white nightgown traitorously revealed never-dangerously-exposed charms." Hoffmann predicts that she will die before the year's delay of her wedding to Don Ottavio is up; her fury/attachment to Don Giovanni will eat away at her, making her incapable of living with a more conventional husband.

The notions that the attack is in fact a rape, that Donna Anna is in love with Don Giovanni because of his violation of her, and that she is a more compelling character because of both these things, have proved remarkably sturdy. Even in the 1970s William Mann, who thought Don Giovanni's assault was probably not consummated, wrote that it would have been beneficial to Donna Anna's "personal growing up" if it had. This is a vulgarization of Hoffmann's mildly erotic description of her fury.[61] Other nineteenth-century writing about her was more inclined to note her nobility of character without presupposing that it rested in part on a sick sexual dependence on Don

Giovanni. For example, a Viennese review of an 1818 performance with Madame Grünbaum in the role remarked "Her acting in this role was particularly good, since she was conscious of her nobility and played the raging woman who profoundly recognized the frightful disaster that had befallen her, and transformed her pain on the death of her father to an act of animated radiance."[62] Some modern commentary has essentially agreed with this more sympathetic evaluation; other critics have understood Donna Anna variously as frigid, merely cold, or a superannuated opera seria heroine, and have turned to the more *mezzo carattere* (somewhere between buffa and seria) Donna Elvira as the "heart" of the opera. Both, in any case, have long been hailed as masterpieces of characterization.

Despite the strong characterization of these women, they are, paradoxically, defined almost totally by their relationship to Don Giovanni. And this paradox intensifies the question of whether Don Giovanni is really a symbol of desire, yearning, life-force, music, etc., or a more socially-grounded representative of humanity. As philosopher Bernard Williams notes, the answer to this question affects the meaning of the ending, and in particular, whether it can be understood as an act of divine vengeance or something more trivially supernatural, and how it connects to the society which Don Giovanni exploits but is not really part of.[63]

All versions of this opera include Don Giovanni's demise, and it has always been considered an opportunity for at least some level of theatrical effect: the chorus of demons may or may not be visible; the flames may rage more or less realistically; Don Giovanni may disappear in a puff of smoke or slide downwards through a trap door; there may or may not be explicit religious symbolism; he may or may not reappear to preside over the *scena ultima* (the last scene of the opera, after Don Giovanni's demise). Recent scholarship has situated this opera not only in the tradition of operas on the same theme but also in a more religious, or supernatural context.[64] This kind of contextualization diminishes the idea that Mozart's and Da Ponte's opera is unique in operatic history, at least with respect to its outlines. However, it leaves open the question of whether the extraordinarily powerful music of Don Giovanni's last moments is a kind of happy accident – namely, that Mozart could not help himself from writing music that would stir generations of listeners to their bones, even though he "only" wanted to create an audience-gripping special effect – or whether he understood the story in a way that led him to write music with an intentionally profound spiritual and psychological resonance. This is obviously not a simple opposition; spectacular theatrics can certainly lead an audience to deeper reflection. Certainly the use of the Commendatore's arrival music at the beginning of the overture suggests at the very least that Mozart was sufficiently pleased with this material that he wanted to use it more than once; it is inconceivable that as a genius of the theater he would not also realize that this double usage would lend extra weight to the moment. Beyond that, the opera leaves performers, critics and audiences to judge the significance of the effect.

Not all versions of the opera, even in Mozart's lifetime, included the *scena ultima*. The libretto from the Vienna 1788 performance omits it, though it is debatable what this meant. Generally speaking, it was more often omitted in the nineteenth century and since the later twentieth century it has more often been included. Mozart himself included a choral "Ah" on the tonic, D major, as Don Giovanni disappears, though he also scribbled it out; clearly he was working on how it would be possible to end the opera at the moment of the Don's demise, with the spectacle of the flames and demons, but also with the customary choral singing.[65] It has also not been unusual in the past decades, at least, to include a cut version of the last scene, proceeding more quickly than the original libretto allows to the "antichissima canzon" (the old, old, song) which pronounces the rightness of Don Giovanni's end.

It is not inconceivable that Mozart's chief, or even only, concern was with theatrical effect: how best to ensure a spectacular end.[66] But since his death, directors, critics and audiences have read much more into the choice of ending than this. In a general way, it may be that those with the most "cosmic" view of the opera's meaning are most likely to want it to end either with Don Giovanni's death or as shortly thereafter as decently possible. That is, if Don Giovanni does in fact represent a primal force, life-energy, or the essence of music, then his death renders the other characters not only irrelevant but in fact dead themselves. On the other hand, in an equally general way, those who see the opera as more grounded either in a social world or in its genre may prefer the inclusion of the *scena ultima* because it obeys the historical convention of ending a comic opera with a *lieto fine* (happy end), or at least with consensus and some sense of a better future, as well as with a substantial ensemble. To end with the *scena ultima* also asserts that society continues as before (or at least as it was represented at the beginning of the opera) once disruptive elements have been removed: Leporello looks to repeat his relationship with another master; Zerlina and Masetto expect to live a cozy bumpkin life; Donna Elvira makes the socially acceptable move of the dishonored woman by moving to a convent, and Donna Anna, only twenty-four hours after the death of her father, continues betrothed to Don Ottavio but not yet ready for a wedding. The fact that these endings are "clapped on," to use Wye Allanbrook's felicitous phrase,[67] and barely conceal the probability that Zerlina will be tempted again, that Donna Anna may never get over the events of the opera, and that Leporello will continue the cycle of evil, is simply the comic norm; it is not a feature particular to this opera. After all, we don't really expect that the Count will stay faithful to the Countess for any appreciable length of time, but that does not diminish the satisfactoriness of the ending to *The Marriage of Figaro*.

A third common ending to this opera involves including the *scena ultima* but representing some or all of the characters as irrevocably altered by Don Giovanni's blitz through their lives. This seems to be a commonplace in modern productions; it is also what E. T. A. Hoffmann seems to have witnessed (or at least so reports in *Don Juan*); "How charitable seems now the appearance of the remaining characters, who vainly seek Don Juan, who has been dragged away by subterranean powers. It is as if one has only just escaped the clutches of the hellish spirits. Donna Anna appeared completely changed: a deathly pallor overtook her face, the light in her eyes was extinguished, her voice [is] trembling and uneven, and makes the most heartrending effect even through the little duet with the sweet bridegroom, who, after Heaven has luckily relieved him of the dangerous office of revenge is ready expeditiously to wed." The persistence or revival of this reading after nearly two centuries, as well as its co-existence with both more comic and more symbolic versions of the ending is testament not only to the obvious staying power of this work, but also to the many ambiguities and unresolved questions posed by this "opera of operas."

Così fan tutte (*Thus do they all*) Dramma giocoso. Libretto by Lorenzo Da Ponte. Vienna, Burgtheater, 26 January 1790.

CHARACTERS

Fiordiligi and Dorabella, Ferrarese ladies and sisters living in Naples	Sopranos
Guglielmo and Ferrando, lovers of the above	Bass, Tenor
Despina, chambermaid	Soprano
Don Alfonso, old philosopher	Bass

SUMMARY

The opera plays out an experiment instigated by Don Alfonso, in which the fidelity of the two young women is tested by having their lovers return in disguise and each seduce the other's beloved. Despina assists Don Alfonso in running the experiment, which fits with her own ideas about love, but she also learns a lesson.

SYNOPSIS

In a coffee shop, Ferrando and Guglielmo praise the constancy of their lovers. Don Alfonso is skeptical because their reasons for believing in the women's fidelity are not particularly relevant or convincing. They agree on a bet to prove the ladies' constancy and the gentlemen agree to do everything Don Alfonso tells them.

In a seaside garden, the ladies look at lockets with pictures of their lovers and admire them. Don Alfonso bursts in in dreadful agitation to tell them that their lovers have been called away to war. The gentlemen enter and the lovers sing about the misery of parting while Don Alfonso chuckles in the background. A military march calls them away, and after promising to write every day, the men are torn away from the women. The ladies and Don Alfonso wish them a safe journey. Left alone, Don Alfonso opines that putting one's faith in the constancy of woman is like trying to catch the wind in a net.

In a genteel room, the chambermaid Despina complains about the life of a chambermaid. The ladies enter, distraught and prostrate with grief. Dorabella compares herself to a grief-stricken heroine, and after some prompting, the ladies tell Despina the cause of their misery. She cannot believe the fuss: after all, men are all alike, plus deceitful, and women should love at their own convenience. The ladies leave. Don Alfonso arrives and lets Despina in on the plan to introduce the ladies to new lovers, paying her for her troubles. The gentlemen enter dressed as Albanians and pay elaborate court to the philosopher and the servant, who is highly amused. The disguised gentlemen start to court the ladies as they enter, and the grief-stricken pair repulses them angrily. Fiordiligi sings proudly about the strength of her constancy to Guglielmo. Guglielmo asks the two ladies to look with favour upon them: Fiordiligi on Ferrando and Dorabella on Guglielmo. The ladies leave in high dudgeon.

Left alone, the gentlemen are delighted with the ladies' fortitude. Don Alfonso says that there is yet more to the trick, and Ferrando looks forward to its happy resolution. Don Alfonso enlists Despina's help to try to soften up the ladies. The first act Finale begins with the two ladies reflecting on how quickly life can change. The gentlemen rush in in mock despair, drinking "arsenic" as proof of their attachment to the still-chilly ladies. The ladies call in Despina, who goes to call a doctor. Don Alfonso confirms the ladies' sense that this could be fatal for the men. In the meantime, the ladies have gingerly touched the men to take their temperatures, and begin to find them interesting in their newly passive condition. The doctor (Despina in disguise) arrives, spouting mumbo jumbo and carrying a large magnet. She has the ladies hold the gentlemen's heads while she performs the cure. The magnet restores the men to their former amorous condition, but the ladies still reject them.

Act II begins in a room, where Despina plays on the women's weakening resolve, and explains to them how to flirt – telling them things any ordinary fifteen-year-old female should know. When she has left, the ladies decide that it might not be so terrible to have a little fun with the visitors. Dorabella is more eager than Fiordiligi. Don Alfonso arrives to usher them to the garden, where all the amenities for courting (including the gentlemen) have been set up. Despina and Don Alfonso manipulate the young people like puppets to engineer proper wooing behaviour. He and Despina leave the couples alone to promenade: awkward conversation ensues. The two couples separate, and Dorabella and Guglielmo make quick work of falling in love; he gives her a heart-shaped necklace that Fiordiligi had given him. Guglielmo feels slightly sorry for Ferrando, since his fiancée deserted him so quickly. The scene shifts to Ferrando and Fiordiligi. He presses his suit with vigor; she refuses him. Left alone, though, she realizes that she is falling in love and asks her absent beloved for forgiveness for what she is about to do. Ferrando and Guglielmo meet to check in: Guglielmo is delighted to hear about Fiordiligi's continuing resistance; Ferrando is furious and ashamed to hear of Dorabella's capitulation to Guglielmo. Guglielmo rubs it in by addressing the ladies in the audience, in effect having them agree that they are deeply and hopelessly fickle and manipulative. He leaves and Ferrando reflects on his fury; Don Alfonso and Guglielmo join him to tell him that this is the way of the world.

In another room, the ladies and Despina also check in with each other: Fiordiligi confesses that she has fallen in love with Ferrando; Dorabella responds by describing love as an irresistible little rascal. Fiordiligi decides to resist her inclinations and go to the battlefield disguised as a man to join her Guglielmo; she hopes that Dorabella will join her. Ferrando and Guglielmo watch this decision with differing feelings: Ferrando decides to redouble his efforts, not out of love for Fiordiligi, but out of jealousy of Guglielmo, whose fiancée seems to be more faithful than his own. In an elaborate duet, Fiordiligi breaks down and agrees to be with Ferrando. She leaves: Guglielmo is horrified. Don Alfonso says that the solution is simply to marry the original women – if that's not what they want, then they can remain forever celibate. He persuades the men that they really do love their "plucked hens", and they should take them as they are; these ones have only done what all women would do under the same circumstances, since "Così fan tutte."

In the second-act finale, the wrong double wedding is about to take place: the wrong lovers (with Guglielmo grumbling in the background) sing a toast to the future. Despina, dressed as a notary, starts the formal proceedings. All of a sudden a military band announce the return of the original lovers. The men rush out in the ensuing confusion. They return dressed as themselves, and pretend surprise at the pale faces and horrified expressions they find.

Despina reveals that she is not a notary; the men find the half-signed wedding contract, the ladies confess, the gentlemen reveal their part in the trick. Don Alfonso points out that although they were deceived, the deceit revealed some truths, and that now they can marry with some accumulated wisdom. Despina says that she's ashamed of how far the trick went. The original couples re-unite and sing a maxim about the importance of approaching life from the perspective of reason.

COMMENTARY

Origins

The facts about the commission and compositional process of this opera are at least as sketchy as, if not more so than, those for the other two Da Ponte operas. Mozart was clearly working on the opera in late 1789, since he mentioned it in a begging letter to a generous fellow-Mason, Michael Puchberg, in late December, saying that he would shortly receive a 200-ducat fee for the work, and that this should serve as a kind of collateral for the loan he was requesting from Puchberg. On 31 December there was a rehearsal of the work to which both Puchberg and Joseph Haydn were invited; they were also invited to the orchestral rehearsal on 20 January. That is the entire extent of Mozart's own mention of the work. Da Ponte also says less about it than about either *Figaro* or *Don Giovanni*, mentioning only that it holds "third place among the sisters" born of Mozart with Da Ponte's assistance, and implying in an early, and factually problematic, version of his memoirs that the success of *Don Giovanni* in Prague stimulated Mozart to ask Da Ponte for another libretto.[68] Contextual sources, however, tell us more about the origins of the work. It seems, for example that Da Ponte originally wrote the libretto (then entitled simply *La scuola degli amanti* ["The School for Lovers"]) for Salieri, not for Mozart. Salieri's sketches for a couple of numbers survive in the Austrian National Library, and these confirm the account of Vincent and Mary Novello, who visited Mozart's widow in 1829 and learned that Salieri was particularly jealous of Mozart's success in setting this libretto.[69] Manuscript detective work also tells us that (at least in Act I) Mozart composed the ensembles first – probably not to test the abilities of his singers, since he knew all the voices pretty well – but perhaps, since the opera contains so many of them, to form a kind of frame for the arias.[70]

Not atypically, either for Mozart himself or for operatic life in general at this time, the final stages of the opera's preparation seem to have been hectic and politically complicated. Mozart's student Joseph Eybler left an account (in his 1826 autobiography) of the late stages of preparation:

For when Mozart wrote the opera *Così fan tutte*, and was not yet finished with the instrumentation, and time was short besides, he requested that I rehearse the singers, and in particular the two female vocalists Fer[r]arese and Villeneuve; whereby I had opportunity enough to become acquainted with theater life, with its disorders, cabals and so forth. . . .[71]

The premiere of the opera took place in January 1790, but after only five performances the theater closed to honor the death of Joseph II, and the opera did not reappear until the summer, when it received another five performances. It was well received: audiences seem to have been sizeable for those performances.[72] The initial cast included Adriana Ferrarese del Bene as Fiordiligi; she was Da Ponte's mistress, and also played Susanna in the 1789–90 revival of *Figaro*. Her place of origin (Ferrara) might also account for the libretto's description of the two ladies as "donne ferrarese". Louise Villeneuve, sometimes (without evidence) referred to as Ferrarese's sister, sang the part of Dorabella: Mozart had written concert arias for her but she had not appeared in any of his operas before this. The Ferrando was Vincenzo Calvesi, a longstanding member of the Burgtheater's opera buffa troupe, and the Guglielmo was Francesco Benucci, Mozart's first Figaro and perhaps the best-loved basso buffo of his time. Don Alfonso was played by Francesco Bussani, a Mozart familiar; he had premiered the doubled roles of Masetto and the Commendatore in the 1788 *Don Giovanni*, and of Bartolo and the gardener Antonio in *Figaro*. Despina was played by his wife, Dorothea Bussani, the first Cherubino, and a gifted comic actress.[73] The audience would, then, have had "histories" for each of these characters that would doubtless have played into their understandings of the new roles.

Of the three works Da Ponte wrote for Mozart, *Così* is the only one not based on a single previous source. It is, rather, a compilation of references to and glosses on a variety of previous sources from both the recent operatic tradition and the more highbrow world of Italian and classical literature. Such sources include the Ovidian myth of Cephalus and Procris, in which a husband tests his wife's fidelity by appearing to her in disguise; and various cantos of Ariosto's pastoral epic *Orlando furioso*, in which the elements of the bet and the doubling of the men and the women are both anticipated.[74] Da Ponte's language, full of both mythological references and paraphrases of sentences in *Orlando furioso* – a lot of learning very lightly worn, it must be said – provide the clues to these sources.[75]

The recent operatic repertory in Vienna also provided either points of reference or sources (it's hard to know which). The most striking and politically pertinent comparison is the opera *La grotta di Trofonio*, by Salieri and the librettist Giambattista Casti, Metastasio's successor as imperial court poet.

Salieri was a rival of Mozart, and Da Ponte makes it quite clear in his memoirs that Casti was his rival. In this opera, whose libretto wears its learning quite heavily (with footnotes, no less) two young women, sisters, one serious and bookish and the other trivial and light-hearted, have their temperaments changed by entering the cave of Trofonio, a kind of wizard. Their lovers are confused by this change, and ask the magician to change their temperaments as well, but by this time the girls have had their characters returned to the original. The confusions are sorted out in short order. This opera was premiered in 1785, and stayed in the Burgtheater repertory until 1788. The two operas shared singers, though mostly in different kinds of roles: Benucci (Guglielmo) played the magician Trofonio, Calvesi (Ferrando) played Artemidoro, the serious male lover, and Francesco Bussani (Alfonso) played Plistene, the less serious male lover. In other words, there were enough connections in both the material and the presentation of this work to make the audience aware of the comparison; they may or may not have known that Da Ponte's *La scuola degli amanti* had first been offered to Salieri; those in the know would certainly have found the connections between *Trofonio* and *Così* particularly delicious. Another, older opera in the Viennese repertory that audiences could have connected with *Così* was *Il curioso indiscreto* by the composer Pasquale Anfossi and possibly the librettist Giovanni Bertati, author of the most immediate source for *Don Giovanni*. In this opera, performed at the Burgtheater in 1783, and for which Mozart wrote two substitute arias, a marquis persuades the younger (and presumably more appealing) Contino to test the fidelity of his wife, a test which, of course, she fails.

Reputation

As the previous paragraphs suggest, *Così* had multiple layers of resonance for its first audiences. And its first Viennese performances, though not tremendously numerous, were well received. Even the diarist Count Zinzendorf, who did not fail to comment when the music did not please, called the work "charming." Early Northern German reception was less enthusiastic: the Berlin *Annalen des Theaters* of 1 May 1791 famously reported on a German language production that it was "a miserable Italian product with the powerful, sublime music of a Mozart." And from then on, throughout the nineteenth century and into the twentieth, the opera was dogged by the notion that Mozart was burdened by a second-rate, silly, trivial, immoral, Italian, libretto. Richard Wagner in 1851 admired Mozart's "incapacity" to write music as good as that for *Figaro* and *Don Giovanni* to such a shameful libretto, opining that had the music been as powerful, it would have desecrated the art.[76] It was performed much less frequently than either of the other two Da Ponte operas, and when it was performed it was not infrequently announced as a revival. Numerous attempts were made to bring the words into line with the perceived beauty and moral purity of the music, including an 1863 French adaptation of Shakespeare's *Love's Labour's Lost* to the music of *Così*. An English review of this version commented, "What think you of Shakespeare's *Love's Labour* [sic] *Lost* tormented into a libretto to suit Mozart's music?"[77] The grounds for objection here are not entirely clear, but the writer was certainly busier defending Shakespeare against the assaults of the French arrangers than Da Ponte against alteration. Indeed, an earlier English version entitled *Tit for Tat* had some success; here the women know that the men are tricking them and play along as revenge.[78] This version was said to do more justice to "the sex" than the original, to demonstrate that women "had their share in the general moral improvement" of the nineteenth century, and to be respectable enough for the English stage. A similar attempt to ennoble the opera and be less "degrading" to women than the original was made in Stuttgart in 1858 (this followed four previous adaptations in the same theater); in this version the gentlemen in disguise seduce their own girlfriends, which allows the women to be in fact faithful, and their "psychological motives agree with truth." This alteration was also thought to make the opera more appropriate both for young people and for the German nation overall.[79]

By the end of the nineteenth century there were increasing attempts to perform the opera with Da Ponte's text, but it did not join its "sisters" in the canon of routinely performed Mozart operas until three decades into the twentieth century; it is generally agreed that the Glyndebourne production of 1934 was the turning point, especially in English-speaking countries. Since then, it has become increasingly appreciated. Nevertheless, it is still also regarded as exceptional among Mozart's mature operas: it is described as everything from the "most enigmatic," the "most disturbing," and the "most artificial" to the "most beautiful"; and directors and producers have not hesitated to change the ending so that the "wrong" pairs (Dorabella and Guglielmo, Fiordiligi and Ferrando) end up coupled, or, as in the Peter Sellars production of 1986, (filmed a few years later) any kind of coupling seems like an impossible feat, and the characters whirl around as isolated monads.

Libretto, music and the truths of Così

Whether or not critics, audiences, and directors find it troubling any more, there is without doubt a tension between the extraordinary and conspicuous beauty of Mozart's music, which most listeners take to be emblematic of some kind of deep emotional truth (whether ironic or literal), and the neat symmetries, pat conclusions, psychological implausibilities and cold-blooded experimentation of Da Ponte's libretto. And this tension is felt all the more because it is only one of a series of more or less explicit tensions or oppositions which in a sense constitute one of the main topics of the opera.

Da Ponte's libretto is in fact anything but trivial. It is both a brilliant display of wit and learning on its own terms and the perfect frame for Mozart's music. Its glassy surface seems to conceal, but in fact reveals its larger points, and it is this play of surface and depth to which Mozart's music so perfectly responds. The set-up of the story seems entirely conventional: two young ladies, one more serious/seria, the other more frivolous/buffa, and a corresponding pair of young gentlemen with whom the young ladies are in love. A maidservant provides both a social and a dramatic foil to the young ladies; and an older man provides the preventative to the marriage that would otherwise take place immediately. This sets the drama in motion. But right away the very perfection of this set-up reveals a problem, which is that the older man is not the conventional guardian or father figure interested either in snaring a girl for himself or ensuring that she marries money or status. He is an "old philosopher," whatever that means. And without a father figure the ladies are, in eighteenth-century terms, remarkably cast loose from the normal social context that would define them. Nor is it explicitly a fantasy or fairy tale, like Salieri's *La grotta di Trofonio,* in which the ladies are equally unmoored from their social location, but where the frankly mythological setting makes that ungroundedness more plausible (if that is the word). *Così* is set in Naples, and the sisters are said to be from Ferrara, so the setting is quite determinedly realistic. However it is not clear what the characters are doing in Naples, and why they are without the normal structures of family or other social authority within which women usually lived. Cultural historian John Rosselli has suggested that the ladies are singers living in temporary lodgings while they perform at the famous opera house there; he bases this idea on their Ferrarese origins (the pun on the name of Da Ponte's singer-mistress, who played Fiordiligi) and on the self-reflexivity of the work as a whole.[80] However, the complete lack of any reference to a theatrical context makes this a bit far-fetched. It seems more likely that the apparent realism of the setting was actually intended to point out the "problem" of the ladies' position in society, and thus to indicate the libretto's status as a game or puzzle rather than a depiction of reality.

Da Ponte's use of language is similarly subtle and complex. On the one hand, the work sets up a closed system consisting of the wager, the seduction of the opposite girlfriends, the dramatically necessary contrast between Dorabella's speedy change of heart and Fiordiligi's slower and more painful conversion, and the placing of the young people's passions between Don Alfonso's elevated philosophy and Despina's worldly-wise cynicism. On the other hand, as mentioned above, the libretto makes frequent, conspicuous, funny and sometimes out of proportion references to a whole world of literature and archetypical human experience. Dorabella invokes the Eumenides, or Furies, in her first response to the gentlemen's departure; Guglielmo says he would rather marry Charon, the keeper of the Underworld, than Fiordiligi, once she has betrayed him; in an earlier moment of optimism, however, he refers to her as a Penelope, Odysseus's faithful and long-suffering wife. Don Alfonso's statement that female fidelity is a phoenix is on the one had an obviously mythological reference, but also invokes specific Metastasian texts, thus calling up opera seria's elevated world of love and duty. One could simply take these references as a sign of (especially) the young people's overblown sense of their own emotions, and indeed on the superficial level, this reading works perfectly well. But one can also read the substrate of reference to life-and-death matters as a sign of the thin ice on which the whole edifice of the opera (and by extension the whole edifice of social life) is precariously balanced.

The *lieto fine* (happy end) is similarly clever. Buffa operas all end with weddings, and many of the couples hitched together in those conclusions seem less than well-matched. Even within Mozart's operas, one might well wonder about the Count's capacity to stay faithful to the Countess in *Figaro*, or Zerlina's interest in an exclusive bond with Masetto in *Don Giovanni*, let alone the promise of a happy life to Violante and the Contino in *La finta giardiniera*, when the latter has already beaten the former senseless and left her for dead. But the presumption in these cases, as with the vast majority of opera buffa happy ends, is that both the characters and the audience paper over the troubles revealed in the body of the opera and that the end is about society's capacity to repair itself, right its imbalances, and produce manageable lives for most people. The end of *Così* may seem to say the same thing, but its relation to the ending-conventions of the genre suggests that its message is more complicated. For example, most operas in the repertory immediately surrounding *Così*, – a repertory that formed the audience's expectations – allowed a relationship that was the result of a "conversion experience" to stick. In *Così* that would mean that Fiordiligi would marry Ferrando and Dorabella would marry Guglielmo. A return to an original pairing whether happy or unhappy, was in these other operas usually the result of class considerations, whereas that is quite clearly not the case in *Così*. The end in *Così* is about affection rather than class, but it is not about blind passion, and it is not about making a convenient end by clapping the lid on the cauldron of problems implicit in human relations, whether intimate or more broadly social. Rather, it speaks in favour of the more honest but also more painful attitude of acknowledging and accepting the impossibility of perfection – or even of real goodness. It is not a cynical end, though, despite Don Alfonso's skepticism about human and especially female nature and Despina's disillusioned opinions about men. Despina's admission at the end of the opera that she herself was duped, which Mozart sets in a completely different rhythm from everyone else's vocal line at the same moment, so that it is as clearly audible as possible, is the key to this. Throughout the opera she has been the personification of "free love" (some have read her as Cupid, or Nature itself). She argues earlier in the opera that love is about "pleasure, convenience, taste, joy, diversion, passing time, [and] jollity"; that men selfishly use women so they can enjoy those things, and that women should follow their own whims for the same reason, discarding partners whenever they happen to feel like it. But when the couples return to their original partners, as Don Alfonso knew they would, Despina's philosophy of throwaway relationships, of the pursuit of immediate and selfish pleasure, is rendered as useless as the lovers' original philosophy of pure, intense, exclusive and permanent passion, and her comment at the end that she has a future in further trickery rings rather hollow. The correct attitude, according to Da Ponte, is perfectly explicit on the surface of the opera and recited by everyone at the end: "Happy is he who can take everything for its opposite and let reason guide him through events. Those things which make others weep are for him a reason for laughter, and in the middle of the tumult of the world, he will find lovely calm."

But even here, there is more than one layer. Don Alfonso has no apparent personal interest in love of any sort; he may be happy, but his happiness is unlike that of most people – when he tells the gentlemen that looking for perfection in a woman is recipe for a life alone, he is not recommending that life. Although he is much more explicit about the reasons for his actions than is Don Giovanni, like that character he remains a psychological blank. Don Giovanni desires all women, makes distinctions among them only to the extent of being able to assume appropriate "voices" for the prosecution of his aims, and thus has no core "personality" beyond his desires. Don Alfonso is similarly unable to make distinctions between actual people, but it is not because he is desire incarnate; rather it is because he is the opposite. He has no personal desires beyond proving his theorems. Neither character has a self-expository aria; both reveal themselves only in relation to others; both are motivated by a principle, whether reason or pleasure, and evidently neither Mozart nor Da Ponte saw fit to have them solicit the audience's sympathy by explaining themselves alone on stage. The point here is not that Don Alfonso's superficial contentment masks a deep unhappiness, but rather that the libretto seems to say that the simultaneous awareness and control of passion – the interaction between surface calm or smoothness with deeper tumult or complication – is the ideal. (The point is also not that Don Alfonso was a consciously-crafted "anti-Giovanni," but rather that both figures explore in remarkably concentrated ways the nature of power, which had long been at the centre of opera buffa's concerns.)

This reading suggests not that the libretto simply "left room" for Mozart's music, but rather that it demanded the overflow of beauty that Mozart provided. That is, the often-perceived mismatch of the music's "excesses" of feeling with the libretto's celebration of disinterested reason and its spirit of pure experimentation is in fact analogous to the ideas of surface and depth that are central to the libretto itself. Three moments of "excessive" musical beauty illustrate this point. They are the two ensembles of the farewell sequence, the quintet "Di scrivermi ogni giorno" (Write to me every day") and the trio "Soave sia il vento" ("Let the breeze be gentle"), and the canonic "champagne" quartet "E, nel tuo, nel mio bicchiero" ("And in your, in my, glass") in the second act finale. Each of these ensembles halts the action and expresses sentiments that are in one way or another more than the occasion demands. In the quintet, the ladies are more grief-stricken than they have any reason to be, and the gentlemen are inevitably caught up in their misery, partly to play along with the trick, but partly out of a mixture of worry at the outcome of the trick and no-doubt genuine sympathy at the ladies' grief. In the trio, the murmurings of the strings as the gentlemen sail out of sight invoke a world of mythological forces – breezes with good or ill intentions, for example; and the twice-heard painful dissonances on the word "desir" (desire) suggest a scope of feeling far beyond the house in Naples accommodating two silly young women and their servant. The "champagne" quartet (inexplicably cut by Mozart for the first performance) does not express feelings in excess of what we now know the characters are capable of, but it is excessive in that it holds the action up at a crucial moment, and suspends the characters in a moment that at least two of them and the audience know must be broken. Each of these numbers has some musical feature that makes its beauty conspicuous – that is, they don't just happen to be lovely pieces because Mozart couldn't help himself. In the two farewell ensembles, the accompaniment is unusually atmospheric: the murmuring strings in the trio, in the quintet the combination of continuous long notes suggesting an infinite trajectory and the more metronomic short notes in the other parts, and in the final quartet, the use of canon (round). These moments are all poised on the hinges of the action, as the trick begins and ends, and Mozart's music makes it entirely clear that the superficial logistics of the trick are only a small part of the real action of this opera.

Within the experiment itself, Mozart uses the well-understood conventions of opera buffa to develop gradations of irony, which also link the quality of the music with the potentialities of the libretto. Dorabella's "Smanie implacabile" ("Unappeasable ravings"), sung immediately she learns of the gentlemen's departure, is usually taken as an unambiguous parody of a seria rage aria. The critical tradition is more ambiguous about "Come scoglio" ("Like a rock"), Fiordiligi's equivalent to "Smanie implacabili," where she asserts the eternal unchangeability of her affections; some critics have seen it as pure parody, others have seen it as a more transparent sign of Fiordiligi's integrity and purity. It does, however, clearly make use of the seria tradition of the simile aria, as well as of the buffa tendency to lampoon that tradition. And although Fiordiligi is indubitably sincere as she sings it, it is hard not to see in its vocal and textual excesses the signs of her undoing. Her second act Rondò, "Per pietà ben mio" in which she begs the absent Guglielmo's pardon for the infidelity she knows she will commit, is rarely taken as ironic. However, it takes the longstanding tradition of the serious aria with obbligato wind instrument to unprecedented extremes, both of vocal effort and of instrumental prominence, with the French horn both serving to support and decorate Fiordiligi's vocal line, and punningly reminding the audience of the cuckoldry that is about to ensue. (Cuckolds – men whose wives cheat on them – were said to grow horns.) The ambiguity of the horn in this aria is emblematic of the delicate balances of musical meaning throughout the opera; and the way it refers to various traditions simultaneously is closely analogous to the witty and profound referentiality of Da Ponte's text.

The nineteenth century found the opera immoral because it "degraded" women. More recent criticism has tended to avoid the question of morality, finding largely aesthetic pleasure in the work. Another reading might return to moral questions and find this work perhaps the most morally engaged of all the Mozart operas because to a unique extent the music suggests its own point of view, independent of the characters' superficial interactions or trajectories, and we perceive that point of view with an emotional immediacy that lends it the force of a lesson. This lesson suggests first of all that beauty (and thus the good that beauty may symbolize) is always fleeting and precarious. The most conspicuously beautiful moments are both brief and at the most delicate moments in the plot, for example, and the conspicuously "beautiful" device of the obbligato horn at a moment of extreme sentiment is both beautiful *and* potentially comic. The lesson thus also suggests, in close collaboration with the libretto, that the fully human life requires a perpetual double consciousness – a capacity to be seduced into a heedless state of being by beauty (or love) and an equal capacity to step back from that state and take heed of social norms.

CHAPTER 6

A BRIEF NOTE ON THE UNFINISHED AND MISCELLANEOUS OPERAS

Apollo et Hyacinthus. Latin intermezzo to the drama *Clementia Croesi.* Libretto by Father Rufinius Widl. Salzburg University, 13 May 1767.

CHARACTERS:

Oebalus, King of Lacedemonia	Tenor
Melia, Oebalus's daughter	Soprano
Hyacinthus, Oebalus's son	Soprano
Apollo, guest of Oebalus	Alto
Zephyrus, friend of Hyacinthus	Alto
Two sacrificial priests of Apollo	Basses
Chorus	

This three-part work would have been performed between the five acts of the Latin play (hence the generic title intermezzo, or intermedium). The first act preceded the beginning of the play.

SYNOPSIS

The opera opens with preparations for a sacrifice to Apollo. Zephyrus lists a series of gods he would as soon worship. The chorus offers its prayers to Apollo, but a storm gathers and destroys the altar; Oebalus and Melia understand this as a sign of Apollo's displeasure. Hyacinthus, however, has a more nuanced understanding of the way the gods rule; sometimes by fear and sometimes by love. Apollo appears in shepherd's clothing. He expresses affection for both Melia and Hyacinthus, and Zephyrus is worried that Apollo will take away his friend. Apollo then sings an aria explaining that like a shepherd he protects his people.

Act II (performed between Acts II and III of the spoken play) opens with Oebalus and Melia celebrating Apollo's affection for them. Melia sings a virtuoso aria expressing her happiness. Zephyrus announces that Hyacinth has been felled while playing discus with Apollo and Zephyrus. Zephyrus attributes the accident to Apollo, who made a bad throw, but in fact he himself is guilty of the accident. He hopes by this lie to wrest Melia's hand from Apollo. Apollo appears, however, accuses Zephyrus of lying, and sends him to the winds. Apollo and Melia sing a duet in which she is still furious and he tries to convince her of his innocence.

Act III (performed between Acts IV and V of the play) begins with Oebalus finding Hyacinth, who is not yet quite dead. With his last breaths he confirms that it was Zephyrus who killed him. Oebalus sings an aria comparing himself to a ship tossed around on a turbulent sea. Melia and Oebalus worry that they will lose the protection of Apollo and sing a duet to that effect. Apollo, however, appears, and makes a flower grow where Hyacinth fell. The opera ends with the three remaining characters celebrating the return of peace after so much turbulence.

COMMENTARY

Apollo und Hyacinth was Mozart's first opera. He wrote it during the brief period of time between returning from the family's first "prodigy tour" (1763–6) and their second extended visit to Vienna (1767–9). Although it is in many ways like a small opera seria it does not really fall into any of the three genres that encompass the rest of Mozart's operatic output. It is a "school drama," part of an annual celebration at the Salzburg *Gymnasium* (high school) where the students of each class performed Latin dramas to show their proficiency in the language. The libretto, like the play performed in conjunction with the opera, was written by Father Rufinius Widl, the teacher of the third-year class (the "Syntaxisten"). Father Widl presumably chose the opera's story and wrote the text in part to reinforce the Ovid story that the students had probably read, and in part to forge a connection with the accompanying play; both dramas feature the accidental killing of a friend, for example.[1] Widl's version differs from Ovid's tale in the *Metamorphoses* in which neither Zephyrus nor Melia appears, and where Apollo does in fact kill Hyacinth. Zephyrus is found in other ancient texts, but Melia is Widl's own addition, perhaps to make a parallel with a female character in *Clementia Croesi*,[2] or perhaps to make the work more conventionally operatic.

The first performers included a 23-year-old theology student playing Oebalus, and boy singers from the court chapel singing the other roles. It is striking that other than the boy who sang Hyacinthus, who was 12, the singers (two altos and a soprano) were 16, 17 and 18. Puberty occurred considerably later then than it does now, so these singers had the advantage of five or six more years of vocal training than a boy singer today might have, and the expectation of such training shows in some of the vocal writing – Melia's aria of jubilation, "Laetari, iocari" ("He continues to rejoice and be mirthful") is an obvious example of this. It would also not have been particularly unusual to have a boy playing a female role; church and chapel choirs were all male, and in Rome it was still the norm to have male singers playing all the female roles in opera. Castrati were still an essential part of the operatic scene and thus, overall, gender was construed in less rigidly binary ways than it is in most circumstances today.

The music of *Apollo und Hyacinth* is a mixture of astonishing competence for an 11-year-old, and lovely by any standards. There was not a lot of dramatic tension for Mozart to work with; the highest drama occurs when Zephyrus lies about who killed Hyacinth and then admits the truth in an aside, and then when Apollo appears to accuse him of the deed; all these moments occur in secco recitative (recitative with only keyboard and cello as accompaniment),[3] and so the possibilities for musical embodiment of the drama are extremely limited. Apollo's thunderbolt at the beginning is a stage effect with no reflection in the music. Nevertheless, the opening choruses show Mozart's experience writing church music: the vocal parts are largely homophonic (hymn style, with everyone singing the same rhythm), but the orchestral parts elaborate this relatively simple music with significant rhythmic variety and a little colorful chromaticism (notes not in the basic key of the piece). Most of the arias have some fairly difficult coloratura towards the end of sections; this kind of writing, which was more common in opera seria than in comic opera, suits the "high style" – that is, mythical, distant in time and place, noble in theme – content. The final duet between Oebalus and Melia, "Natus cadit" ("My son is felled"), where they imagine that Apollo will no longer protect them, is the most beautiful number in the opera. It shows Mozart's melodic gift, but perhaps more presciently, it shows his capacity to make an idea grow; Oebalus's opening tune is very appealing, but slightly fragmentary; when Melia enters, she sings a varied version of it that coheres beautifully, and provides a wonderful commentary on the material that Oebalus has presented. The texture of the accompaniment is also strikingly gorgeous – muted strings with the first violins playing the tune, second violins playing harp-like chords on the offbeats, divided violas providing a gentle murmuring background, and the cellos plucking the bass line. A pair of horns glues the sound together with the background harmonies. It is the kind of moment that would turn into the slow movement of the C major piano concerto, K. 467 ("Elvira Madigan") or, from a melodic point of view, the "Laudate dominum" from the Solemn Vespers, K. 339.

THE UNFINISHED OPERAS

Mozart left three operas unfinished: the Singspiel *Zaide* of 1779/80, and two buffa operas: *L'oca del Cairo* (The Goose of Cairo) from 1783, and *Lo sposo deluso* (The Deluded Bridegroom) of 1785. *Zaide* is almost complete. *L'oca del Cairo* has a complete trio and another six numbers sketched, and *Lo sposo deluso* has only the overture and two ensembles complete, plus two partial arias. Mozart's work on the two buffa operas show his continued interest, following on the success of *Die Entführung* (1782) in writing another opera for the Burgtheater.

Zaide

This work was started in 1779, and evidently written "on spec". Mozart's correspondence suggests that he initially hoped that Joseph II's National Singspiel enterprise would stage it, but he got no response;[4] when he was in Munich writing *Idomeneo* he asked his father to send it to him, hoping that someone there would be interested,[5] and then finally, once he was living in Vienna, he thought that the intriguers and cabals in Joseph's theatrical establishment had nixed it, but also that it was probably not suited to the more comic taste of that city.[6] By that time, he and Stephanie were in any case negotiating about the libretto for *Die Entführung aus dem Serail*, and *Zaide* never saw the light of day during Mozart's lifetime.

The libretto is an adaptation by the Mozarts' family friend Johann Schachtner of *Das Serail*, a Singspiel set by Joseph Frieberth in 1777. Mozart himself never mentioned the opera by name, and the title *Zaide* was first applied by the publisher Johann Andre in 1838 when he brought out the first available score of the work. The story is set in an Oriental seraglio. Zaide is the Sultan's favourite, who falls in love with Gomatz, a slave, who reciprocates her love. They escape, aided by the Sultan's slavemaster, who is a renegade (that is, a defected or captured Christian working for the Ottoman rulers). All three are recaptured, thanks to the Sultan's faithful Turks, but in the denouement it turns out that the renegade saved the Sultan's life some years ago, that Gomatz and Zaide are brother and sister, and, indeed, the children of the renegade, who turns out to be Prince Rothschiero, captured at sea when Zaide and Gomatz were children.

Mozart wrote fifteen numbers from this work, with the usual eclectic stylistic mixture of Singspiels, ranging from Zaide's gorgeous song-like lullaby, "Ruhe sanft" ("Rest peacefully"), which is often sung as a separate number,[7] to the bass-voiced renegade Allazim's quite virtuosic music, to Gomatz's two "melologhi"— numbers like accompanied recitative but with the voice part spoken rather than sung. This latter is a technique used in some of the more ambitious North German Singspiels by Georg Benda and others. *Die Entführung* includes no such advanced techniques, perhaps out of a concern for Viennese taste.

L'oca del Cairo

This opera buffa was started in 1783, after Mozart had reportedly looked at "at least a hundred and more" Italian libretti, finding none to his satisfaction.[8] This libretto was written by Giambattista Varesco in Salzburg, presumably at Mozart's request, so there is considerable correspondence about it: Mozart wrote to his father, who passed on the information to Varesco. The correspondence shows the extent to which Mozart was willing to insist on changes in the libretto in order to get what he wanted. His primary criteria for this libretto, as for all his operas, were dramatic effect, not boring the audience, and the "naturalness" that would help achieve these two aims. Thus he objected to Varesco's device of having the two principal female characters locked up in a tower, visible but without any music, for the majority of the opera – one act's worth of that would be enough, but nearly two was out of the question.[9] In the same train of thought, he confessed some trepidation about the device of having one of the characters disguised in a mechanical goose: whatever disguises were necessary would be more pleasing and natural if they were human.[10] He also had trouble with the notion that the two captive females would sing the same aria one after the other, preferring an ensemble. About two months into the project, it is clear he was pretty much giving up, partly because of lack of opportunity, and partly because of dissatisfaction with the libretto. He writes "At present I haven't the slightest intention of producing [the work]: I have works to compose which *at the moment* are bringing in money, but will not do so later. The opera will always bring in some; and besides, the more time I take, the better it will be. As it is, the impression I have gained from Varesco's text is that he has hurried too much, and I hope that in time he will see this himself. That is why I should like to see the opera *as a whole* . . . Then we can make drastic alterations. If you were to hear what I have composed, then you would wish, as I do, that my work should not be spoilt! . . . I guarantee that in all the operas [by other composers] which are to be performed until mine is finished, not a single idea will resemble one of mine."[11]

The story of this opera takes place in the household of Don Pippo, who believes himself a widower, his wife Pantea having disappeared some years ago. He has locked his daughter Celidora up in a tower with a companion, Lavina, in order that she not also disappear. Celidora has had an offer from a Count Lionetto, whom Pippo wants her to marry because this Count claims to be able to offer her the famous golden goose of Cairo. Celidora, however, already has a lover, Biondello, as does Lavina – hers is Caladrino. Biondello has a bet with Don Pippo that he will be able to rescue Celidora within a year: it is now the last day of that year. A first escape attempt is foiled in the first act finale. In the second act, Pantea returns, in disguise, with a large mechanical goose, in which Biondello hides, which allows him into the tower. Don Pippo is foiled and the lovers are united. A servant couple consisting of the manipulative minx Auretta, and the lovesick bumpkin Chichibio, complete the cast.

Mozart wrote some of a buffa duet for the two servants, part of an aria for Auretta, in which she pretends to pine, part of a buffo aria for Chichibio in which he complains about the infidelity of women, the beginning of a buffa aria for Don Pippo in which he prepares for the wedding of Celidora and the Count Lionetto, a lovely quartet for the two pairs of lovers, and a draft of the exciting first act finale. Most of these numbers are not fully orchestrated; there have been several attempts to flesh them out to make a complete first act.

Lo sposo deluso

Written in 1783–4, this work is based on the intermezzo *Le donne rivali*, possibly written by Giuseppe Petrosellini, and set by Domenico Cimarosa in Rome in 1780. There is no clear reference to this work in Mozart's correspondence. The story is a conventional buffa intrigue involving an older man, Bocconio, to whom the young and beautiful Eugenia is engaged, despite being in love with Asdrubale. Asdrubale is also loved by the vain Bettina. Eugenia's tutor Geroglio is in love with Metilde, a diva, who is also in love with Asdrubale. She feigns friendship with Eugenia. The cast is completed by Pulcherio, a mocker of women. The outcome is clear from this arrangement of characters: Eugenia and Asdrubale overcome Bocconio's objections by a mixture of trickery and fidelity, Geroglio and Metilde match up at the last moment, and Bettina extends her hand to Pulcherio. Bocconio is left alone, blessing the unions once the young folk have agreed to keep loving him.[12]

In addition to the overture, Mozart wrote a jolly buffo opening quartet, which prominently features Pulcherio's laughter at the idea of Bocconio's marriage; a draft of a seria aria for Eugenia, for which role Mozart imagined Nancy Storace, his first Susanna; part of a wonderful mocking aria for Pulcherio, who was to be sung by Francesco Bussani, the Bartolo and Antonio in the first *Figaro*; and a beautiful trio for Eugenia, Asdrubale and Bocconio sung after Bocconio has offered Eugenia a ring, Asdrubale has entered unexpectedly, and everyone is confounded. (Bocconio was to have been sung by the inimitable buffo Francesco Benucci, the first Figaro, and Asdrubale by Stefano Mandini, the first Count in *Figaro*.)

CHAPTER 7

MOZART'S THEATERS

Mozart's operas were produced in circumstances that in some respects seem perfectly familiar today, and in others seem so different as to be almost incomprehensible. Among the more familiar features are the use of star singers collected at considerable expense from geographically distant places to grace a particular stage; the audience's interest in spectacle and vocal prowess; and the endless jockeying for power and authority among the administrators, creators and performers of opera. Among the larger number of unfamiliar elements are the often loud and inattentive behavior of the audiences, combined with raucous demands for encores when an aria had gone well; the economic underpinnings of the theaters, which relied on the aristocracy to rent (or occasionally purchase) boxes for an entire season or more; the physical set-up of the theater, in which the boxes had a better view of each other than of the stage; the formulaic and exaggerated acting style; and the relatively dim lighting throughout the stage and the auditorium.

Mozart's operas were premiered in a wide variety of locations: the University at Salzburg (*Apollo et Hyacinthus*) the Archbishop's palace (Residenz) at Salzburg (*La finta semplice, Il Sogno di Scipione*), the Teatro Regio Ducal in Milan (*Mitridate, Ascanio in Alba, Lucio Silla*), the Residenz (Cuvilliés) Theater in Munich (*Idomeneo*), and the Salvatortheater in the same city (*La finta giardiniera*), the Burgtheater in Vienna (*Die Entführung aus dem Serail, The Marriage of Figaro, Così fan tutte*), the Orangerie at Schönbrunn Palace (*The Impresario*), the Nostitz Theater in Prague (*Don Giovanni* and *La clemenza di Tito*), and the Freihaus Theater auf der Wieden (*The Magic Flute*). Few of these locations still survive: the Residenz palace at Salzburg has been lovingly restored in rococo style, but we do not know in which room(s) the operas were performed, and the Cuvilliés Theater in Munich, though destroyed during World War II, was rebuilt afterwards to the original auditorium specifications and using some of the original fittings, which had been stored during the war.[1] The Nostitz Theater in Prague (now renamed the

Estates Theater) remains in something like its original condition.[2] However, the Teatro Regio Ducal in Milan was destroyed by fire in 1776, to be replaced by the still-extant La Scala; the old Burgtheater in Vienna was demolished in 1867[3] and replaced by a newer structure in the 1880s, of which the current Burgtheater is a postwar rebuilding; and the Theater auf der Wieden was replaced in the early nineteenth century by the Theater an der Wien. Even the extant theaters, however, have preserved only the general appearance of the eighteenth-century theaters; candle fittings were of course replaced, first with gas and then with electricity; seats have been added in the parterre where there may have been only benches; the boxes were redesigned, and the stage machinery was modernized. Fortunately, several small eighteenth-century theaters (none directly associated with Mozart) remain in their original condition because the aristocrats on whose estates they lay lost interest and walked away from them leaving the original materials in place. The most famous of these is the 1766 Drottningholm theater just outside Stockholm; Ingmar Bergman's famous 1975 film of *The Magic Flute* was filmed there, and there have been numerous productions from there recorded on video. There is also good documentation about the theater.[4] Another Swedish theater from this period is the one at Gripsholm castle, built in 1782. There is also a relatively recently discovered theater (built 1766) at Český Krumlov in the Czech Republic, which provides more information about eighteenth-century theatrical practice.[5] Much information about Mozart's own theaters and the physical circumstances of production, then, must be gleaned by inference from these indirectly related sources and from the contemporary context. We do, however, know some particulars of some of the theaters in which he worked, and it is worth laying some of those out before proceeding to a more general picture of operatic theater life in the late eighteenth century.

THE TEATRO REGIO DUCAL

The first theater in Mozart's life about which we know quite a lot is the Regio Ducal in Milan. This theater was built in 1717 as part of the Ducal Palace complex, replacing a theater that had burned down in 1708. It was pervasively renovated in 1771, but there continued to be complaints about its inadequacy for the task at hand until 1776. Its stage was about 22.5 meters wide and about 45.5 deep, which was unusually long and narrow for the time.[6] Moreover, the arrangements for scenery were such that the placement of the flats may have forced the performers to the front of the proscenium.[7] Like most European theaters at the time, its auditorium was a horseshoe shape, with vertically-stacked rows of boxes around the horseshoe.[8] Unlike in other theaters, each of these boxes had its own antechamber where servants could assemble meals (cooking was forbidden because of the danger of fire, though this rule was clearly ignored, as demonstrated by the management's frequent reiterations of it.)[9]

In additional contrast to other theaters, many of the boxes were owned outright by some of the most important aristocratic families in Milan; they were the ones who had helped fund the 1717 construction, and the ownership of the boxes passed down through generations, much as subscriptions to popular sports teams do in the U.S.A. today. The Regio Ducal also included a number of other public spaces for amusement; at some periods it contained a restaurant, and throughout its history it had a gambling salon, which in fact provided nearly half the establishment's yearly income. From 1773 on, gambling was restricted to the nobility and the mercantile class in two segregated spaces; games at the door and in the cheap seats in the fourth tier for the servants and lower classes were expressly forbidden.[10] The Regio Ducal also made significant money by holding balls on some evenings on which opera was not performed. A final specialty of the Milanese theater during Mozart's time was the splendid ballet company, which routinely performed entr'actes within the operas, thus extending an evening's entertainment to six hours. Other than the balls, the theater was devoted entirely to opera, with opera buffa being played throughout the year, and opera seria only during the carnival season (after Christmas until Lent).

Charles Burney, an older English contemporary of Mozart, and important musical scholar who made several extensively documented trips to investigate the musical life of continental Europe, attended a performance of the opera buffa *L'amore artigiano* by Goldoni and Florian Gassmann at the Regio Ducal in 1770, a couple of months before Mozart arrived to write *Mitridate*. His description covers much of the information mentioned above:

> In the dance the stage was illuminated in a most splendid, and to me a new manner – with *Lampioni coloriti*, or coloured lamps which had a very pretty effect. The theater here is very large and splendid: 5 rows of boxes on each side, 100 each row with a room behind every one for cards and refreshments. In the fourth gallery was a pharo [game of chance] table. There was a very large box, bigger than my dining room in London[,] for the Duke of Modena, who is Governor of Milan, and the principessina his daughter, who is to be married to the second brother of the present emperor.[11] There was an abominable noise except during 2 or 3 arias and a duet, with which every body was in raptures. During this last, the applause continued till the performers returned to repeat it. . . . Each box of the 3 first rows contains 6 persons who sit 3 on each side facing each other. Higher up they sit 3 in front and the rest stand behind.[12]

A few nights later, Burney went again to the opera, possibly to the same work, and his description of this occasion gives some insight into the vicissitudes of a company that performed every night come what may:

> The 1st tenor and the only good singer in it was ill – all his part was cut out and the baritono, who did a blustering old father's part that was to abuse his son violently in the first scene and song, finding he had no son there, gave a turn to the misfortune which diverted the audience very much and made 'em submit to their disappointment with a far better grace than they would have done in England, for instead of his son, he fell foul on the prompter, who here as at the opera in England pops his head out of a little trap door on the stage. The audience were so pleased with this attack upon the prompter that they encored the song in which it was made. However after the 1st act and the dances I came away, as the lights at the opera house here affect my eyes in a very painful manner. . . .[13]

Burney's calculations about the boxes suggest that at full capacity they would hold 600 people; assuming the parterre would hold about half as many again (though with no restrictions on numbers, it might have held many more than that) it is possible that the total capacity of the theater was something like 900 people. For comparison, the Metropolitan Opera in New York holds just under 4000, and the renovated Royal Opera House in London something over 2200.

THE BURGTHEATER

Something around 1000 seems to have been a relatively normal capacity for an opera theater during Mozart's lifetime. The theater which saw the largest number of his premieres, namely the Burgtheater in Vienna, seems during the 1770s and '80s to have been capable of holding around 1300 souls, though one has to remember that these calculations are always approximate, both boxes and the parterre having variable capacity, and there being no fire codes to legislate the degree of crowdedness permissible.[14] Partly because of Mozart's association with the Burgtheater, and partly because by good luck significant records survive, we also know quite a lot about this theater. Like the Regio Ducal it was essentially a horseshoe shape with rows of boxes around the walls: here four storeys rather than the Regio Ducal's five.[15] As in most European theaters at the time, the majority of the boxes were rented by the season to prominent aristocratic families, who often kept the boxes for generations. The remainder of the theater was also divided by price and class. The cheapest seats were in the fourth balcony (the "Paradise") and the second parterre – the back part of what today would be called the stalls (or orchestra): these were sold by the evening to anyone who could afford them. Between the boxes and the cheapest seats were seats in the third balcony, which did not have boxes; these went to members of the high bourgeoisie (bankers, rich merchants, etc.) and the "second aristocracy" (the newly ennobled), and places in the *parterre noble* (the front part of the orchestra) went to the aristocracy, theatrical personnel, and the military.[16] The house was renovated several times between the founding of the theater in 1748 and the end of the eighteenth century; the majority of changes involved the disposition of boxes.[17] The stage was about 56 feet wide, with a proscenium opening of something like 30 feet, and about 40 feet deep, with extra space at the back.[18] It had five triple tracks for wings, and two more double wing-tracks.

The décor of the Burgtheater seems to have been more neo-classical than rococo; the one picture of its stage during Mozart's lifetime, an engraving by J. E. Mansfeld from a parodistic collection of "worldly abuses" by journalist Joseph Richter, shows a very plain set of wings and remarkably unadorned boxes (ill. 6). The original design of the proscenium was also strikingly plain compared with the rococo extravagances of the Cuvilliés theater in Munich or of the Regio Ducal.[19] Aesthetic severity notwithstanding, it was still a kind of pleasure palace; gambling was available in specially-outfitted gaming rooms, despite Maria Theresia's moral objections,[20] and individuals could rent tables and lights for card playing on an evening-by-evening basis. Unlike the Regio Ducal, which played only operas, the Burgtheater offered both spoken and sung entertainment. During Mozart's decade in Vienna, for example, operas alternated with German-language spoken theater.

The Burgtheater orchestra was smaller than that of the Regio Ducal. It consisted of around 35 players – violins, violas, cellos, basses, oboes, flutes, clarinets, horns and bassoons – in contrast with the 50-plus of the Italian theater, though it seems clear that extra players (like trombonists, trumpeters and timpanists, not to mention mandolinists and Turkish percussionists) were hired as needed. But despite its somewhat smaller size, the Viennese ensemble was remarkably stable over Mozart's time in the city, and the players were clearly capable of negotiating even Mozart's exceptionally demanding scores.[21]

Both the Regio Ducal and the Burgtheater were owned by their respective courts. The Regio Ducal was run by an impresario appointed by the court; this person chose repertory, hired personnel, and assumed the financial risk of the enterprise. This had been the system in Vienna until 1776; from that time on, Joseph II ran the Burgtheater directly, with help from Count Orsini-Rosenberg, who held the position but not the title of *Musikgraf* (Count of Music).[22] Joseph had strong opinions about singers and repertory, and even helped scout for performers, while his younger brother Ferdinand in Milan also took a close interest in the choice of repertory and general running of the theater, even with an impresario on hand.[23] From 1776 onwards, the Burgtheater was given the additional burden of being declared a *Nationaltheater*. Joseph II was interested in using the theater as a site where German national character and bourgeois mores could be taught. Thus from 1776 until 1778 the repertory was all German spoken theater[24] (ironically enough, many plays were translations from the French); from 1778, these plays alternated with Singspiel, most newly composed for the venue. The nobility, however, missed their Italian opera and demanded its reinstatement, which happened in 1783. Opera buffa at the Burgtheater, then, had the reputation among Joseph's Germanifying apologists of being aristocratic frippery. Joseph himself, however, was evidently as enthusiastic about it as his nobles, but it is important to remember that it could not have quite the same position in Vienna as it had in Italy.

THEATER AUF DER WIEDEN

In contrast to the courtly context of the Regio Ducal and the Burgtheater, the Theater auf der Wieden, in which *The Magic Flute* was premiered, was run entirely by its impresario, Emanuel Schikaneder (the author of the libretto to *The Magic Flute* and also the first Papageno), with the backing of Joseph von Bauernfeld, a rich officer.[25] Suburban theaters began to flourish around Vienna in the early 1780s after Joseph had negated the court's exclusive right to run theaters. The Theater auf der Wieden was founded in 1787 in a housing complex, the Freihaus, and showed German-language comic opera (much of this being Italian opera in translation or pastiches cobbled together from bits of different operas, or new works composed quickly and more or less collaboratively),[26] as well as spoken drama of a variety of sorts, including a smattering of grand and serious plays by Schiller and Lessing.[27] Tickets were somewhat cheaper than in the Burgtheater: the cheapest places (standing room in the balcony) in the Wiedner Theater, as it was known, were seven kreuzer,[28] whereas a place in the top balcony at the Burgtheater cost twenty kreuzer.[29] The more expensive tickets seem to have been closer in price in the two theaters, however. Unlike at the Burgtheater, it seems not to have been the habit for aristocrats to rent boxes for the season, though we do not know this for certain. This theater, like the other German-language suburban theaters, certainly catered to a less thoroughly aristocratic public than the court theaters, but equally certainly the Viennese nobility attended with some regularity.

Physically, the Wiedner Theater was rectangular rather than horseshoe-shaped, and there were only two rows of boxes. Scholars estimate that the room held something like 1000 people; such estimates are necessarily approximate, given the flexibility of both bench seating and standing room.[30] The stage was proportionately large, however, (ca. 40 feet deep and between 33 and 56 feet wide, with a proscenium opening of about 31 feet) and extremely well equipped for special effects, which Schikaneder delighted in, in part because of their box-office draw.[31] The normal orchestra at the Wiedner Theater seems to have been about 10 players smaller than that at the Burgtheater, though the pit was the same size.[32] However, Schikaneder would hire extra players when necessary, and the first performances of *The Magic Flute* seem to have been such an occasion, as one account describes an orchestra of 35 for this work.

As the above accounts of some of Mozart's theaters suggest, the social stratifications of his age were displayed and enforced in the theaters. The first stratification was simply who could pay for a ticket. At the Burgtheater before 1776, for example, the cheapest ticket was equivalent to a full family midday meal for the middle classes, or a mason's salary for a day, or a suburban seamstress's weekly wages.[33] On the other hand, the aristocrats brought their servants and lackeys, so the theater was not completely empty of the less privileged. Joseph II lowered the ticket prices considerably in 1776 in order to bring more people into his educational experiment, but even though tickets for the theater remained cheaper than those for opera, the prices crept up again over the last decades of the century, and the court theater remained an essentially high-middle and upper-class entertainment. Even given the de facto exclusion of the poorest people, theaters still divided the audience up by rank, with the divisions enforced not only by pricing policies but also by rules about who might inhabit which spaces. Military sentries were not unusual in theaters; they were there in part to enforce moderately respectful behavior and to break up brawls, but they could also be used to keep the audience properly parceled out into their constituent parts.

The extant eighteenth-century court theaters – Drottningholm, Gripsholm and Český Krumlov, which are significantly smaller than the theaters associated with Mozart (Drottninghom holds about 450) have most of the seats on the floor, and a single, undivided balcony around the back and sides of the theater. This may be because, as court theaters, they were not open to a paying public, and the social organization of the court, which would be well understood by all, would simply be replicated in the theater.

The behaviour of the audience, though noisy throughout the auditorium, differed from group to group. In the Burgtheater, the third balcony, which was the province of the upper middle class and second aristocracy, was also the site of the most lively (and loudest) critical discussion of the work at hand. One contemporary commented that there he could learn the value of the work before the curtain had even risen.[34] But in addition to what we would now find unacceptably intrusive commentary on the work itself, there was also the continuous noise of gossip, courting, gaming, eating, brawling, and more. In Vienna the continuous chatter was (stereotypically enough) attributed chiefly to the noblewomen in the boxes,[35] but it is clear from contemporary accounts throughout Europe that boisterous inattentiveness was all but the rule for most people most of the time in the opera house. Premieres and particularly favoured numbers seem to have been an exception to this. One reason for this was the prevalence of seasonal box-rental at most European theaters. Aristocrats used their boxes essentially as extensions of their salons and living quarters at home, entertaining guests in a variety of ways, keeping in touch with the social world, and simply being seen. They would thus attend the same opera multiple times: Count Zinzendorf in Vienna, for example, attended the 1789 revival of *The Marriage of Figaro* 18 times – the total run between August 1789 and February 1791 being 29 performances.[36] Even with the inevitable and relatively frequent substitutions of understudies and alternate singers[37] it would surely be hard to remain equally interested for all 18 performances. And Zinzendorf's comments, which often concern his immediate social situation in the theater or the physical charms of the female singers, may reflect the kinds of attitudes common among the Burgtheater's aristocratic attendees.

LATE EIGHTEENTH-CENTURY ACTING

Operatic acting even today tends to be less naturalistic than most stage, and all film acting, though the trend towards naturalism has on the whole been accelerated as more operas get filmed or videorecorded in some way. But even given our modern comfort with the idea that opera singers on stage will make bigger and more extravagant gestures than regular actors, we would probably find eighteenth-century acting paradoxically both stiff and overdone. One reason for this was that in a dimly lit theater (see below), subtleties of gesture and expression would simply not communicate. Another reason was the basis of much serious acting in the oratorical tradition. And yet another reason for this acting style was the general understanding of art as the clear communication of conventional and readily-legible affects rather than of the complexities of individual psychological motivations.

Acting in opera seria was, not surprisingly, given the genre's higher intellectual status, better-documented than that in comic opera. The sources include pictures of singers and productions, and also acting and oratory manuals. The basic style seems to have been quite consistent across Europe and persistent over several centuries. The actor's basic posture was a stance, with more weight on one leg than the other (one leg would often be in front), with the elbows away from the body, and the arms and hands slightly bent, and balancing each other asymmetrically. (A common posture had the right arm up and the left one down, for example.) It was not unusual for the head to face in a different direction from the body. The total effect, then, was of elegant asymmetry, with the asymmetry giving life to the elegance.[38] This effect was frequently called "decorum." Gestures could involve the whole body, or simply the arms and hands or the face; they communicated a series of stock mental states: grief, surprise, terror, anger, contempt, jealousy, aversion, disparagement, shame, and welcome were among the more common.[39] Gestures could indicate an interlocutor or enact the beginning or end of a speech, and they were also used to describe or imitate an object or condition indicated in a speech.[40] These gestures were closely tied to, and illustrated, the actual words of the text in an almost pantomimic manner. In opera, this kind of acting took place in the recitatives; for seria arias the singer would stand downstage in an appropriate posture and deliver the aria without much bodily movement. Described this way, the acting style sounds rather cold and formulaic – almost puppet-like. But acting that conveyed the essence of a character was as valued by eighteenth-century commentators as it is today; it is just that what counts as the "essence" of a character may have changed between then and now.

Pietro Metastasio, as prolific a letter writer as he was a librettist, wrote a letter to Johann Adolf Hasse, one of his favorite composers, that sheds light on the way acting, music, and character were thought to relate during this period. The letter concerns Metastasio's libretto *Attilio Regolo*, which Hasse was in the process of setting. It is the historically-based story of Marcus Attilius Regulus, who has been taken as a slave by the Carthaginians. Returning to Rome with the Carthaginian ambassador to negotiate a peace whose price is essentially his life, Regulus persuades the Senate to vote for the good of Rome rather than his own well-being, and returns to Carthage to die. Metastasio begins his letter by describing the characters in the opera as a way of helping Hasse imagine the appropriate music for each one. Regolo he describes as follows:

A Roman hero whose virtue is consumed no less by maxims than by practical matters, and is secure in its capacity to be tested by the whims of fortune; he is thus a rigid and scrupulous observer of justice and honesty in the laws and customs consecrated in his country by the progress of the years and by the authority of the populace; sensible of all the permitted human passions but superior to them all; a good warrior, good citizen and good father, but accustomed to considering himself as inseparable from his country . . . eager for glory, but only as the reward to which private people should aspire when they sacrifice themselves to the public good. Given these internal qualities, I attribute to my protagonist an exterior majestic but without pomp, thoughtful but serene, authoritative but human, steady, considerate, and composed. However, it would not please me if he never became excited in voice or movements; two or three places in the opera stand out by means of their palpable difference from the constant tenor of the rest of his behavior, in their distinct liveliness in expressing his dominant affects, which are his country and glory. Now don't worry, my dear monsieur Hasse: my descriptions of the other characters will be shorter.[41]

Later in the letter Metastasio describes a particularly intense solo scene for Regolo, where he derides himself for worrying about his own fate; the librettist instructs Hasse both about how the music should accompany this moment and about how it should look onstage:

This [recitative] should be spoken while seated, until the words *Ah! no, This is the language of cowards . . .* and then the rest [spoken] while standing. But if the set designer has the liberty to make the two scenes in the loggia and in the gallery either long or short [that is, with the backdrop further back or further forward], if by chance the change from short to long is not difficult, then Regolo could appear seated [from the beginning of the scene]. If this is not possible, however, he could go to the seat slowly, stopping from time to time, and showing himself to be immersed in grave reflection; saying, perhaps, if he wants, a few words from the beginning of the scene. The orchestra will need to help and follow him, until the character sits down. All he says are reflections, doubts, interruptions; which will give way to impromptu modulations prompted by the text, occurring in the orchestra at discrete intervals. But as soon as he rises [once more] to his feet, the entire remainder of the speech demands resolve and energy. Here my above-mentioned desire for a moderate tempo recurs.

Regolo's character, then, is primarily an accumulation of observable behaviors rather than a modern tangle of personal history and semi-conscious desires. Even what Metastasio describes as "inner" may seem quite "outer" to a modern sensibility: being superior to the passions and a good father, etc,. are qualities of behavior at least as much as of interior disposition. Acting was thus a matter of clarifying and intensifying the behaviors that formed the character. And whereas today we sometimes rely on subtle twitches of lips and eyebrows to tell us the truth *behind* what a character might be saying, for most of the eighteenth century, acting was more about the truth *of* the speech; it served as amplification of the language rather than a counterpoint to it.

Metastasio's description of the stage movement during the scene is striking for its single-minded focus on one (or possibly two) basic actions: sitting and standing. Of course he would naturally have expected the actor to make smaller gestures with his hands and arms, but the cataclysmic effect of so simple a movement as sitting or standing cannot be over-estimated if the general context is one of relative stasis.

In general there seems to have been considerably less stage movement (that is, characters walking around the stage) than there is today;[42] this may very well have been due in part to the dim and spotty lighting on most stages (see below), and perhaps in part also to the need to declaim directly at the audience to be heard above the general din. Interlocutors, at least in opera seria, also seem not to have moved very much; when an aria needed to be addressed to another character, the singer would usually point at that character (or to a group, if the situation demanded),[43] he or she might make a single move nearer the addressee (or vice versa), the interlocutor might position him or herself slightly downstage of the singer, and the singer could have his or her body and face pointing towards the audience while his or her hands and eyes were pointed in the direction of the interlocutor.[44] All of this meant that the interlocutor was basically locked to the singer for as long as he or she was being addressed.

Given that stage movement was employed with great economy, the positioning of characters on stage took on a particular importance, not only with respect to making the words and notes audible and comprehensible, but also with respect to indicating the relationships between the characters. As mentioned, characters would often indicate those whom they were addressing with a gesture, but it was position rather than gesture that indicated relative rank or importance – rank being at least as important onstage as it was off. Just as the right hand was considered more important than the left in the formation of gestures, so to be on the right-hand side (stage right) of a pair of people indicated higher rank (with the exception of female confidantes, who were normally placed to the right of their mistresses).[45] When there were more than two characters on stage, the highest-ranked person stood in the middle. This placement reflected actual social practice, and its importance and relevance to opera seria is indicated in a letter from Metastasio to the Dresden court poet Giovanni Pasquini, describing in detail the correct placement of characters in his *Demofoonte*, which Pasquini was adapting.[46] The same instructions caused difficulties with Hasse's wife, Faustina Bordoni, the prima donna in this production, who found herself in a less prestigious stage position.

Acting in comic opera was less well-documented than seria acting. There were certainly many overlaps with the seria conventions. The relatively few pictures of scenes from comic operas show postures and gestures very much in line with the principles of rhetorical style promoted in opera seria: wide, slightly off-centre stances and exaggerated expressive gestures. The frontispiece for one of the very few published buffa operas, Antonio Salieri's *La grotta di Trofonio* (Vienna, 1785) is particularly interesting. The story involves changes of character in two girls and two boys, one pair serious, the other pair not. The engineer of these changes is the magician Trofonio, shown on the right of the picture; he is a grotesque mixture of comic and supernatural. While the two young ladies are shown in familiar rhetorical gestures of surprise,[47] the magician has his right arm crossed all the way over his body, a gesture which would have been considered graceless or unpleasing by the rhetoricians, and which thus immediately marks him as outside the normal limits of decorous behavior. In the context of the ladies' more acceptable gestures, this failure of decorum on Trofonio's part is clearly no accident and equally clearly meaningful.[48]

But comic acting also had roots in the various kinds of street theater that preceded both opera buffa and Singspiel. Commedia dell'arte and its offshoots, like the Hanswurst ("Jack Sausage") entertainments in Vienna, were full of physical comedy and pratfalls: misapplied slaps and kisses, exquisitely timed entrances and exits, and silly walks. By the time Mozart was writing comic operas, the most violent and physical gags from the commedia had generally been excluded from the genre, but stage directions in comedies in general in the eighteenth century (as well as the plots themselves) suggest considerably more physical movement and more complex blocking than was the case in opera seria.[49]

STAGE DIRECTIONS IN MOZART'S LIBRETTOS

The stage directions printed in the librettos to Mozart's operas do not contradict the picture painted above. Their exact relation to performance, of course, cannot be determined, since singers and actors would always do what was necessary to make themselves look good and to make a good theatrical effect, and the these indications may in any case have been designed to assist reading rather than acting. Many such stage directions are reproduced in Mozart's scores, but score and libretto rarely match exactly in this respect. Nevertheless, the general picture presented by the librettos' directions fits remarkably well with the oratorical rules described above. They fall into three main (and somewhat overlapping) categories: entrances and exits, stage business including indication of addressee, and expressive indications.

Entrances and exits are virtually always noted clearly and in full, since the division of a work into scenes was based primarily on changes in the onstage personnel. Ceremonial or dramatic entrances are also typically described in some detail: at the beginning of *La finta giardiniera*, for example, the serving-girl Serpetta, the Mayor and the seria lover Ramiro are described as descending the staircase of the Mayor's villa as Nardo and Sandrina are busy in the garden; this arrangement clarifies instantly who belongs in the garden and who is merely "visiting" from his or her proper place indoors.[50] Don Giovanni and Zerlina leave the stage "abbracciati" (in an embrace) after the seduction duet "La ci darem la mano" ("There we shall exchange vows"), which communicates in no uncertain terms what the duet has been about; and Tito's first entrance in *La clemenza di Tito,* which is accompanied by a chorus, is announced as follows: "Publio [a character], Roman senators, and the delegates of the subject provinces, arriving to present their annual tribute taxes. While Tito, preceded by bodyguards and followed by Pretorian guards, and surrounded by a large crowd, descends from the Capitol, [the chorus] sings the following." In essentially all such cases, the description of the entrance or exit establishes or clarifies the status of the character(s) involved, or explains the dramatic action. The librettos are also very clear in indicating who remains (or arrives) onstage unseen by the other characters, and who make as if to go but does not; this again, is usually an essential part of the stage action.

The simplest kind of stage business involves address, which is often indicated in the librettos, especially when there are more than two people on stage and the addressee may not be clear from the words alone, when in the course of a recitative or an aria the addressee changes, or when a character is speaking to him or herself. It seems likely that such directions in the text would be performed either as gestures of indication (see above), or would be preceded by the character moving closer to the one s/he was about to address.[51] The most interesting libretto with respect to addressee indications is *Ascanio in Alba,* the *festa teatrale* written for the Milanese wedding of the Archduke Ferdinand and Beatrice d'Este. This is a work in which almost nothing "happens," but the outcome – the coupling of Ascanio and Silvia, who are obvious analogues for Ferdinand and Beatrice – was of enormous political and social significance. The stage directions describe with unusual completeness who is looking at whom, who moves near to whom, and who addresses whom, such that one can almost deduce the story from the stage directions alone. Indeed, the minuteness of the stage directions suggests that they were a complete record of the stage movements, and that the visual spectacle of the characters' relationships was at least as important as the words sung.

Other stage business routinely noted in these librettos may involve props: in *La finta giardiniera* Ramiro gives the Podestà the letter that reveals the Contino's attempted murder of his fiancée; in *Mitridate* swords are drawn and confiscated as signs of honor and the loss thereof; in *Figaro,* the pin that seals Susanna's letter of assignation with the Count has to be seen to change hands;

in *The Magic Flute*, Papageno has to have the rope with which he makes as if to hang himself, and so forth. Stage business directions also describe the relative positions of characters: in *Figaro* Susanna and Cherubino need to be in and out of the closet at precisely the right moments, and in the famous trio "Cosa sento," the movements of Susanna, Cherubino, the Count and Basilio need to be precisely indicated (and followed) for the comedy to work. Not surprisingly, the comedies have considerably more such directions than the seria operas. However, the indications in the seria operas suggest that crucial moments were emphasized by stage movement. In *La clemenza di Tito*, for example, there are almost no stage directions other than entrances and exits until Tito has to decide whether to execute his friend Sesto. Their dialogue (Act II scene 8) is marked by Sesto kneeling and rising, and being led out by the guards. Tito's subsequent recitative of decision (Act II scene 9) involves his sitting down, writing, tearing up the page on which he has written the decree of execution, and throwing the torn-up document to the floor. All of these actions, particularly if they occurred at the end of a performance with relatively little stage movement, would be quite striking, and would intensify the audience's appreciation of the agony of the moment for Tito.

The most interesting stage directions in the librettos have to do with expression, because they are rarely as obviously necessary to articulate the plot as are indications of address or the descriptions of stage business, and thus may give a slightly more direct sense of the relations between eighteenth-century and modern acting. "Expression marks" are by far the rarest kind of stage direction; some of Mozart's librettos have none at all. But when they do occur, the range of affects indicated overlaps markedly with the common expressive gestures noted in the acting and rhetoric manuals. Fear, agitation, anxiety, grief, disgust and anger are the negative emotions found in these librettos; in addition to these we find transport, tenderness, laughter, irony, vivacity and fire, especially in the comic texts. *The Marriage of Figaro* is particularly full of such indications, and among the more striking aspects of this libretto is the way Lorenzo Da Ponte has indicated expression even during the arias and ensembles. These expressions must have been indicated gesturally, since communicating them vocally in a fully-realized musical number (as opposed to a recitative, where the singer has much more freedom with tempo and inflection) would have been quite difficult and unlikely to have been noticed. Perhaps the most remarkable stage direction, at least from the point of view of articulating the distance between 1786 and now, is the indication that, having discovered the Count's untoward interest in Susanna, Figaro's betrothed, Figaro is shown "pacing furiously (con foco) around the room, wringing his hands." (An equivalent direction is also in the Beaumarchais play [Act I scene 2].) Modern productions quite often have Figaro pace, but handwringing would seem under most modern circumstances ridiculously melodramatic. However, in an acting style where intense conventional gestures were the means for communicating affect, handwringing was the obvious and appropriate response to potential betrayal.

LIGHTING

It is essentially impossible today to imagine, and usually illegal to have an audience in, a candlelit theater, but candles, along with oil lamps in certain situations, were the lighting technology for Mozart's operas. Beeswax or sper-maceti[52] candles were preferred because they were less smoky and smelly, but tallow (rendered beef or pork fat) candles were cheaper. The auditorium was usually lit with several chandeliers, and the pillars between the boxes often had double or triple sconces (or more) attached. If the estimate that 8 wax candles equal about a 7-watt electric light bulb is approximately right,[53] then even a couple of hundred candles would shed not a lot more light than one 150-watt bulb. Contemporary prints of librettos are often spotted with candlewax; one wonders what else the dripping wax may have hit. In addition to their relative dimness, candles produce smoke and heat. Eighteenth-century men and women sometimes complained about the air quality in the theater as well as about the quality of light, just as they complained about constipation and catarrh, but because these things were unavoidable they marveled at the spectacle regardless. Candles were dangerous as well as nasty to be around. Theaters – largely wooden interior structures with upholstery and oil-painted flats – burned like kindling time after time, and were re-erected just as often.

The amount of light in theaters varied enormously, with the Comédie Française and a couple of grand Italian opera houses as models of brightness, with candles and oil lamps to the equivalent of two-thousand-plus candles, and some German and English theaters particularly dimly lit.[54] Unfortunately we have very little information on the lighting situation at the theaters for which Mozart wrote, beyond the fact that candles were one of the largest single expenses at the Regio Ducal.[55] The stage was typically only slightly brighter than the auditorium, though the Italian tradition was to darken the auditorium more than the French did, usually by hoisting the auditorium chandeliers closer to the ceiling for the duration of the performance.[56] This was evidently also done in the Burgtheater.[57] Many stages had several chandeliers, either in a row along the front, or more deeply distributed up the stage. Wing-flats may have had candles on reflective sconces, or "trees" of lights hidden behind them, and some theaters also had standing candelabras at either side of the stage. Many stages had footlights; these were more often oil-lamps than candles, and they could include literally hundreds of wicks.[58]

The Argand lamp – an improved oil lamp that burned more brightly and steadily and with less smell – revolutionized stage lighting, but it was only invented in France in 1783. As the theater historian Evan Baker has noted, the Burgtheater was unusually well equipped, but it is not clear that this technology would have reached Vienna in time for Mozart's operas.[59]

The older candle and oil-lamp system was, however, capable of a variety of effects, and the light of the candles was increased by the use of prisms in the chandeliers, as well as various other reflectors. Lights could be dimmed in various ways: footlights were often on a platform that could be raised or lowered, light "trees" could be turned so that the reflector faced away from the stage, and some theaters had a system for lowering open-ended canisters over the candles. Coloured fabrics and glasses were also used as filters for special effects.

The stage directions in Mozart's librettos sometimes indicate what must have been a lighting effect. Night, for example, which most famously occurs at the beginning and end of *Don Giovanni* and in the fourth act of *The Marriage of Figaro*, would have involved some kind of dimming. In the second act of *La finta semplice*, the second set calls for "A room with seats and lights, it being night," which presumably meant that whatever stage-wide lighting there was, was dimmed, and that candelabras were set up to make pools of light in the general darkness. This lighting set-up holds for the scene when Rosina and Cassandro speak to each other in pantomime (see pp. 120–21 for synopsis); the spottily illuminated stage must have made this scene all the more remarkable. In *Lucio Silla* the scene in the sepulchre is described as "molto oscuro" (very dark); again, even if the wings and backdrops themselves were painted in dark colors, there may well have been some dimming of the lights. *The Magic Flute* has two night settings, in the second of which (Act II scene 7) the moon is said to illuminate Pamina's face; presumably a moon would have been suspended from the flies (the Theater auf der Wieden was well-equipped for flying machines) and some candles or oil lamps behind it would have provided the light.

COSTUMES

Costuming for late eighteenth-century opera is not a well-understood subject. We do know, however, that the lighting, the acting style, and the costumes worked together in many ways. Especially in opera seria, costumes were designed both to catch the light as much as possible and to magnify the effect of every movement. Many costumes were highly reflective, so they shimmered in what light there was. Sequins, mirrors, gold and silver thread, and so on, were the norm, especially in the costumes of grand personages. Headdresses were similarly designed to catch the light. Ostrich feathers, shiny elements, and other size-enhancing and quivering decorations were routine. The size and design of the headdresses also ensured that they trembled as the actor moved, thus lending a kinetic shimmer to the reflective one. Hooped skirts, or side panniers were normal for women; these also magnify motion. And there are many pictures of castrati in a kind of stylized Roman costume in which the part of the "tunic" that fell below the breastplate was supported underneath by an inverted-boat shaped hoop, making a wide but relatively flat skirt that fell to mid thigh. In line with the general principles of seria costuming, this provided both an expanse for the application of glitter, and a structure that reflected the movement of the singer.[60]

Costume as a design feature of the whole production seems to have been more prevalent in ballet than in opera. The extant pictures of costumes from this period are often for dancers, and librettos in general more often designate a costume designer for the ballets than for the opera with which they were performed. (The libretto for Mozart's *Mitridate, re di Ponto* is a case in point. *Lucio Silla*'s libretto, on the other hand, lists a costume designer on the same page as the other creators of the opera itself.) In opera the female principals were often expected to provide their own costumes, and the whole visual aspect of the production was often cobbled together from more or less stock materials (see below). The accuracy of costumes with respect to the place and era of the action was highly variable. In general, male costume seems to have been more different from everyday dress than female. For operas set in ancient Rome and Greece, for example, men would sometimes wear breastplates, helmets, bare (or stockinged) legs below the tunic, and sandals with calf-high straps (ill. 7). Women, however, would wear the usual long-waisted dress with a hooped skirt and the usual kind of wig; and the evidence of Roman origins would be in the fabric design of the overskirt, or a bodice with elements that might be reminiscent of a breastplate. For operas set in exotic places, men would quite often wear turbans, longish overcoats, and harem pants, often in the most elaborately woven and embroidered fabrics; women's costumes would adapt those fabrics to their usual slim-waisted, décolleté, wide-skirted profile.

As with every other visual element, the costumes for comic opera are less well-documented than those for opera seria. One of the incredibly rare direct visual records of Mozart's comic operas is a 1787 engraving of Luigi Bassi as Don Giovanni. Here he is wearing a standard late eighteenth-century overcoat, though with a puff at the top of the sleeve reminiscent of sixteenth-century breeches. His dress under the coat is unclear, but it might be "slops," the short Elizabethan-style breeches suggested by his sleeves.[61] In any case, clearer indications of costume from the several decades after 1787 show that this historical dress for males may have been the norm for this opera, which may be an acknowledgement of the fact that it was an old Spanish story. More intriguingly, the famous set of engravings of the Beaumarchais play *Le marriage de* Figaro also show some characters wearing a less extreme version of this costume, so it is possible that this was a relatively standard indication of stage-aristocrat status. In contrast, the original libretto's picture of Emanuel Schikaneder as Papageno show him completely kitted out in a feathered body-suit with a birdcage on his back (see ill. 3). It seems clear from subsequent paintings and engravings of *The Magic Flute* that extravagant costume was part of the appeal of the piece, along with fantastic scenic effects.[62]

SCENERY AND SCENIC EFFECTS

The basic stage set-up during Mozart's life was a series of pairs of wing flats placed increasingly close to the centre of the stage as they got closer to the backstage, providing an intensified sense of perspective. A backdrop completed the effect. Trompe l'oeuil paintings on the flats could give a sense that the stage was bounded by two flat surfaces, or that there were several vanishing points rather than the single central one (ill. 8). Many theaters had several places for the backdrop, so the stage could be variably deep for different scenes. There was often machinery, as well as both small props and practicable pieces of scenery.

One of the staple effects in this kind of set was the transformation: scenes could change from one into another before the audience's eyes by means of the parallel tracks on which the wings ran. That is, one scene would slide in as the other one slid out, all effected by invisible winches and ropes. The back-drop and ceiling strips could change at the same time. Trapdoors in the stage floor allowed for magical appearances and disappearances (Don Giovanni must have met his demise in Vienna via one of the seven traps on the Burgtheater stage). And mechanisms in the ceilings of many theaters allowed for a variety of drops, flying chariots, and imitation hot-air balloons.[63] Gunpowder could provide flashes of light, and thunder machines – large tippable pans filled with rocks – were not uncommon.[64]

Most operas were staged with stock scenery, the sets representing "a street," "a room," "a piazza," "a delightful copse," and so on. Alternatively, stock scenery would be used for some sets, and new sets would be made for partic-ular scenes. Some librettos from the period announce the "painters and archi-tects" of the operas they represent; others don't. Generally speaking, the choice to announce these members of the theatrical team was made theater by theater. Thus librettos from the Regio Ducal in Milan regularly announce the Galliari brothers as responsible for the visual aspects of the production;

librettos from the Burgtheater during Mozart's stay in Vienna are silent on the subject of set design. The surviving records of the two establishments match the attention given in the librettos: many drawings by the Galliaris survive, including one of the sepulchre scene in *Lucio Silla*, but one can only deduce the scenic habits of the Burgtheater from the occasional engraving of a given opera, or from reviews.

The scenery indications in most of Mozart's operas suggest that most scenes could have been played with stock scenery. Even *The Marriage of Figaro*, whose stage directions for the actors are more detailed than in any other opera, is set in a series of rooms and outdoor settings that could easily have been found in existing holdings. The chief specific needs for this opera are practicable (i.e. usable) doors, and one window, all of which could easily have been produced without need for an overall aesthetic design. Similarly in *Don Giovanni*, the only scenes that might have needed to be specially designed were the cemetery scene with the statue of the Commendatore (a piece of scenery quite easily produced), and some machinery to produce the hellfires that consume the hero at the end.

Mozart's two most elaborately-conceived operas with respect to sets are *Idomeneo* and *The Magic Flute*. The former was designed by Lorenzo Quaglio, who was employed at the Munich court; the set included a magnificent Temple of Neptune[65] as well as a variety of more and less stormy seascapes. *The Magic Flute* was so complexly designed that in 1792, the year after the opera's premiere in Vienna, the co-director of the Berlin National Theater wrote, "It seems to have been the author's intention to crowd together every conceivable difficulty for the stage-designer and technicians, and a work has thus been created whose sole merit is its splendor."[66] Emanuel Schikaneder, the author of the libretto and the first Papageno, seems to have imagined the sets himself, but the playbill for the first performance mentions Messrs. [Joseph] Gayl and Nesslthaler as, respectively, the scene painter and set designer; these men were presumably the regular set designers of the Wiedner Theater.[67] The sets for this opera followed in the emerging tradition of exotic and magic operas in that theater. Indeed, the Berlin commentator was responding to something real in his evaluation that the merit of the work was intended to be judged on the basis of its spectacle. Schikaneder needed to draw in the crowds, and spectacle was a pretty reliable way to do that. The unusually large number of transformations from one scene to another was certainly part of the appeal; the settings themselves were another. These settings included mountains that opened (Act I, scene 6), a harem-like oriental setting (I, 9), exotic temples (I, 15), a carriage drawn by lions (I, 18), a silver and gold palm forest (II, 1), a flying chariot bedecked with roses (II, 13), and of course the spectacular trial scene (II, 28) with two mountains, one containing an audible waterfall and the other a spitting fire; in both cases a horizon of sky is visible past the mountain.

THE ORCHESTRA

The norm across Europe in Mozart's time was to have the orchestra on the floor in front of the stage, separated from the parterre by a chest-high barrier. The "pit" occupied the full width of the stage (usually over 30 feet) and could be as little as seven feet deep.[68] Quite often the string and wind players would read off a single double-sided desk that ran nearly the length of the pit, so that half the players would be facing the stage, and half the audience. Orchestra size could range from the low 20s to nearly 60; the orchestra in Milan was exceptionally large at 57, and Mozart's Viennese orchestras seem to have been around 35 players strong. The single largest group of instrumentalists in the orchestra was always the violins: in Milan for Mozart's operas there were 28; in the Burgtheater there were 12.[69] Overall, violas got fewer in number proportionate to the violins as the century wore on; however, in Milan in 1770 there were 6, and in the Burgtheater in the 1780s, 4.[70] The number of cellos (usually 2–4) was often either equalled or exceeded by the number of double basses, but since these instruments were sometimes smaller and lighter than modern double basses,[71] the sound would not have been as bottom-heavy as those proportions suggest. (For comparison, the Royal Opera House orchestra has 34 violins, 13 violas, 11 cellos and 9 basses on their roster, though presumably not every player plays for every performance.)[72] These figures should be understood in the context both of modern instruments on the whole being louder than they were in the late eighteenth century, and the orchestra also now being placed in a pit underneath the stage. Eighteenth-century opera orchestras usually had a couple of oboists, a couple of bassoonists for the bass lines, and at least a couple of horn players on their regular rosters; oboists could often play flute parts as well, allowing for some variety in colour. Mozart's Viennese orchestra had pairs of flutes, clarinets and trumpets as well as oboes, horns and bassoons.[73] Extra instrumentalists would be hired in for special effects.

The continuo group – the keyboard (harpsichord or fortepiano), cello, bass, and sometimes bassoon, which would accompany the simple recitatives, and would play throughout the other numbers as well – was often placed at the end of the pit to far stage right. The leadership of the ensemble was often entrusted to the keyboard player, though the first-violin-playing concert-master could also co-ordinate entries and set tempos. When the composer himself directed the performance, as was the case for all of Mozart's premieres, he would probably have done so from the keyboard. The movie

Amadeus's representation of Mozart standing in front of the orchestra beating time is thus most likely not accurate, though it is certainly visually more compelling than a cornered harpsichordist would be. Italian theaters often had two continuo groups, one at each end of the pit. The first harpsichord (stage right) would play the recitatives, and it seems that the second would play along during the other musical numbers, perhaps to help the singers on stage left, a long way from the first harpsichord, and perhaps simply to provide more volume and thus a better chance of togetherness in a noisy auditorium.[74] Today a single keyboard is the norm.

CHAPTER 8

MOZART'S SOCIAL WORLD

Mozart's operas depict worlds that, like other aspects of their content and context, seem in some respects familiar to us, and in others quite foreign. Among the familiar elements, their concentration on appropriate and successful mating and marriage have been the stuff of Western drama since at least the Renaissance; in addition, we still admire qualities like generosity and constancy, we still laugh at characters who cannot rise above their immediate needs, and we continue to feel that characters who misuse their power or betray their friends or family should be punished. At the same time, the conflict between love and duty that animates the seria operas, the preoccupation with nobility in both comic and serious works, and the structures of entrenched power based both on rank and gender, are not so readily recognizeable to us. Modern productions negotiate in a variety of ways with the historical circumstances represented by these structures of power and habits of mind; the most frequent form this negotiation takes is to assume that the dramatic context will make the underlying social structures clear, and to make little specific effort to clarify or explain them. Another method is to contextualize the characters' interactions with the social context in which they could have originated. David McVicar's acclaimed 2005 production of *The Marriage of Figaro* at Covent Garden, for example, always shows a corridor or other space outside the room where the action occurs, and has a cast of servant extras, dressed very much like Susanna, doing the endless household business and, of course, in the process, eavesdropping. The effect is to suggest the (historically supported) intimacy between masters and servants, which makes Susanna's closeness to the Countess in some ways less remarkable if no less touching, and it also makes sense of the pervasiveness of rumor and intrigue in the opera. Yet another kind of negotiation with history, especially in performances not set in the eighteenth century, or some version of an eighteenth-century conception of the ancient world, is to suggest modern analogues or symbols for the structural situations of the characters. Thus in

Peter Sellars' famous 1980s production of *The Marriage of Figaro*, set in Trump Towers, the Countess is costumed and coiffed to look remarkably like Princess Diana: a caged and unhappy noblewoman whose plight many modern Western spectators would feel in their bones.

This chapter begins with a description of Mozart's operatic social world as a more or less self-contained system; the second portion of the chapter relates this to the real world of eighteenth-century social relations.

THE RANKS OF CHARACTERS IN MOZART'S OPERAS

The social worlds within Mozart's operas vary by genre, but all the works share certain attitudes about rank and stratification, and the range of possibilities for social organization is relatively limited. The seria operas, set in ancient Rome, Greece or a timeless pseudo-classical pastoral world, represent only high-ranked characters; even the retainers and confidantes are from the same social milieu as the rulers. Opera buffa and Singspiel represent a wider range of social strata, and the relations between these strata are typically of central interest in the plot.

All Mozart's operas except *Bastien und Bastienne* have some noble or gentle-born characters. The seria operas include emperors, kings, princes and princesses, and the patrician class if the setting is ancient Rome. The buffa operas tend to represent a lower level of the nobility: the Count and Don Giovanni are masters of considerable estates, but they do not rule a country or an empire. The more middling nobility is represented by Donna Elvira, the cast of *Così* except for Despina, the noble characters in *La finta giardiniera* and, probably, Belmonte and Constanze in *Die Entführung*. Mozart's two full-length Singspiels include higher-ranked personnel than his buffa operas: Tamino is a prince, Pamina, being the daughter of the Queen of the Night, is a princess; Sarastro is a kind of king, and the Pasha is clearly an important ruler. But whereas the royalty of opera seria is in some sense a reflection of the presumed (or desired) virtues of the ruler paying for the opera, the royalty in *The Magic Flute* is a side product of the fairy-tale setting: fantasy kings and queens represent an abstraction of power rather than its exercise in any real-world domain. The concentration in Mozart's buffa operas on the middling level of nobility rather than royalty is characteristic of the genre as a whole; it both avoided potential problems with royal censors and allowed the action to take place in a world more recognizable to the majority of the audience.

The next significant social layer in the comic operas consists of servants and peasants: Zerlina and Masetto in *Don Giovanni*, Susanna and Figaro (and Antonio and Barbarina) in *The Marriage of Figaro*, Despina in *Così*, Monostatos in *the Magic Flute*, Blonde, Pedrillo and Osmin in *Die Entführung*.

These characters are all bound to their masters or the lord of the manor by a web of obligations that is almost never spelled out, but is, nevertheless, powerfully felt. Servants keep the households going and peasants (implicitly) till the land and produce the food. The rulers, in turn, provide for and protect the servants, and often serve as the local judiciary. We do not see most of this work going on; Zerlina and Masetto do not till, while Leporello's complaints about keeping guard for Don Giovanni all day and all night and Despina's displeasure with serving but never tasting the cocoa are only tokens of the work the audience knows they do. Both the Count in *Figaro* and the Mayor in *La finta giardiniera* exercise their judicial functions, but other privileges and obligations of their rank are not made explicit. The Count's (historically unsupported) "right" to sleep with Susanna before her marriage is one exception to the unspoken nature of noble privilege, as is Sarastro's right to have Monostatos punished in any way he sees fit.

STRATIFICATION

The social stratification in Mozart's comic operas is represented as mostly clear, absolutely immutable, and generally desirable, whatever the failings or foibles of the individuals within the strata. Social mobility via extraordinary work or marriage is simply not in evidence: Tamino, for example, matures in the course of *The Magic Flute* to earn a position at the head of Sarastro's brotherhood, but he is a prince at the outset of the opera, and the story is about growing up and assuming a position destined for him, not of changing rank. The gardener-girl Sandrina does marry the Contino in *La finta giardiniera*, but the point is precisely that she is really the Marchioness Violante disguised as a humble gardener. (Why she wants to marry a man who has stabbed her and left her for dead is another question.) The Count's attentions to Susanna are simultaneously inappropriate and unsurprising because she is in no position either to consent or refuse with any degree of autonomy. And Don Giovanni's interest in Zerlina can never be seen as anything other than a passing lust, not only because we know his history of conquests, but also because as an operatic nobleman he would not marry a peasant.

THE CHARACTERISTICS OF RANK AS SHOWN IN THE OPERAS

This rigid stratification is supported by the ways the operas make class differences part and parcel of the characters' personalities. Papageno's and Leporello's cowardice in the face of the supernatural contrasts with Tamino's and Don Giovanni's bravery (or foolhardiness); Zerlina's sexual cosiness with Masetto is intentionally distinct from Donna Anna's honorable distance

from Don Ottavio; Despina's earthily pragmatic attitude to love is differenti-
ated from Fiordiligi's and Dorabella's high-flown romantic notions. The
servants set into relief the nobility's capacity for deeper and more refined
sentiment and their capacity for self-sacrifice. Although these aspects of
personality are expressed first in the texts of the operas, Mozart's music also
emphasizes (and sometimes complicates) them in various ways.

Noble characters

The central issue for characters in the highest social layers in Mozart's as in
all eighteenth-century operas is their ability (or lack thereof) to live up to the
ideals of nobility, some of which are gendered, and others of which pertain to
both sexes. One primarily masculine ideal as shown in these operas is self-
conscious gravitas, or a concern with honour. The emperor Tito in *La
clemenza di Tito*, for example, is possessed by the question of how to rule his
people with honour. For women, on the other hand, honour usually means
fidelity and/or chastity; underlying even the late-eighteenth-century ideal of
female nobility is the old story of patient Griselda, who submissively accepts
her husband Gualtiero's apparent plan to snub her and marry another
woman, accepts the task of making up their marriage bed, but then greets her
husband's "return" to her with joy once she learns it was "only" a test, instigated by Gualtiero's vassals as a response to Griselda's humble origins.[1]
Mozart's and Da Ponte's Countess has more agency than poor Griselda, but
some of the same notions of self-abnegating fidelity apply.

Another element of operatic nobility is the capacity for self-sacrifice, and
this is shared by both genders; indeed, the Griselda story is a model example
of female self-sacrifice. In *Mitridate, re di Ponto* the good son Sifare is nobler
than the bad son Farnace in part because he is willing to give up his true love
Aspasia to his father, to whom she has already been promised; Aspasia herself
is willing to die in order to remain faithful to Sifare. In *Idomeneo*, the title
character's ignoble bargain with Neptune (namely that he will sacrifice to the
god the first person he sees if Neptune will only save him from drowning) is
not atoned for until he is willing to sacrifice his throne to Idamante, his
son. Meanwhile, Idamante's nobility is demonstrated by his wholehearted
willingness to die to save his father and the city of Crete from the depredations
of the god. His betrothed, Ilia, a Trojan princess, offers to die in his stead,
demonstrating a characteristic form of noble female self-sacrifice.

Generosity is also a noble characteristic: it is the character's acknowledgement of social advantage and his or her use of it to beneficent ends. Tito's
decision to forgive Sesto and the other traitors is a signal example of this, but
his request at the beginning of the opera that his people "regift" their tributes

to him to the victims of a recent eruption of Vesuvius is an early sign that he is an exemplar of beneficence. Among women, the Countess is the best example of generosity, as she touchingly forgives the Count his philandering at the end of the opera. Operatic nobility is also characteristically eloquent: it manifests itself as the ability to turn strong feelings into metaphorical or other abstract language, or musically to use the conventional signs of high style: accompanied recitative, majestic tunes, coloratura.[2]

Personal restraint is the final standard characteristic of true nobility. In *The Magic Flute* Tamino is required to be able to keep his counsel to join Sarastro's brotherhood, and in *Don Giovanni*, Don Ottavio (who is the male counterweight to the decidedly ignoble title character) exercises restraint both in his willingness to wait for Donna Anna, and in his deliberation about taking revenge on Don Giovanni. Restraint is a more masculine characteristic among Mozart's nobles; the female equivalent is a capacity for greater inwardness and more refined sentiment than others, usually demonstrated in particularly touching arias. The Countess's sorrows, for example, are evidence of her refinement, and in *Così* Fiordiligi's anguish at her betrayal of her first love functions similarly.

Some of these characteristics, of course, are ripe for mockery or betrayal. Eloquence easily turns into pomposity, as evidenced in both Dorabella's and Fiordiligi's first reactions to the departure of their lovers: Dorabella invokes the Eumenides in her high-flown anguish, and Fiordiligi sings an elaborate simile comparing her constancy to a rock buffeted by storms. Gravitas and concern with the appropriate behavior for one's rank can easily turn into braggadocio or inappropriate self-regard, as when the Contino in *La finta giardiniera* describes his implausibly ancient bloodlines. Characters who are of noble birth but not behavior demonstrate the mismatch by violating several of these ideals. The Count and Don Giovanni, for example are both notably ungenerous and unrestrained. And Don Giovanni is in some ways ineloquent; he has no aria or accompanied recitative describing his feelings, and "Fin ch'han dal vino" ("When they have had wine"), the one aria in which he is not assuming a persona to seduce or persuade someone else, is remarkably poverty-stricken in invention.[3]

Although the elements of nobility (or its mockery) are present in the texts of the operas, Mozart's music emphasizes them. Sarastro's hymns are models of musical restraint, particularly in contrast to the extravagant and hysterical coloratura of the Queen of the Night, which takes the elements of seria eloquence and power and exaggerates them to prove her inability to be truly noble. Tito's arias, with their crystal clear structures and majestic opening melodies, are models of eloquence. And the Countess's two arias, with accompaniments that (in the slow sections) provide a steady pulse underneath her vocal line, and wind-instrument lines that suggest a kind of parallel consciousness, have a richness of texture and color that gives the impression of great depth and sincerity.

Serving-class characters

There is no serving-class "ideal" comparable to the noble "ideal" in these operas; characters generally make no particular effort to live "up" to their servant status. Indeed, the ideals of nobility shape even the profiles of the serving-class characters: part of the humor typically attaching to them involves their mockery (both conscious and unconscious) of those noble forms and ideals. Papageno's suicide "attempt" in *The Magic Flute* is funny in part because we know that he does not have the idealism to go through with it; in *Die Entführung* Blonde's pride in her English heritage as she gives Osmin a piece of her mind is funny because even though she uses that heritage to prove herself superior to the "oriental" Osmin, she is still only a servant to Constanze.

Even though there is no serving-class or peasant ideal for which to strive, these roles nevertheless demonstrate consistent characteristics that mark their social station. Servants and peasants – especially women – are typically clever, or at least sly. Susanna is part of a long chain of quick-witted serving girls who save not only their own skins and reputations, but also those of their lovers and betters. Despina's play-acting abilities (she appears as both a doctor and a notary in the execution of the plot to deceive the ladies) are part of the same tradition. And in *Don Giovanni* even Zerlina's not-quite-truthful and not altogether successful attempts to deflect Masetto from his suspicions about her, belong to the same tradition. Serving-class men tend to be less sly – certainly less cleverly manipulative – than the women; even Figaro, the cleverest of the lot, is not the one who comes up with the successful plan to thwart the Count, and he is in the end duped by his own betrothed. Serving class men in Mozart's operas tend to bumble about the stage, blurt out their feelings or suspicions with remarkable directness, and either ape or criticize their superiors more straightforwardly than their female counterparts. Thus, as noted in Chapter 2, buffo arias – the comic arias sung mostly by serving-class men (or by the likes of Dr. Bartolo in *Figaro*) – often begin with a majestic-sounding tune to a noble march rhythm, often expressing a maxim or other generalized sentiment, but typically devolve into confusion or spluttering. Figaro's "Aprite un po' gli occhi" is a classic example of this kind of aria; in it, the singer aspires to the eloquence of the nobility but fails to achieve it.

The servants in Mozart's comic operas are more carnal than their superiors, with the obvious exception of Don Giovanni, who degrades his status at almost every step by satisfying his bodily needs. Papageno and Leporello delight in food: Leporello steals a bit of meat from Don Giovanni's final banquet, while Papageno joyfully eats the food sent to tempt him and Tamino on their trials. Serving-class characters are also more explicit about sexual pleasure: Papageno's and Papagena's plans for hundreds of little Papageni are clearly not only about the pleasures of parenting, and Zerlina's balm for Masetto's wounds after he has been beaten up by Don Giovanni is openly erotic. Even Figaro's and Susanna's measuring their room for a bed is more explicit than anything concerning the sex lives of the noble characters. And while chastity remains a virtue for serving-class women, there is not the same emphasis on honor there is for noblewomen: Zerlina's obviously consummated relation with Masetto occasions no comment, and in *The Marriage of Figaro* Barbarina's already considerable sexual experience is not in itself a matter for punishment. Despina's insouciant attitude to love puts no premium on chastity; it is, rather an economic bargain: give the men what they want, get what you want, and be done with it. In another version of bodiliness, the Pasha's servant Osmin's astonishing litany of proposed punishments for the invading Westerners ("first hanged, then beheaded. . .") shows a bloodthirsty delight in broken bodies, and in the same opera, Pedrillo's plan to get Osmin drunk on forbidden wine to facilitate the escape of the Westerners, relies on a physical response to alcohol as well as playing on the Western obsession with the Islamic rules against it.

Both the servants and the peasants in Mozart's comic operas are largely absolved of moral responsibility: Papageno is given his wife even though he cannot live up to the tests of Sarastro's brotherhood; Monostatos is beaten for his near-assault on Pamina, but he describes his desire for her as only natural, and nothing in the opera contradicts that. Masetto's jealousy (however justified) is mocked but there are no real consequences for it, while Leporello's assistance to Don Giovanni in his nefarious schemes goes largely unpunished (the fury of the other characters in the second-act sextet is more an expression of their frustration than a global moral judgment on his actions). Despina learns a lesson when she discovers that the "Albanians" are in fact the original lovers, but that discovery only stimulates her desire to take revenge by engaging in more trickery herself. Even Osmin, the "wickedest" of the servant characters, is only doing what the Pasha requires of him. Unlike the nobility, who are clearly either good or bad, these lower-class characters are, if not amoral, then something less than either moral or immoral.

Finally, serving-class characters in these operas are typically not gifted with particularly deep feeling; with the obvious exceptions of Susanna and Figaro, they do not engage our sympathies in the same ways as the noble characters, and they typically deflect the sympathies of the audience rather than inviting them. That deflection can take the form of making accusations rather than describing the character's own situation or feelings (Figaro's "Aprite un po" is a prime example of that), of taking on an inappropriately high-class manner or form at a moment when sympathy would otherwise be forthcoming (Papageno's suicide attempt) or expressing a set of values that resist sympathy (Despina's two arias). Servant-class characters also tend to assert themselves through activity rather than expression, and wit rather than sentiment, which may not exclude a sympathetic response, but it does not invite it as openly as a self-revelatory soliloquy.

HOW REALISTIC ARE THE SOCIAL ARRANGEMENTS IN MOZART'S OPERAS?

Stratification

The distinctions between the ranks in Mozart's comic works are clearly related to the world in which the operas had their origins. As we have seen in Chapter 7, theaters were organized to keep the various social layers in their particular places, and contemporary writers and commentators – even the ones dedicated to the bourgeoisification of society – were profoundly and intensely aware of rank and status. Johann Pezzl, for example, a writer and apologist for the Habsburg emperor Joseph II, who penned a detailed demographic, social and cultural description of late eighteenth-century Vienna, and who firmly espoused the bourgeois values of hard work and advancement by merit, nonetheless clearly grouped the population into ranks, and ascribed quite different behaviors to people in those ranks.[4]

Mozart's comic operas, however, represent the principle rather than the reality of stratification. One striking difference between the social picture in the operas and Mozart's real world is the lack of economically autonomous artisan and professional classes in his operas – of what today we would call the middle classes. (The minor characters Bartolo, Basilio and Don Curzio in *Figaro* are the exception to this absence.) The lack of such a class in the Mozart operas is striking for two reasons. First is that the tradition of opera buffa and (to a lesser extent) Singspiel within which Mozart was working had long had plots set in essentially middle-class venues (town squares, shops, etc.) and had included substantial numbers of merchants, milliners, shoemakers, and innkeepers. Unfortunately Mozart himself never commented about the social composition of his operatic casts, and there is no contemporary commentary about it, so we cannot speculate about why he chose libretti essentially without such characters. The second striking thing about the lack of middle-class characters in his works is that the eighteenth century saw a significant rise in the powers and proportion of this stratum of society, and one might reasonably expect to see this mirrored in the entertainment – especially the apparently realistic genres – of the time. Indeed, Mozart himself lived essentially a bourgeois life, once he moved to Vienna in 1780. That is, he made a living by teaching, performing and from the commissions on his larger works (including the operas) and by the sale of his published music. He did not obtain a position at court until 1787 and that position, *Kammermusicus*, did not pay a wage on which he could live. On the other hand, as an artist, Mozart also had freer access to the court and to the aristocrats who patronized music than did most middle-class entrepreneurs.

Setting aside the question of why there are so few bourgeois characters in the operas, it can be said that one effect of their absence is that the stratification is much clearer and more emphatic than in real life, where the boundaries between (say) rich bankers and the aristocracy could be quite thin, where Joseph II in particular liked to ennoble his civil servants, who came from various levels of society, and where, lower down the social scale, servants (especially men, for whom marriage did not end their careers) might move in and out of service, spending periods exercising a profession as well as periods under obligation to a single master.[5]

The serving classes

In addition to representing a very clearly demarcated society, Mozart's and his librettists' concentration on the noble and serving classes also allows the representation of a remarkable familiarity or intimacy between the ranks based on an implicit and absolute understanding of the fundamental gulf between them. The striving entrepreneur, always hoping for social advancement, could not be so easy in either direction; terrified of being treated like a servant by his superiors s/he was also desperate to be treated by the servants with the kind of respect accorded a noble. Hester Thrale Piozzi, a friend of Dr. Johnson in late eighteenth-century England, noted with great astuteness on her visit in the mid-1780s to a still largely feudal Italy that the servants there were much more intimate with their employers than was the case in an increasingly middle-class England, where social mobility was much more possible and acceptable.[6] Sarah Maza's work on servants in pre-Revolutionary France also describes the familial intimacy between masters and servants, especially those who stuck with their employers for many years.[7] In this context, Susanna's friendship with the Countess, and Despina's, Leporello's and Papageno's freedom of address with their superiors can be seen to reflect something real about the world that Mozart and his audience would have known, even though it does not show the whole picture. Don Giovanni's abuse of Leporello is also historically plausible; in an age where the corporal punishment of children was entirely normal, the physical abuse of servants was equally unremarkable. Indeed, servants were often considered like children: part of the household, in need of moral guidance with the rewards and punishments that this implies, deserving of basic food and shelter, and in return expected to be loyal to the family even after leaving the household.[8] The historical realism in the operatic depiction of servants works to dramatic advantage, in that it allows the serving-class characters to interact in varied and interesting ways with their superiors without challenging the basic social structures that frame the action. Indeed, one of the hallmarks of the comic operas as far as the representation of the serving classes is concerned, is that the lower-class characters tend to run the local action: Despina pushes her mistresses around, Susanna confounds the Count and Countess by substituting herself for Cherubino, Leporello occupies Donna Elvira while Don Giovanni is on another pursuit. But these local actions are all framed by, or contained within, actions initiated by their social superiors: Despina is part of Don Alfonso's plan to prove something about women, Susanna would not have to hide in the closet if the Count were not so suspicious, and Leporello is only with Donna Elvira because Don Giovanni has ordered him to be. We might thus say that the incompleteness of Mozart's operatic social world reveals an ideal in which the levels of society are both perfectly distinct and perfectly interdependent. Whether this was primarily a social ideal or a dramatic goldmine is essentially impossible to determine except in very specific instances.

The representation of the peasantry is both less accurate and less complex than that of the serving classes. Peasants in eighteenth-century Europe, even after the abolition of serfdom (which in Austria did not happen until 1781), typically lived short, miserable lives on the edge of starvation. The prettified rural jollity shown both in *Don Giovanni* and in the choruses of *The Marriage of Figaro* has no pretension to accuracy, but it served the purposes of the primarily aristocratic sponsors of opera buffa, who would probably not want their entertainments to remind them of the truth about the economics of rural life. One accurate aspect of Zerlina's and Masetto's relationship is the implication, noted above, that they are already sexually comfortable with each other. Since peasant society relied on the labour of every member of the household, including children (who died in enormous numbers), it was paramount that a wife be proved sexually compatible and fertile, and it was not unusual to test this before a marriage contract was signed.[9] Also factually plausible in a world where serfdom was an active memory and the unending misery of peasant life was surely known to everyone, at least to some extent, is the wealthy Don Giovanni's ability to arouse Zerlina's interest and to compel her submission.

Finally, the absence of moral responsibility in the lower-class operatic characters may or may not be true to real life: servants were certainly regularly punished for a variety of infractions. But the sense in the operas that, unlike the noble characters, they do not pass or fail a basic moral test, corresponds directly to the position of servants as pseudo-children in their households, and to the paternalism of the feudal lord's responsibilities to his peasant workers.

To summarize, then, the serving-class characters in these operas do represent a set of social relations and values that Mozart's audiences could have recognized; and the inaccuracies – in particular their prettification – served to assure the main target audience for these works that whatever the particular frictions between the nobility and their inferiors, the system was not fundamentally unjust.

The nobility

The rhetoric of nobility in Mozart's world was that nobles as a group were distinct from all other segments of society and that they were born into privileges that usually included at least some kind of exemption from state taxes, the possession of noble estates, the ability to dispense justice, the opportunity to hold important public office and to avoid certain kinds of penalties.[10] This rhetoric was largely mirrored in Mozart's operas. In *Don Giovanni*, for example, Don Ottavio and Donna Anna make common cause with Donna Elvira because she is one of them, regardless of the fact that they do not know her, and her actual circumstances could be quite different from theirs. (They offer Zerlina their protection, but they do not form a united front with her.) And Don Ottavio is slow to pass judgment on Don Giovanni explicitly because he is nobly born.

The reality was much more complex and various, however. Far from being an immutable caste, made up of the same families over the course of centuries, all with the same kinds of rights and powers, the European nobility in the eighteenth century (as in periods before and since) was an immensely adaptable and flexible phenomenon. Jonathan Dewald and Michael Bush have recently detailed the variety of ways people could become ennobled, which multiplied during the eighteenth century in most places. In addition to inheriting it, which was touted as the principal method, nobility could be assumed by buying it, acquiring a landed estate that included it, taking up an office which granted it, doing service which merited it, and simply pretending to it, hoping that the pretense would not be discovered for some number of generations, by which time it would be fact. This last was a rural strategy rather than an urban one. This social stratum thus had all kinds of ways in, earned and unearned, honest and dishonest. But it also had many ways out: families died out, not all patents of nobility were inheritable, and women in many cases could not inherit family estates. In addition, in places where primogeniture was not the law, estates became increasingly divided up among the sons over the course of generations, until next to nothing was left. The many ways in, then, were a boon to the institution, though they were also easy to mock.

If the nobility was not a caste, guaranteed by birth, it was also not a class, economically distinct from the rest of society. Particularly in places like Poland and Russia, which had an unusually high proportion of nobles, it was not unusual for members of the nobility to be utterly impoverished and earning a living by artisanal or other subsistence activities.[11]

Mozart's comic operas also reflect – at least to some extent – the variety of the nobility. The levels of aristocracy in these operas range from the Commendatore, obviously an immensely important figure, to Don Anchise, the Mayor in *La finta giardiniera*, who seems to come from the bottom end of the nobility; he is portrayed very much as a parvenu, whose father or grandfather may very well have simply asserted his status by buying a bit of land or "living nobly." As Jerzy Lukowski notes, "much of the nobility of Italy was noble because it was reputed as such."[12] Also, just as in the real eighteenth-century world, not all the nobility in the operas live on landed estates. Arminda in *La finta giardiniera*, for example, is a "Milanese" lady, which means that whether or not her family owns land, they live an urban life, as did much of the nobility in Mozart's Vienna.

The nobility in the seria operas obviously cannot demonstrate the same kind of literal historical accuracy as those in the comic operas; the plots are set in ancient historical or mythological places, and the kinds of distinctions between landed nobility and urban aristocrats, or between families of ancient lineage and parvenus are simply not relevant. Nor, indeed, is the relation between the nobility and other classes, since there is no significant social stratum other than the nobles. What is historically relevant about the characters in the seria operas is the ideology they share, whether or not the individuals live up to it. As noted above, "good" nobles in Mozart's operas are concerned to behave with dignity, they preserve their honor however that is defined, they are capable of self-sacrifice for a greater cause, and they are generous. They are also (implicitly) sufficiently educated to be eloquent.

Although virtues like honor and heroic self-sacrifice had long been hallmarks of nobility, and it is thus not surprising to find them modeled (both positively and in the breach) in Mozart's operas, the concept of nobility was undergoing a sea change during Mozart's lifetime, and this is reflected to a remarkable degree in the operas. This change was both aesthetic and political (as well as moral and economic). It was related to the much debated

Enlightenment question about whether merit should play as significant a part in ennoblement as heredity, but the change most obviously reflected in Mozart's operas is more about how nobility was demonstrated once achieved than how it was to be earned in the first place. Until the middle of the century, as historian Norbert Elias demonstrated in a groundbreaking study,[13] noble status was demonstrated by display: nobles competed with each other in conspicuous consumption and patronage, and a noble who did not dress, spend and eat the part was in danger of losing the respect of his peers and thus status in his social world. By the 1760s, such conspicuous display was beginning to be considered tasteless, and a sign of mere pretension.[14] The aesthetic concept of "noble simplicity" and the personal/political idea of "true nobility" evidenced in the soul of a man rather than his dress began to replace display as signs of elevated social status.

The idea of noble simplicity came from Heinrich Winckelmann's study of ancient Greek art and sculpture, and in particular from his evaluation of the statue of Laocoön and his sons battling the serpent; what Winckelmann saw in that statue was "the pain [of the snake's bite] expressing itself with no sign of rage in his face or in his entire bearing."[15] In other words, noble simplicity was extraordinary restraint in a situation where extravagant expression – rage, revenge, fury, ecstasy, etc. – would be the obvious response. This aesthetic had immediate resonance in the world of opera, notably in Christoph Willibald Gluck's "reform operas," including *Orfeo* and *Alceste*, which Mozart knew, and which left their traces on *Idomeneo*. The more social or political notion of true nobility, which suggested that an elevated character would show itself in action rather than appearance was by no means new in the eighteenth century, but it was enthusiastically taken up by some thinkers and aristocrats at this time, including Joseph II in Vienna, who behaved with conspicuous informality, espoused the bourgeois virtues of rewards for merit and work, and moved around Vienna in ways that did not set him apart from the lower nobility and upper bourgeois.[16]

Mozart's seria characters track this change with remarkable fidelity. His early seria operas feature arias for his heroes (usually sung by castratos) and heroines in which virtuosity is at a premium. Today we think of the Queen of the Night's arias (not to mention the competing soprano arias in *Der Schauspieldirektor*) as parodies of seria pyrotechnics, but the arias in the early operas – for both male and female characters – are only minimally less high for their respective voices, and the coloratura work is no less difficult. Opera seria was quite explicitly a genre that supported aristocratic values and demonstrated the buying power of the noble purses paying for the virtuoso singers; the extraordinarily and conspicuously difficult arias were both a sign that the patron(s) could afford the best singers, and an analogy for the eloquence and power of the ruler himself (who was usually allegorized in the opera's hero).

Mozart's later seria characters and his seria operas step back from this level of display. The king Idomeneo has only one pure display aria, and Idamante's arias, while entirely compelling from a vocal point of view, do not engage in the show-stopping passagework of the early operas. Ilia's arias in that opera are strikingly plain from a vocal perspective. The emperor Tito's arias include some passagework, but they are quite short (as are most of the arias in this opera), and vocally considerably plainer than the comparable pieces in the early operas. And arguably Mozart's most "noble" character of all from the point of view of her inner life – namely, the Countess – has almost no strikingly virtuosic moments.

SOCIAL DISTINCTIONS IN PRODUCTION

Servants and peasants

For most modern audiences, the serving-class characters in Mozart's operas do not seem to need much "translation." These characters typically have greater immediacy than do their social superiors, due in part to their active stage presence, their comic riffs, which connect directly to riffs we can see in modern comedies, and their concern with the dailiness of living, whose essentials – food, sex, chores, companionship – seem to have persisted across the centuries. Productions that stress the immediately comic aspect of these characters may, however, overlook the structures of power that keep them in their places and miss an edge to the humor. Productions that take a more tragic attitude to the material often highlight the social inequalities at the expense of the comedy. (For example, Peter Sellars's Despina has a long and difficult history with Don Alfonso, in which she is the permanent underdog and victim, and her arias are bitterly cynical rather than insouciant.) In such versions – particularly if the settings are modern or without recognizable historical context – we may want to ask why Leporello or Susanna and Figaro don't just leave if their bosses are so deeply corrupt and abusive, why Blonde doesn't intervene on Constanze's behalf if she has leverage with Osmin, or why Papageno follows Tamino into the trials when he's expressed a positive lack of interest in doing so. Having raised these issues, thoughtful productions then present power relations that illuminate the structural constraints upon these characters. (Sellars' productions, for example, typically rely on a feminist notion of the patriarchy to explain the women's inertia.)

In contrast to the obviously and immediately "human" servants, and also in contrast with the aristocrats who behave ignobly, Mozart's admirable noble characters tend to need more translation, or justification, or a greater effort to identify with. The difficulty with "true" nobility on the modern stage is that the idea that admirable personal traits (generosity, self-sacrifice, eloquence, etc.) are (or should be) a by-product of privileged social status has very little resonance for us today. Indeed, democracies tend explicitly to downplay the idea that a whole social layer of people "should" be both socially privileged and morally superior. It may be that one reason for the modern appeal of the Countess as an exemplar of what many have called "inner nobility" is that she exemplifies the noble traits of generosity, a kind of eloquence, and minor self-sacrifice while still in a subordinate position in her household, thus conforming to modern sensibilities about the moral power of the downtrodden.

Given the lack of modern interest in nobility as, in principle, a integrated system of social status and moral qualities, it is no surprise that opera seria is still regularly decried as stiff and dessicated with respect to dramatic rhythm or simply silly with respect to the plots, even though Mozart's later works in the genre are now quite regularly staged. Even a production like Ursel and Karl-Ernst Herrmann's Paris production of *La clemenza di Tito*, which clearly takes the genre and the issue of nobility entirely seriously, still relies on Susan Graham's incandescently agonized reading of the adolescent lovestruck traitor Sesto to hold it together. Tito and Sesto in this production do not represent failed and successful examples of nobility, respectively, but relate on the level of personal need.

Don Ottavio in *Don Giovanni* is an interesting case with respect to nobility. As early as the early nineteenth century he was seen as a hopelessly ineffectual character: E. T. A. Hoffmann's long-lasting notion that Donna Anna was infatuated with Don Giovanni put the noble lover in competition with the demonic seducer, and not surprisingly, the latter won.[17] Echoes of this reading are to be found in productions up to the present day. But readings that take account of late eighteenth-century ideas about nobility, and/or present Don Ottavio as an admirable exemplar of a social type rather than an insufficiently manly man, can at the very least re-balance the dramatic weight of the opera, and may also suggest something about the relation between personality and the expectations of certain social circumstances.

Don Ottavio does in fact embody many features of the "true" nobility of Mozart's time, despite lacking Tito's or even Idamante's power and despite being asked to sacrifice less than Idamante, Sifare, or even Idomeneo. He clearly takes the obligations of his status very seriously; it takes him a while to realize that someone of his own social station could behave as badly as Don Giovanni evidently has. This connects with historian Michael Bush's comment that even given the vast differences among members of the nobility, they typically coalesced and spoke as one in the face of attacks on their status or dignity.[18] His offer, first and foremost, of protection to Donna Anna immediately after her father's death also demonstrates an awareness of his capacity to substitute for the Commendatore and ensure her continued social viability. This need not, however, mean that he is cold or without love; indeed, in the real world, Joseph II's first marriage, to Isabella of Parma, was arranged for purely dynastic reasons, but when she died of smallpox only two years after the wedding he was devastated.[19] Contemporary audiences may well have understood Don Ottavio's feelings for Anna – and hers for him – as real love, within their social boundaries.

Perhaps more importantly, Don Ottavio demonstrates the restraint that goes with the "noble simplicity" so important in the late eighteenth century. As mentioned above, he is extremely deliberate in deciding to avenge himself on Don Giovanni; he exemplifies the capacity to hold his counsel that is asked of Tamino as he goes through his trials. More operatically interesting than that, he has only one aria. In the first version of the opera, written for Prague in 1787, he waits until the very end of the opera to sing a virtuoso aria ("Il mio tesoro intanto") asking the other characters to comfort Donna Anna while he takes revenge on Don Giovanni. The virtuosity of the aria, which is far beyond anything Don Giovanni sings, and which originated in a world where male vocal pyrotechnics still functioned as a metaphor for power, finally allows Ottavio's dignity and eloquence to shine through. This aria is obviously not simple in itself; the noble simplicity of this version of the opera is evident primarily in Ottavio's previous deliberation despite his obvious distress at the assault on Donna Anna's honor. In the version of the opera performed in Vienna in 1788, however, Mozart omitted "Il mio tesoro" and inserted the quite different aria "Dalla sua pace" much earlier in the opera, right after Donna Anna has narrated the full story of Don Giovanni's assault upon her. It has long been assumed that this substitution was made because the Viennese tenor could not manage the difficulties of "Il mio tesoro." This may very well be true, but "Dalla sua pace," in which Ottavio says that his peace of mind depends on Anna's, deploys a guilelessly beautiful and apparently artless melody in a dramatic situation where fury and agony would not be out of place; it is a paragon of noble simplicity. Having stated his case in this way, Ottavio does not need another aria to prove his sincerity or capacity to deal appropriately with Don Giovanni.

Many modern productions have Don Ottavio sing both arias. As far as drawing an audience is concerned this makes perfect sense: if a famous tenor is to play the role (and it is the only tenor role in the opera now that the nineteenth-century practice of casting Don Giovanni as a tenor is well and truly dead), then obviously an audience would rather hear him sing two great arias than one. From a historical/dramatic perspective, though, the presence of the two arias weakens the sense of continence and restraint that would historically have been part and parcel of this character's noble soul. Some productions stick to the Prague version and do only "Il mio tesoro," which allows this aria to work as an eruption at the end of a process of consideration and deliberation. Few modern productions make the arguably strongest move towards "noble simplicity" and do only "Dalla sua pace."

In conclusion, considering the meaning and manifestations of nobility in Mozart's time can raise new and potentially fruitful questions for both producers and audiences in the third century of his operas' lives. More broadly, an awareness of the historical contexts of these operas does not have to result in painful and un-entertaining historical "reconstruction," but can add depth to our understanding of the range of meanings possible in these works, and make us think about the relations – both of similarity and difference – between Mozart's social world and ours.

CHAPTER 9

MOZART OPERAS IN PRODUCTION

Thanks to the proliferation of videorecordings easily available both for purchase and for rental, it is easier today than ever before to watch multiple productions of the Mozart operas repeatedly, and/or in quick succession. Most of these recordings document stage productions.[1] They are, however, not mere echoes of the stage, but also interpretations in their own right, with a variety of camera angles, close-up views impossible in the theater, their own subtitles, and even some occasional special effects or filmic moments. Some are spliced compilations of the best segments of a series of live performances; some document a single live performance; some are filmed in the theater but without an audience present; some may be a mixture of the two; and some are filmed in the studio. It is often possible to distinguish studio recordings from those filmed in the theater (the presence of an audience is something of a giveaway), but the different kinds of theater recordings are difficult if not impossible to identify, and the recording process is not advertised in the packaging. More recent video-recordings of productions tend to be both more inventive and more tactful than older ones; they make much use of close-up shots, but they do not explore the vocal organs and the sweat of the singers in the ways that some older videos do. At the same time, singers' acting techniques and bodies have changed in response to the television-like expectations of the screen; gestures tend to be smaller and less melodramatic, and the singers themselves tend to be less over-weight and more subtly made-up than some of the stars of a few decades ago. The predominance of close-up shots may make the screened versions more appealing as video, but they sacrifice the large stage picture – that is, the rela-tionships between the characters and the characters' relation to their environ-ment – in favor of a more individual and psychological take on the works. It is thus important to remember that although screened performances are a real benefit to the majority of people out of reach of opera houses, they do not replace live performance, either with respect to the thrill of being in the room with the voices, or with respect to seeing the whole stage picture all the time.

It has always been the case that the differences between productions have raised crucial questions about the meanings of these works. However, having so many productions available to so many people makes public discussion of those meanings both easier and more needed than ever before, as it becomes unavoidably obvious that any given production is not "the" work, and, indeed, that "the" work is not a simple or single phenomenon. This chapter suggests some ways of thinking about how productions shape our sense of these operas, particularly with respect to their status as both historical and living objects, but also with respect to what they are most centrally about.

As far as the overall meanings of these operas are concerned, certain operas, and certain places or questions in those operas, have long been focal points for different interpretations. One such is the ending of Così fan tutte. The three most common stagings of the denouement are: a) reuniting the original couples, as the text pretty clearly indicates; b) ending with the "wrong" couples united, as the text can be read to permit; and c) to have no coupling at the end, but rather to have the young people either reject or ignore Don Alfonso's attempt to pair them off, which takes a creative reading of Da Ponte's words. Each of these endings can be played more or less definitely and more or less cheerfully, so that they create a continuum of possibilities rather than three mutually exclusive endings. Thus if the original couples reunite, for example, they can either look perfectly satisfied with their lot, as in Michael Hampe's 1989 La Scala production, conducted by Riccardo Muti,[2] or there can still be glances and other indications that the "wrong" couples remain at least somewhat interested in each other, as in John Eliot Gardner's 1992 Théatre du Chatelet production.[3] Alternatively, if there is no final coupling, the young people can be played as permanently damaged and incapable of love, as in Peter Sellars' 1986 Pepsico Festival production, filmed several years later, or simply uncertain, as in the production by Ursel and Karl-Ernst Herrmann from Salzburg in 2006.[4] The decision about the final disposition of the couples in this opera is a clear statement about the director's understanding of the work. It suggests whether it is understood as a comedy or something darker; whether the romantic feelings engendered by the experiment in seduction are thought to be more real than the ones with which the opera starts; whether anyone in the opera truly loves anyone else; whether the opera is about women or makes a broader point about society, and if the latter, what that larger subject might be.

Another example of directorial choice that profoundly affects the work's meaning is the way Don Giovanni is played, both as a character in his own right and in relation to the rest of the cast. Is he plausibly charismatic, as is Rodney Gilfry in the 2001 Zürich production conducted by Nikolaus Harnoncourt,[5] or is he a thoroughly repellent character, as in Calixto Bieito's modernized production from the Teatro del Liceu, Barcelona?[6] Is he clearly of a social class set apart from the mass of humanity, as in Joseph Losey's 1978 film of the opera,[7] or is he a "regular guy," as in Peter Sellars's 1990 video-recorded production?[8] These choices influence whether the opera comes across as closer to comedy or a darker kind of drama; they also affect whether the title character is understood as an incomplete or damaged soul looking obsessively for completion or repair, or a product of a particular social system.[9] These are of course not the only ways to understand this character and his fate; my points are rather that particular choices (and happenstances, for that matter) in production can have profound resonance for the meanings of these works in performance, and that there is much to be learned about the potential meanings of these works by comparing productions.

A second benefit of having a variety of videorecordings easily to hand is that it is easier than ever before to think about trends and ideologies in production overall – i.e. not tied to single works. There are many different kinds of production, some of which I will discuss below, but one element they all share is an awareness of Mozart's almost unique stature in the musical canon and the profound cultural familiarity of his operas. Even the early seria works , which may not in themselves be well known, are treated as though they belong in the modern world in ways that could not happen with the comparable operas of Mozart's lesser-known contemporaries. The much-loved status of Mozart's operas means that on the one hand outré modern productions are often greeted with roars of outrage, and a conviction that "Mozart" has been horribly betrayed;[10] but on the other, that attempts to reconstruct the historical circumstances of performance in Mozart's time have typically barely scratched the surface of "authenticity" because too much attention to historical veracity would render the work uncomfortably unfamiliar. The rest of this chapter discusses the ways in which Mozart's historical and canonic status play into production choices.

Many productions project an aura of familiarity, which guarantees that the audience feels they "know" the characters and their circumstances. Many also convey a sense that the meanings of the work are "universal," stretching beyond the time and location in which the work is set. Using familiarity and universality as touchstones, it becomes clear that while many productions make the operas seem both entirely familiar and timelessly relevant, others make a point of defamiliarizing their settings. Some "defamiliarizing" productions emphasize the "universal" or archetypal meanings of the works in question, while others set the operas in locations intimately familiar to a modern audience, thus suggesting that their meanings make most sense in the particulars of certain social settings.

Familiarizing techniques in productions range from the most global to the most local, and affect everything from costumes and sets to musical performance practices. Among the most global familiarizing moves are the use of wigs and makeup – especially for the female characters – that approximate the hairstyles and cosmetics of the audience's own time. It is a truism about historical epics on film that one can always tell when the film was made by the hair and lipstick of the characters: these are essentially invisible to the audiences of that time, and then become crashingly obvious to later audiences as fashions change. Elizabeth Taylor as Cleopatra in Joseph Mankiewicz's 1963 film of the same name, for example, screams of the 1960s with her overemphasized eyes and pale lipstick.[11] Similarly, Frieda Hempel as Susanna and Geraldine Farrar as Cherubino, with Giuseppe De Luca as Figaro, speak more loudly to us about the 1917 date of this Metropolitan Opera production that about the eighteenth century (ill. 9). This impetus to make the characters look natural to a given audience is much more striking with female characters than with males, though males are obviously not exempt from it. Even though the singers in historically-costumed Mozart operas almost always wear wigs, the women have not since the eighteenth century worn the elaborately-built, often very high, white-powdered edifices that were the norm at that time, however lovingly replicated is the rest of the costume. Men, on the other hand, are quite frequently dressed in plausibly authentic periwigs, but the principal male characters typically have at least one wigless scene, especially if they have some romantic interest. Interestingly, the principle of fashion "naturalness" with women seems to have operated in Mozart's time, though the results were precisely the opposite of modern ones. One of the 1795 illustrations to *The Magic Flute* by Joseph and Peter Schaffer, for example, shows Papageno in his feathered bird suit and Tamino in a theatrical tunic, while Pamina is dressed in a contemporary hooped skirt and grand wig (ill. 10).[12]

If women have long looked more "natural" (i.e. familiar) than men, it is also the case that some productions distinguish between the women, deploying less conspicuous coiffure and/or costumes for characters who are supposed to excite more audience sympathy. For example, in the 1981 Drottningholm production of *The Marriage of Figaro*, Susanna and Marcellina are mostly costumed in very plausible replicas of eighteenth-century dress, but the Countess – the figure whom modern audiences typically find the most "human" – is dressed throughout in costumes with more modern touches, thus, presumably, bringing her subliminally closer to "us."[13] And at the end of the opera, when Susanna sings her ravishing love song, "Deh vieni non tardar" ostensibly to the Count but actually to Figaro, whom she knows to be eavesdropping, she is costumed in a sleeveless white underdress, with the bodice-lacing increasingly loose, which departs quite radically from eighteenth-century norms. This is a moment full of theatricality, of course, but it is also where Susanna reveals her true feelings for Figaro: the costume is clearly intended not only to thematize revealing-ness, but also to bring her closer to a modern audience.

Another familiarizing strategy in many productions is to adhere to the conventional (but usually unmentioned) ways of representing particular situations and characters. For example, in productions of *The Marriage of Figaro*, Susanna is almost always shorter, and never significantly taller, than the Countess. There is no historical record about the relative heights of the original singers, and it is not clear when this convention was instigated if it was not part of the original performance practices. But it is most certainly the norm in later twentieth, and early twenty-first century performances. Of course such a disposition of bodies also reflects a centuries-old expectation that people of greater social status should occupy more physical space; and even modern people feel unconsciously more comfortable about having larger bodies occupy more elevated positions: the taller candidate usually wins the U.S. presidential elections, for example. However, in the modern world, where inherited or otherwise unearned social status is not advertised as admirable, and where the relation between Susanna and the Countess is most often described as an intimate friendship, it seems most likely that this difference in size is maintained as much to retain the familiar lineaments of the work as to impress their difference in rank upon the audience. Similarly, in *The Magic Flute* it is quite customary to have Papageno extremely mobile on stage: he runs, jumps, and in some productions is almost acrobatic, in contrast to Tamino's more deliberate motions. In *Così fan tutte* Fiordiligi and Dorabella usually have different-colored hair (despite being sisters), in *Don Giovanni* Leporello is a fundamentally cheerful presence on stage despite his complaints, and in *Idomeneo* the title character is typically played in a rather statuesque way. Some of these conventions have obvious justifications in the texts of the operas; others do not, but they are all part of the "default" conventions of staging that remind us of what we already know, even in productions that are in other ways highly unconventional.

There are also conventions in the broader staging of these operas, not indicated in the librettos, that find their way into the most disparate productions, and that over time seem to have become almost part of the works: to repeat them is (consciously or unconsciously) to assert the familiarity of these operas. For example, the three characters who sing the farewell ensemble "Soave sia il vento" ("Let the breeze be gentle") in *Così fan tutte* (Don Alfonso and the two young ladies) almost always stand still throughout the entire (short) number. Vitellia often sits down towards the front of the stage at some point during her regretful aria "Non più di fiori" in *La clemenza di Tito*; and the Countess often wears white in her opening scene in *The Marriage of Figaro*.

To make the less palatable aspects of these works more acceptable in the modern world is also a form of familiarization. *The Magic Flute* is a particular case in point. Many of the attitudes expressed in the work's spoken dialogue, and even in the sung text, count as racist and sexist today. Monostatos is an uncomfortable figure in modern Western and Westernized societies; the sentiments Sarastro and his "brothers" express about women would be unacceptable in the homes of most audience members. Modern productions do not typically change the words to which Mozart's notes are sung, but it is standard practice to omit bits of the spoken text, and to sub- or surtitle selectively. Monostatos is some other colour than black in many modern productions of *The Magic Flute*, rendering the racial comments literally invisible. And where the social contexts of Mozart's work are problematic for modern audiences, they can also be made more palatable: for example, in the Drottningholm theater, where much is made of its eighteenth-century ambience, every member of the orchestra wears a kind of period livery – wig, knee breeches, long waistcoat white stockings and shirt. But this orchestra includes women, which is a distinctly modern practice. It is easy to see why the orchestra is mixed: it would be completely unacceptable, if not illegal, to deny women admission to the ensemble. The mixed orchestra is surely not the result of a conscious attempt to whitewash Mozart's world, to make it just like ours in all the potentially uncomfortable respects. Nevertheless, it has something of that effect, intended or not.

Defamiliarizing strategies typically involve either failing to make the familiarizing moves or actively doing something different. They can involve making the characters look and move in ways foreign both to the norms of the opera and to the daily lives of the audience: Graham Vick's production of *Mitridate*, with its use of white face paint, exaggerated versions of eighteenth-century panniered skirts for characters for both sexes, Asian dance and gestures from rhetoric or melodrama, does exactly that. Defamiliarizing can also involve radically re-interpreting the text of stage directions: for example having Don Giovanni's banquet in the second act finale be a Big Mac and fries, eaten on the front step of a broken-down house in the Bronx, as Peter Sellars does. Another example of that strategy is Calixto Bieito's production of *Die Entführung*, which includes Quentin Tarantino-like bloody violence and explicit sex onstage. The reported cries of "That is not Mozart!" in response to this production proves that defamiliarization worked: this was certainly not the "Mozart" with which this audience was familiar.[14] On a less crudely controversial level, "authentic" performances using instruments like those of Mozart's time, lighter voices than the big-opera-house norm, and tempos different from (usually faster than) usual were considered profoundly defamiliarizing in the 1970s and '80s. However, now that style of playing is embedded in our culture, the defamiliarizing effect has largely disappeared. "Familiarity" is, after all, entirely relative and by definition variable in its manifestations.

Universality as a principle offers less room for play than familiarity; simply doing these works in the modern world is an assertion that they are relevant beyond the immediate circumstances of their origin. Nevertheless, we can distinguish between productions that present themes and characters as more or less abstract human archetypes, and those that connect the big themes to particular and recognizeable historical circumstances. The most obvious opera for decontextualized, or archetypal, readings is *The Magic Flute*, which is already highly symbolic, and not located in any readily recognizeable time or place. Productions like Axel Manthey's 1992 interpretation for the Ludwigsburger Schlosstheater[15] emphasize this aspect of the opera: it takes place on a largely empty white stage with shadowy surroundings; the characters are dressed in primary colors and the costumes are wildly various: Sarastro and the brotherhood wear cassock-like tunics and bald caps and resemble science fiction cult members. The Queen of the Night has an astonishing balloon-like star-studded skirt; Papageno wears Boy Scout-like shorts decorated with a rooster tail; his head is decorated with a large beak. Pamina wears something like 1990s semi-formal wear. Monostatos is in blackface with grotesquely exaggerated red lips and a leopardskin tunic. The few props and the animals in Tamino's enchantment scene are brightly colored two-dimensional, child-like abstractions. The total effect is not only timeless and placeless, but everything seems projected on the "screen" of the white stage, as though the story and characters were figments of the audience's imagination. The message here is clearly that this work deals in universal themes of good vs. evil, love vs. hate, enlightenment vs. obdurateness, and spiritual striving vs. earthly complacency. One feels very little for the characters as psychological beings: a sense of the dream-like intersection of more or less abstract issues pervades the whole.

Obviously most of the Mozart operas do not lend themselves so easily to symbolic interpretations. But various kinds of modern productions of works other than *The Magic Flute* do engage in universalizing moves, if on a smaller scale. Color-coding is such a move; certain colors have had the same connotations for centuries and over a broad geographic span. Women in white indicate purity, for example, and green has long been the color of envy. The Countess, Susanna, Konstanze, and Pamina all quite routinely wear white at some point in their respective operas; and Farnace's livid green costume in Graham Vick's *Mitridate, re di Ponto*[16] makes his envious character clear to everyone in the audience regardless of what else they may know or understand about this work. In addition, productions that set the works in spaces with no clear temporal identification, with costumes that either indicate no particular period, or that refer to an "incoherent" mishmash of periods, also seem to be saying that the social locations of the characters are of little importance; what matters is the psychological or political or spiritual action – Mozart's exploration of the "human heart," as though that were an entity recognizeable to, and agreed-upon by all people in all ages and places. Ursel and Karl-Ernst Herrmann's production of *Così* is somewhat of this sort, with remarkably empty sets, and costumes that refer to various times and locations in the twentieth century. Ursel Herrmann herself remarks that the opera is about "learning to know oneself" – a theme presumably thought to be relevant in many different historical and social circumstances.[17]

A production's use or avoidance of familiarizing techniques, and its communication of historical and geographical particularity or dislocatedness can suggest a good deal about how the director views the enterprise of performing much-loved works by an unassailable composer who lived in a world very different from our own. Using this framework one could propose four basic categories of production, with the caveats, of course, that these categories overlap, are not fixed, and are more useful as sets of questions than as reified or permanent pigeonholes. The first category, then, is the "classic" production. This is the most familiar sort: such productions hew closely to the "default" interpretations of these works (which of course changes over time), and assert in a variety of ways that the "then" of the production's setting is also integrally part of the audience's "now." "Reconstructed" performances make greater efforts to suggest the work's historical circumstances. "Modernizing" productions do the opposite; they bring the work into a particular time and location familiar to the audience. Finally, "postmodern" productions combine a variety of historical and cultural references to create a completely unfamiliar venue; this is often balanced by the generalized and familiar "message" of the whole. Obviously, not all productions fit easily into these four categories, but all do deal in some way or another with the unavoidable questions of familiarity and universality.

Michael Hampe's 1989 La Scala *Così*, conducted by Riccardo Muti, is a perfect "classic" production. It is set in a ravishing eighteenth-century set, and uses largely plausible eighteenth-century costumes, with a serious Fiordiligi, a playful Dorabella, and a skeptical but avuncular Don Alfonso. It is entirely familiar on several levels. Its visual accoutrements remind the audience of the much-repeated dictum that this is an exceptionally beautiful work, even among the Mozart operas. The characters fill the roles that anyone even minimally familiar with the opera would expect from previous productions. The orchestra uses modern instruments and makes the sound we expect from classical music on the radio or in the background of advertisements or cartoons.

The tempos, conducted by Riccardo Muti, are on the slow side, reminding us that *Così* is a Great Work. The female characters' hair and make-up are essentially modern, as are the young gentlemen's when they are not dressed up as Albanians. Everyone's physical gestures are entirely of our time, with the possible exception of Despina's in her turns as the Doctor and the Notary in the two finales, and then, of course, she is acting. In other words, not only is the work presented in its most familiar guise, but the characters within it are also represented as human beings whom we might know; the work is made to speak across history as though there were no break between then and now. This production asserts the canonic status of the work by its lavishness: La Scala is one of the great opera houses of the world; Muti is a world-class conductor, and the sets and costumes are obviously enormously expensive. Mozart's status as canonic composer is emphasized during "Soave sia il vento" (the trio where the girls and Don Alfonso bid the boys goodbye) with the image of Muti conducting superimposed on the picture of the stage. Although the sets and costumes carefully represent the eighteenth century, the overall effect is universalizing – in part because of the undisguised modernity of the faces, bodies and gestures of the people occupying them, and in part because of La Scala's place in the entirely modern world of classical music.

The 1981 production of *The Marriage of Figaro* in the Drottningholm theater, done with period instruments, lower lighting levels, sets that are exact copies of the original eighteenth-century stock scenery, and costumes that reflect eighteenth-century clothes to some considerable degree, is advertised on the DVD cover as harking back to Mozart's own time.[18] The theatrical context is indeed largely particular to the eighteenth century, with the exceptions of electric light and women in the orchestra, as mentioned above. And the proportion of the human bodies to the small, steeply-raked stage is quite different from that in the great modern opera houses. However, like the other Mozart productions from that theater, it also engages in a variety of familiarizing moves. Hair, make-up, and gestures are all modern; moreover, the singers, although they may have lighter voices than the superstars who sing in the great opera houses of the world, do not make significant attempts to sing in "period style:" their vibrato is as they will have learned it in modern schools of music, and they rarely add ornamentation. It is hard to know whether these "modern conveniences" are the result of a conscious attempt not to make these works alien to the audience who subsidize the theater, whether the research had stopped at the stage set and the orchestral instruments, or whether those responsible felt that "reconstruction" was simply not what they were interested in. It is instructive to compare these productions with the revivals of Baroque operas done at such venues as the Boston Early Music Festival, which, even at the time of this *Figaro*, were going much further in the direction of a kind of exoticization of old music, with elaborate reproductions of period costumes, and seventeenth- and eighteenth-century singing styles and gestures. The difference may be that these "festival" operas were typically revivals, working against no previous preconceptions about the operas they brought to life. It is much harder to revive a work that is not really dead, and the Drottningholm *Figaro* is a compromise between the defamiliarization of a thoroughgoing reconstruction and the incongruous familiarity of a thoroughly modern-classic performance in this historical location.

Our third type of production involves "modernization." Such productions set the opera in a particular, carefully and completely reproduced, modern environment, usually recognizeable to the audience. Peter Sellars' 1980s productions of the Da Ponte operas – *Figaro* in Trump Towers, *Don Giovanni* in the South Bronx, and *Così* in a diner – are now-classic examples of this strategy. Calixto Bieito's more recent (2004) production of *Don Giovanni* among the twenty-something and thirty-something Eurotrash of Barcelona is another. These productions rely on the familiarity – at least in principle – of their settings. In other words, even though many audience members will not actually have spent time in the 1980s South Bronx or the bars of Porto Olimpico, they "know" from the media what life is like there, and they can instinctively supply a whole set of social particulars that flesh out the opera's action. Both Bieito and Sellars provide back stories that aid in this fleshing out: Bieito's Leporello is an old military buddy of Don Giovanni, while Sellars's Don Alfonso is a still-traumatized Vietnam veteran. At the same time as making the settings and circumstances familiar to modern audiences, these settings radically defamiliarize the works themselves. To have Don Giovanni "phone in" his serenade to Donna Elvira's maid, as Bieito's does, or to have the Countess look like Princess Diana, as Sellars's does, is to bring a whole new range of reference to those moments or those characters. The combination of making the work different from its usual versions, but socially and politically familiar in the circumstances and back story it presents has the effect of universalizing both the work, and, more importantly, the idea of Mozart himself. That is, if Mozart's and his librettists' characters are made to live and act in circumstances that the audience deeply recognizes, it makes Mozart (his librettists are never invoked by the directors of such productions) an essentially modern man – someone who understands the vicissitudes of modern life, and whose vision encompasses the corners of the modern soul. The obsessive particularities of these settings, and the exactitude with which particular circumstances are represented, universalize the spirit of the composer.

Finally Karl-Ernst and Ursel Herrmann's "postmodern" Paris Opera production of *La clemenza di Tito*, conducted by Sylvain Camberling, exemplifies the

ways familiarity and alienness, and universality and particularity can all play
off against each other in a single production.[19] The setting and costumes quite
specifically indicate three periods: ancient Rome, the Napoleonic era, and the
modern world. Ancient Rome, the ostensible time of the action, is represented
by the togas of the populace, Tito's laurel wreath, and Publio's breastplate,
though this is probably more medieval than ancient. These elements do not
simply sit still in a single period, however. The laurel wreath, for example links
the ancient world with the Napoleonic era, as Tito himself resembles
Napoleon, especially in the famous Ingres portrait of that ruler on his imperial throne.[20] The other prominent sign of the ancient world is the statue of
Winged Victory (re-provided with head and arms) at the end of a corridor
of arches.[21] This image also links quite directly to the modern world
of the audience, as the famous Winged Victory of Samothrace (currently
headless and armless) is in the Louvre, in a stairway articulated by arches.[22]
The Napoleonic era is indicated not only by the title character's striking
resemblance to that ruler (Tito is played by Christoph Prégardien) but also by
the 1820s double-breasted waistcoats and greatcoats worn by the male characters. This historical reference signals not only to the kind of power wielded
by the emperor, but also the Herrmanns' idea (stated in the "making of"
section of the DVD) that Mozart was a romantic, ahead of his time, and that
Sesto is like Werther, Goethe's tragic and prototypically Romantic hero.[23]
(Never mind that *Werther* was written before *Tito.*) The modern period is
announced in the women's costumes, which mix Vitellia's formal gowns with
Servilia's child-like smocks, sundresses, and short white socks. Vitellia's wide
floor-length skirts also link back to the eighteenth and nineteenth centuries.

The combination of these periods makes in total a time and place unlike
any experienced by the audience, but since all the particulars are familiar and
identifiable, the overall impression is of a typically postmodern historical
patchwork or collage, rather than the universality achieved in, say, Manthey's
production of *The Magic Flute.* In that respect this production is not unlike
the increasing numbers of (usually European) productions often grouped
together under the heading of *Regieoper* (director's opera), which combine
elements from disparate periods and cultures.[24] One might think that this
setting would defamiliarize the action of the opera, but in fact, that is not the
case. Not only do the usual kinds of familiarity pertain – musical elements,
gestures, hair and make-up, etc. are entirely familiar – but the opera is also
constructed around mezzo soprano Susan Graham's electrifying portrayal of
Sesto. In her reading, he is an exquisitely tortured adolescent – an archetype
entirely familiar in our world of school shootings, substance abuse and young
men's mayhem. In centering the opera on this vision of Sesto, articulated in a
vocal and theatrical performance that overshadows all the others, the work

becomes about psychology and not about politics. Susan Graham herself describes Tito as Sesto's "best friend,"[25] which completely ignores the vast differential in power between them – something that could not have been ignored in either the eighteenth century or the ancient world, however Metastasio plays up Tito's willingness to act on his personal feelings for the younger man. This psychological vision of the opera suits the video screen (small or large) better than a political vision; it also accords with the norm in mainstream film, which tends to focus on the personal even when it also deals with systems and structures. In other words, even as the setting is in a sense defamiliarized, this is balanced by the conscious and powerful device of making the fundamental energy of the plot entirely familiar.

* * * *

At least in the English-speaking world, Mozart's operas took longer than Wagner's and Verdi's on the one hand, and Handel's on the other, to be produced in modernized and postmodern versions, and opera as a whole was slower to undergo such production than canonical spoken drama like Shakespeare. It is hard to say exactly why this is so; there are certainly no definitive answers. One possible answer to the comparison between opera in general and Shakespeare is that music "dates" the work more completely and irrevocably than even Shakespeare's antiquated language, and that twentieth- and twenty-first-century musicians have for various reasons hesitated more to change Mozart's notes than have actors to change Shakespeare's words by actual substitution, by omission, or by ignoring the poetic rhythms in favour of a prosier and more mundane style of declamation. As far as the tardiness of modernized Mozart productions in comparison to some nineteenth century composers is concerned, one answer might be that nineteenth-century music is still a template for certain kinds of film scores or other background music; there is less perceived "dissonance" between that more fluid and more immediate style and a modern setting than there is between Mozart's more "formal" and apparently "historical" style. Another answer might be that some later operas – Wagner's in particular, but also some moments of Verdi – deal more with the other-worldly or the frankly symbolic than most of Mozart's,[26] and when the work does not sit fully in its own age or place it is easier to transpose it elsewhere. With respect to the comparison with Handel – whose music is, if anything, more distant from our modern "soundtrack" than Mozart's – the difference seems to lie in the fact that Handel's operas were largely unknown until the second half of the twentieth century, and have only recently made it into the normal repertory of the biggest opera houses. There was thus no entrenched tradition of production to counter. In addition, producers of the Handel operas struggled to make these works, with their convoluted plots, da capo arias, and alien social worlds, comprehensible to audiences, and modernization may have seemed a way to accomplish this. Thus the combination of the relative particularity and alienness, in an everyday sense, of Mozart's style, and the deep cultural familiarity of the operas, may have been the underlying causes of an unusually conservative attitude toward production, especially in the English-speaking world.

That is changing quite dramatically in the early years of the new century, with modernized and postmodern productions appearing everywhere: Jonathan Miller's contemporary *Così* is making an impact in Seattle and elsewhere, and Hans Neuenfels' and Calixto Bieito's sensational European productions are hotly debated in Berlin, London, Barcelona, and elsewhere. That is surely a good thing; each of us may find given productions unappealing, objectionable, or even immoral, but to argue about them is to keep the works alive in whatever form seems most relevant to the modern world, and if the history of these works shows us any single thing it is that every age has found its own meaning in them.

NOTES

CHAPTER 1 – INTRODUCTION

1. See the account by Daines Barrington, an English lawyer and naturalist, who tested the eight-year-old Mozart during the latter's visit to London. Otto Erich Deutsch, *Mozart: A Documentary Biography*, trans. Eric Blom, Peter Branscombe and Jeremy Noble (London: A & C Black, 1965), 98. The account is quoted below, in the commentary on *La finta semplice*.
2. Mozart, letter to his father, 28 February 1778. Emily Anderson, trans. and ed., *The Letters of Mozart and his Family*, 2nd edn (London: Macmillan, 1966), 497. (Henceforth *Letters*.)
3. See Rudolph Angermüller, *Mozart's Operas*, preface and translation by Stewart Spencer (New York: Rizzoli, 1988), for an exceptionally vivid illustrated history of production for each of these operas.
4. David Cairns, *Mozart and his Operas* (Berkeley: University of California Press, 2006); Daniel Heartz, *Mozart's Operas*, edited, with contributing essays, by Thomas Bauman (Berkeley: University of Califormia Press, 1990); William Mann, *The Operas of Mozart* (New York: Oxford University Press, 1977); Jane Glover, *Mozart's Women: His Family, His Friends, His Music* (London: Macmillan, 2005).

CHAPTER 2 – THE MUSICAL ANATOMY OF MOZART'S OPERAS

1. In "da capo" here I am including all versions of that form, including the more sonata-like one in which the first A section goes to the dominant and the second A section remains in the tonic, as long as the middle section uses a discrete section of the text which does not return in the second A section.
2. Count Karl Zinzendorf, for example, reported quite faithfully in his diary which numbers were encored in the repertory that he saw at the Burgtheater in Vienna, and a good proportion of those numbers are ensembles. See Otto Schindler, *Das alte Burgtheater als Opernbühne* (Vienna: Böhlaus, 1971), passim.
3. Lorenzo Da Ponte, quoted in Daniel Heartz, "The creation of the buffo finale in Italian opera," *Proceedings of the Royal Musical Association*, 104 (1977–8), 73.
4. Quoted in Andrew Steptoe, *The Mozart–Da Ponte Operas: The Cultural and Musical Background to Le nozze di Figaro, Don Giovanni and Così fan tutte* (Oxford: Clarendon Press, 1988), 173.
5. John Platoff, "Musical and dramatic structure in the opera buffa finale," *Journal of Musicology* 7 (1989), 219.

6. See Wye J. Allanbrook, *Rhythmic Gesture in Mozart: Le Nozze di Figaro and Don Giovanni* (Chicago: University of Chicago Press, 1983), for a reading of *The Marriage of Figaro* as a study in pastoral.
7. See James Webster, "The analysis of Mozart arias," in *Mozart Studies,* ed. Cliff Eisen (Oxford: Clarendon Press, 1991), 183.

CHAPTER 3 – MOZART AND OPERA SERIA

1. Reinhard Strohm, "The *dramma per musica* in the eighteenth century," *Dramma per musica: Italian Opera of the Eighteenth Century* (New Haven: Yale University Press, 1997), 12.
2. Roger Savage, "Staging an opera: letters from the Cesarian poet," *Early Music,* 26 (1998), 588.
3. John Rosselli, "Castrato," *Grove Music Online,* ed. L. Macy. <http://www.grovemusic.com> Accessed 29 June 2006.
4. Savage, "Staging an opera," 587.
5. Strohm, "The *dramma per musica,*" 9.
6. Kathleen Kuzmick Hansell, "Mozart's Milanese theatrical works," *Music in the Theater, Church, and Villa: Essays in Honor of Robert Lamar Weaver and Norma Wright Weaver,* ed. Susan Parisi with Ernest Harriss and Calvin Bower (Detroit: Harmonie Park Press, 2000), 198.
7. Strohm, "The *dramma per musica,*" 23.
8. Marita McClymonds, "Opera Seria, § 3: 1740–1770," *Grove Music Online* <http://www.grovemusic.com> Accessed 30 June 2006.
9. Bruce Alan Brown, "Calzabigi," *Grove Music Online,* <http://www.grovemusic.com> Accessed 30 June 2006.
10. Christoph Willibald Gluck [Ranieri Calzabigi], "Dedication for *Alceste*", in Oliver Strunk, *Source Readings in Music History,* vol. 5, *The Late Eighteenth Century,* ed. Wye Jamison Allanbrook (New York: Norton, 1997), 199.
11. The phrase is Leopold's. Leopold Mozart to his wife, 24 November 1770. *Letters,* I, 171.
12. Luigi Ferdinando Tagliavini, introduction to *Mitridate Re di Ponto,* Neue Mozart Ausgabe, series 2/5, vol. 4, viii.
13. Ibid., viii ix. On the Gasparini aria, see *The Cambridge Mozart Encyclopedia,* ed. Cliff Eisen and Simon P. Keefe (Cambridge: Cambridge University Press, 2006), 308.
14. Leopold Mozart to his wife, 29 December 1770. *Letters,* I, 176.
15. "Mithridates VI Eupator," *Encyclopaedia Britannica.* 2006. <http://search.eb.com/eb/article-4911> Accessed 14 June 2006.
16. Tagliavini, introduction to *Mitridate Re di Ponto,* vol. 4, ix.
17. See Chapter 2.
18. DVD: Unitel video 071 507–3.
19. DVD: Kultur, D1490.
20. Leopold Mozart to his wife, 21 September 1771. *Letters,* I, 197.
21. Parini, *Descrizione delle Feste celebrate in Milano per le nozze delle L. L. Altezze Reali l'Arciduca Ferdinando d'Austria e l'Arciduchessa Maria Beatrice d'Este,* Milan, 1825. Quoted in Luigi Ferdinando Tagliavini, introduction to *Ascanio in Alba,* Neue Mozart Ausgabe, series 2/5, vol. 5, ix.
22. Leopold Mozart to his wife, 13 September 1771. *Letters,* I, 196.
23. Kathleen Kuzmick Hansell, "Manzuoli, Giovanni," *Grove Music Online* <http://www.grovemusic.com> Accessed 15 June 2006.
24. Joseph-Horst Lederer, introduction to *Il Sogno di Scipione,* Neue Mozart Ausgabe, Series 2/5, vol. 6, vii.

25. "Scipio Africanus the Younger," *Encyclopaedia Britannica*, 2006. <http://www.britannica.com/eb/article-6520> Accessed 20 June 2006.
26. Kathleen Kuzmick Hansell, introduction to *Lucio Silla*, Neue Mozart Ausgabe, Series 2/5, vol. 7, ix.
27. Stanley Sadie, *Mozart: The Early Years* (New York: Norton, 2006), 230.
28. Leopold Mozart to his wife, 14 November 1772. *Letters,* I, 215–16.
29. Ibid., 18 December 1772. *Letters,* I, 221.
30. "Sulla, Lucius Cornelius," *Encyclopaedia Britannica*, 2006. <http://search.eb.com/eb/article-9070258> Accessed 19 June 2006.
31. Hansell, introduction to *Lucio Silla*, vol. 7, xi.
32. John A. Rice, "De Gamerra, Giovanni," *Grove Music Online* <http://www.grovemusic.com> Accessed 19 June 2006.
33. Hansell, introduction to *Lucio Silla*, vol. 7, ix.
34. Pierluigi Petrobelli, introduction to *Il re pastore*, Neue Mozart Ausgabe, series 2/5, vol. 9, viii.
35. Stanley Sadie, *Mozart: The Early Years* (New York: Norton, 2006), 378.
36. Pierluigi Petrobelli, introduction to *Il re pastore*, vol. 9, ix.
37. Michael Talbot, "Serenata," *Grove Music Online* <http://www.grovemusic.com> Accessed 21 June 2006.
38. Sadie, *Mozart: The Early Years,* 378.
39. See Chapter 2 for more on this aria form.
40. "The much-loved castrato", Mozart to his father, 15 November 1780. *Letters,* II, 664.
41. Daniel Heartz and Paul Corneilson, "Raaff, Anton," *Grove Music Online* <http:www.grovemusic.com> Accessed 6 June 2007.
42. Mozart to his father, 8 November 1780. *Letters,* II, 660.
43. Ibid., 15 November 1780. *Letters,* II, 664.
44. Ibid., 29 November 1780. *Letters,* II, 674.
45. Ibid., 27 December 1780. *Letters,* II, 699.
46. Ibid., 30 December 1780. *Letters,* II, 701.
47. Ibid., 29 November 1780. *Letters,* II, 674.
48. Julian Rushton, *W. A. Mozart: Idomeneo* (Cambridge: Cambridge University Press, 1993), 41.
49. Ibid., pp. 39–40, for more detail.
50. M. Owen Lee, "Only a Matter of Time," *Opera News*, 42, September 1977, 21–2.
51. *The Harmonicon,* January 1832, 9.
52. *The Musical World,* vol. XXIV, no. 6, 10 February 1849, 81–2.
53. *The Musical World,* vol. XXXVII, no. 14, 2 April 1859, 212.
54. *The Harmonicon,* January 1832, 9.
55. "Idomeneo in Vienna," translation in the *London Musical World*; reprinted in *Dwight's Journal of Music*, vol. XXXIX, no. 25, 6 December 1879, 193–4.
56. Review of the 1990 English Bach Festival performance at Covent Garden. *Opera*, 41/9 (September 1990), 1118.
57. Rushton, *W. A. Mozart: Idomeneo*, 45–6.
58. Julian Rushton, review of Mozart, *Idomeneo*, conducted by John Eliot Gardiner (Archiv 431674–2), in *Early Music* 19 (1991): 663.
59. Rushton, *W. A. Mozart: Idomeneo*, 133.
60. Ibid., 134.
61. John Rice, *W. A. Mozart: La clemenza di Tito* (Cambridge: Cambridge University Press, 1991), 64, mentions that the famous phrase has only been traced back to a source from 1871.
62. Otto Erich Deutsch, *Mozart: Die Dokumente seines Lebens* (Kassel: Bärenreiter, 1961), 439.

63. Rice, *La clemenza di Tito*, 104.
64. Ibid., 107–15.
65. Quoted in Rice, *La clemenze di Tito*, 124.
66. See Chapter 3 on opera seria for a comment on reform opera.
67. David J. Baker, "The Reluctant Ruler", *Opera News*, 62 (6 Dec. 1997), 13ff.
68. See Rice, *La clemenza di Tito*, 135.
69. DVD: Opus Arte 0942 D.
70. DVD: Arthaus Musik 102 009.
71. Rice, *La clemenza di Tito*, 155.
72. Nicholas Till, *Mozart and the Enlightenment: Truth, Virtue and Beauty in Mozart's Operas* (New York: Norton, 1992), 268–9.
73. Ibid., 265–7.
74. Heinrich Winckelmann, *Reflections on the Imitation of Greek Works in Painting and Sculpture*, trans. Elfriede Heyer and Roger C. Norton (La Salle, IL: Open Court, 1987), 33–4. See also Chapter 8 on Mozart's social world for more about the concept of noble simplicity.

CHAPTER 4 – MOZART AND SINGSPIEL

1. Anna Amalie Abert and Thomas Bauman, "Hiller, Johann Adam," *Grove Music Online* <http:www.grovemusic.com> Accessed 1 August 2006.
2. Christian Felix Weisse, "Vorrede zu den komischen Opern (1778)," in Renate Schusky, *Das deutsche Singspiel im 18. Jahrhundert: Quellen und Zeugnisse zu Ästhetik und Rezeption* (Bonn: Bouvier, 1980), 51.
3. John Warrack, *German Opera: From the Beginnings to Wagner* (Cambridge: Cambridge University Press, 2001), 93–8.
4. M. Elizabeth C. Bartlet and Thomas Bauman, "Jesuit drama," *Grove Music Online* <http:www.grovemusic.com> Accessed 1 August 2006.
5. James Van Horn Melton, "From image to word: cultural reform and the rise of literate culture in eighteenth-century Austria," *The Journal of Modern History*, 58 (1986): 105–9.
6. John Warrack, *German Opera*, 125–6.
7. These are all titles of works listed as possibly having been given in 1753, in Gustav Zechmeister, *Die Wiener Theater nächst der Burg und nächst dem Kärntnerthor von 1747 bis 1776* (Vienna: Böhlaus, 1971), 440–1.
8. Peter Branscombe, "Music in the Viennese popular theater of the eighteenth and nineteenth centuries," *Proceedings of the Royal Musical Association*, 98 (1971–2), 103.
9. Thomas Bauman, preface to Umlauf, *Die Schöne Schusterinn* (New York: Garland, 1986).
10. John Warrack, *German Opera*, 125.
11. Otto Schindler, *Das Alte Burgtheater als Opernbühne* (Vienna: Böhlaus, 1970), 25.
12. Ibid., 30. Piccinni, Anfossi and Paisiello were composers of opera buffa; Grétry wrote *opéra comique*, whose musical numbers tended to be shorter and less vocally demanding.
13. Warrack, *German Opera*, 137–9, provides the text and a translation of this set of recommendations.
14. John Rice, *Antonio Salieri and Viennese Opera* (Chicago: Chicago University Press, 1998), 295.
15. Bruce Alan Brown, "Vienna, §2," *Grove Music Online* <http:www.grovemusic.com> Accessed 2 August 2006.
16. Peter Branscombe, "The Singspiel in the late eighteenth century," *The Musical Times*, 112 (1971), 227.

17. Dorothea Link, *The National Court Theater in Mozart's Vienna* (Oxford: Clarendon Press, 1998), 496–7.
18. The Starhemberg family owned the Freihaus complex in which the Theater auf der Wieden was built. See Kurt Honolka, *Papageno: Emanuel Schikaneder, Man of the Theater in Mozart's Time*, trans. Mary Jane Wilde (Portland, OR: Amadeus Books, 1990), 76.
19. Rudoph Angermüller, introduction to *Bastien und Bastienne*. Neue Mozart Ausgabe, series 2/5, vol. 3, x–xi.
20. Ibid., viii.
21. Ibid., x.
22. Ibid.
23. Mozart to his father, 8 August 1781. *Letters*, II, 756.
24. See Daniel Melamed, "Evidence on the Genesis of *Die Entführung aus dem Serail* from the Autograph Score," *Mozart Jahrbuch*, 2003–4, 25–42
25. See Thomas Bauman, *W. A. Mozart: Die Entführung aus dem Serail* (Cambridge: Cambridge University Press, 1987), Chapter 2, for a detailed discussion of the opera's relation to the Bretzner libretto.
26. Mozart to his father, 26 September 1781. *Letters*, II, 769.
27. Ibid., 13 October 1781. *Letters*, II, 773.
28. Melamed, "Evidence on the genesis of *Die Entführung*," 34. Also Thomas Bauman, "Coming of Age in Vienna," in Daniel Heartz, *Mozart's Operas* (Berkeley: University of California Press, 1990), 79, n. 20.
29. Mozart to his father, 13 October 1781. *Letters*, II, 773.
30. Mozart to his father, 20 July 1782. *Letters*, II, 807–8.
31. Ibid., 27 July 1782. *Letters*, II, 810.
32. See Thomas Bauman, *Die Entführung aus dem Serail*, 103–4, for a list of these premieres.
33. *The Musical Times*, 461 (1 July 1881), 355.
34. DVD: Image 9312RADVD.
35. Donald Quataert, *The Ottoman Empire, 1700–1922* (Cambridge: Cambridge University Press, 2000), 5.
36. Mary Hunter, "The Alla Turca style in the late eighteenth century: race and gender in the symphony and the seraglio," in Jonathan Bellman, ed., *The Exotic in Western Music* (Boston: Northeastern University Press, 1998), 43–73.
37. Gerhard Croll, introduction to W. A. Mozart, *Die Entführung aus dem Serail*, Neue Mozart Ausgabe, series 2/5, vol. 12 (Kassel: Bärenreiter, 1982), ix–x.
38. Ibid., xi.
39. Christopher Raeburn, review of Otto Erich Deutsch, *Mozart: A Documentary Biography*, *The Musical Times*, 106 (Sept. 1965), 677.
40. Ibid.
41. Ibid.
42. Gerhard Croll, Preface to Mozart, *Der Schauspieldirektor*, Neue Mozart Ausgabe, series 2/5, vol. 15, vii.
43. Mozart to his wife, 8–9 October 1791. *Letters*, II, 969.
44. Peter Branscombe, "Schikaneder, Emanuel," *Grove Music Online* <http://www.grove music.com> Accessed 16 September 2006.
45. Robert Spaethling, "Folklore and Enlightenment in the libretto of Mozart's *Magic Flute*," *Eighteenth Century Studies*, 9 (1975), 49.
46. Ibid., 50–1.
47. Ibid., 55.
48. Julian Rushton, "Die Zauberflöte," *Grove Music Online* <http:www.grovemusic.com> Accessed 17 September 2006.
49. Otto Erich Deutsch, *Mozart: Die Dokumente seines Lebens* (Kassel: Bärenreiter, 1961), 358.
50. Ibid., 360.

51. *Allgemeine musikalische Zeitung, mit besonderer Rücksicht auf dem österreichischen Kaiserstaat*, no. 100, 13 December 1820, 794–5.
52. *Allgemeine Wiener Musik-Zeitung*, 12 July 1842. Zweiter Jahrgang, no. 83, p.338.
53. *Allgemeine musikalische Zeitung, mit besonderer Rücksicht auf dem österreichischen Kaiserstaat*, no. 100, 13 December 1820, 794–5.
54. Michael Freyhan, "Toward the Original Text of Mozart's *Die Zauberflöte*," *Journal of the American Musicological Society*, 39 (1986), 355–6.
55. David J. Buch, "*Die Zauberflöte*, Masonic opera, and other fairy tales," *Acta Musicologica*, 76 (2004), 197–8.
56. Ibid., 200.
57. Georg Nikolaus Nissen, *Anhang zu W. A. Mozarts Biographie, nach Originalbriefen, Sammlungen alles über ihn Geschriebenen* . . . (1828; reprint, Olms: Hildesheim, 1964), 112–14. Quoted in Buch, "*Die Zauberflöte*, Masonic opera," 203.
58. Jacques Chailley, *The Magic Flute: Masonic Opera. An Interpretation of the Libretto and the Music*, trans. Herbert Weinstock (New York: Knopf, 1971).
59. Buch, "*Die Zauberflöte*, Masonic opera."
60. Robert Spaethling, "Folklore and Enlightenment in the libretto of Mozart's Magic Flute," *Eighteenth Century Studies*, 9 (1975), 45–68.
61. Ibid.; and Thomas Bauman, "At the North Gate: instrumental music in *Die Zauberflöte*," in Daniel Heartz, *Mozart's Operas* (Berkeley: University of California Press: 2000), 277–8.
62. This is the main argument in David J. Buch, "*Die Zauberflöte*, Masonic opera."
63. Quoted ibid., translation adapted by the present author. Almost all of this excerpt, with the exception of the first sentence, is also found in an anonymous review of the opera in the *Berliner Allgemeine Musikalische Zeitung* of 1824; whether Nissen simply borrowed the sentences or had something to do with the original article is not known.
64. One well-tried but unsubstantiated story has it that when Mozart saw *Kaspar der Fagottist* (*Kaspar the Bassoonist*) at the rival Leopoldstadt theater, he realized that his work was too close for comfort (both were based on the same story from *Dschinnistan*) and instructed Schikaneder to take the second half in a different direction.
65. David J. Buch, "Mozart and the Theater auf der Wieden: New Attributions and Perspectives," *Cambridge Opera Journal*, 9 (1997), 195–232.
66. Buch, "*Die Zauberflöte*, Masonic opera," 206.
67. Jocelyn Godwin, "Layers of meaning in the Magic Flute," *The Musical Quarterly*, 65 (1979), 471–92. See also Bauman, "At the North Gate," 278, 285.
68. Mozart to his wife, 7–8 October 1791. *Letters*, II, 967.
69. Mozart to his father, 4 April 1787. *Letters*, II, 907.
70. Malcolm Cole, "Monostatos and his 'sister': racial stereotype in *Die Zauberflöte* and its sequel," *The Opera Quarterly*, 21 (2005), 11.

CHAPTER 5 – MOZART AND OPERA BUFFA

1. See the commentary to *Don Giovanni*, p. 149, for a comment about Mozart's libretto designations.
2. Charles Troy and Piero Weiss, "Intermezzo," *Grove Music Online* <http://www.grovemusic.com> Accessed 3 July 2006.
3. Ibid.
4. Piero Weiss, "Opera buffa," *Grove Music Online* <http://www.grovemusic.com> Accessed 3 July 2006.
5. Ibid.
6. Mel Gordon describes some of these in *Lazzi: The Comic Routines of Commedia dell'arte* (New York: Performing Arts Journals Publications, 1983).

7. Carlo Goldoni, "L'autore a chi legge," preface to *Il servitore di due padroni*, in Goldoni, *Commedie*, ed. Guido Davico Bonino (Milan: Garzanti, 1981), vol. 1, 3.
8. Mozart's *La finta giardiniera* is a close descendant of *La buona figliuola*. See the commentary on that opera, p. 129.
9. See Chapter 2, pp. 10–11.
10. Lorenzo Bianconi and Giorgio Pestelli, eds, *La Storia dell'opera italiana*, part II: *I sistemi*, vol. 4, *Il sistema produttivo e le sue competenze*, 61.
11. Dexter Edge, "Mozart's Viennese Orchestras," *Early Music*, 20 (1992), 63–88.
12. Rudolf Payer von Thurn, *Joseph II als Theaterdirektor: Ungedruckte Briefe und Aktenstücke aus den Kinderjahren des Burgtheaters* (Vienna: Heidrich, 1920), passim.
13. Daniel Heartz, "Constructing *Le nozze di Figaro*," *Mozart's Operas* (Berkeley: University of California Press, 1990), 133–56, esp. 140–6.
14. Mary Hunter, *The Culture of Opera Buffa in Mozart's Vienna* (Princeton: Princeton University Press, 1999), Chapter 8.
15. Rudolph Angermüller and Wolfgang Rehm, introduction to *La finta semplice*, Neue Mozart Ausgabe, series 2/5, vol. 2, xviii–xix.
16. Ibid., ix–xiii.
17. See Leopold von Sonnleithner, "Ueber Mozarts Opern von seiner früheren Jugend," *Cäcilia*, vol. 23, no. 92 (1844), 238–41.
18. H. C. Robbins Landon, "Notes from Abroad," *Musical Times*, 97 (March 1956), 152.
19. Daines Barrington, "Account of a very remarkable Young Musician," quoted in Otto Erich Deutsch, *Mozart: A Documentary Biography*, translated by Eric Blom, Peter Branscombe, and Jeremy Noble (Stanford: Stanford University Press, 1966), 98.
20. Rudolph Angermüller and Dietrich Berke, preface to Mozart, *La finta giardiniera*. Neue Mozart Ausgabe, series 2/5, vol. 8 (1978), ix.
21. Ibid., xii.
22. Ibid., xv.
23. Daniel Heartz, "Constructing *Le nozze di Figaro*" in *Mozart's Operas* (Berkeley: University of California Press, 1990), 137.
24. Ibid., 138.
25. Ibid., 142.
26. Quoted in Otto Michtner, *Das alte Burgtheater als Opernbühne* (Vienna: Böhlau, 1970), 208–9.
27. Mozart, letter to Gottfried von Jacquin, 15 January 1787. *Letters*, II, 903.
28. Tim Carter, *W. A. Mozart: Le nozze di Figaro* (Cambridge: Cambridge University Press, 1987), 129–32. Chapter 8 of this guide provides an excellent description of the performance history of this opera.
29. Portions of Zinzendorf's diary are transcribed in Dorothea Link, *The National Court Theater in Mozart's Vienna: Sources and Documents, 1783–1792* (Oxford: Clarendon Press, 1998), 339, 355.
30. See Carter, *Le nozze di Figaro*, 136, for a table of comparative performance numbers (taken from S. Vill, ed., *Così fan tutte: Beiträge zur Wirkungsgeschichte* [Bayreuth, 1978]).
31. See, for example, *The Musical World*, VIII, no. 98 (26 January 1838), 60.
32. Carter, *Le nozze di Figaro*, 134–5.
33. *The Harmonicon*, vol. 1, no. 8, August 1823, 116.
34. *Allgemeine musikalische Zeitung, mit besonderer Rücksicht auf dem österreichischen Kaiserstaat*, no. 32, 15 August 1818, 299.
35. *Berliner allgemeine musikalische Zeitung*, vol. III, no. 4, 25 January 1826, 39.
36. Henry Lunn, in the *Musical Times and Singing Circular*, vol. 12, no. 283, 1 September 1866, 363.
37. Otto Michtner, *Das Alte Burgtheater*, 208.

38. Paul Bechert, "The Salzburg Festival," *The Musical Times*, vol. 66 (1 October 1925), p. 942.
39. Carter, *Le nozze di Figaro*, 140.
40. Nicholas Till, *Mozart and the Enlightenment: Truth, Beauty and Virtue in Mozart's Operas* (New York: Norton, 1993), 167–71; Wye J. Allanbrook, *Rhythmic Gesture in Mozart: Le nozze di Figaro and Don Giovanni* (Chicago: University of Chicago Press, 1983).
41. Johann Pezzl, "Sketch of Vienna" (1786), partly translated in H. C. Robbins Landon, *Mozart and Vienna* (New York: Schirmer, 1991), 111–12.
42. Wolfgang Plath and Wolfgang Rehm, preface to *Don Giovanni*, Neue Mozart Ausgabe, series 2/5, vol. 17, x.
43. This libretto is available in a modern edition in Charles Russell, *The Don Juan Legend Before Mozart* (Ann Arbor: University of Michigan Press, 1993), 407–43.
44. See ibid. for an essay on the history of the story and translations of several pre-Mozart libretti.
45. Kurt Helmuth Oehl, "Die eingeschobenen Dialogszenen in Mozarts Don Juan im 18.–19. Jahrhundert," *Florilegium musicologicum: Hellmut Federhofer zum 75. Geburtstag*, ed. Christoph-Hellmut Mahling (Tutzing: Schneider, 1988), 247–66.
46. Katharine Ellis, "Rewriting 'Don Giovanni', or 'The Thieving Magpies,'" *Journal of the Royal Musical Association*, vol. 119, no. 2 (1994), 212–50, describes this production in considerable detail.
47. Ibid., 221ff.
48. Ibid., 250.
49. James Parakilas, "The afterlife of Don Giovanni: turning production history into criticism," *The Journal of Musicology*, 8 (1990), 254.
50. Rachel Cowgill, "Re-gendering the libertine; or the taming of the rake: Lucy Vestris as Don Giovanni on the early nineteenth-century London stage," *Cambridge Opera Journal*, 10 (1998), 45–66.
51. Bernard Williams, "Don Giovanni as an idea," in Julian Rushton, ed., *W. A. Mozart: Don Giovanni* (Cambridge: Cambridge University Press, 1981), 81.
52. Brigid Brophy, *Mozart the Dramatist* (New York: Harcourt, Brace & World, 1964), 254.
53. Liane Curtis, "On the politics of teaching Mozart's *Don Giovanni*," *NWSA Journal*, 12 (2000), 119–42.
54. Søren Kierkegaard, *Either/Or*, trans. David F. Swenson and Lillian Marvin Swenson, vol. 1 (New York: Anchor Books, 1959), 91.
55. <http://gutenberg.spiegel.de/etahoff/donjuan/donjuan.htm.> Accessed 23 October 2006.
56. Williams, "Don Giovanni as an idea," 82.
57. Williams, "Don Giovanni as an idea," 89, describes comparable "problems" in all the Da Ponte operas.
58. Russell, *The Don Juan Legend*, x.
59. Joseph Kerman, "Reading Don Giovanni," in Jonathan Miller, ed., *The Don Giovanni Book: Myths of Seduction and Betrayal.* (New York: Schocken Books, 1990), 108–25.
60. Kierkegaard, *Either/Or*, 100.
61. William Mann, *The Operas of Mozart* (New York: Oxford University Press, 1977), 468.
62. *Allgemeine musikalische Zeitung, mit besonderer Rücksicht auf dem österreichischen Kaiserstaat.* August 1818, 297.
63. Williams, "Don Giovanni as an idea," 89.
64. Edmund Goehring, "Don Juan at the Feast of All Souls," paper delivered to the American Musicological Society, 2005.
65. Michael Robinson, "The alternative endings to *Don Giovanni*," in Mary Hunter and James Webster, eds, *Opera Buffa in Mozart's Vienna* (Cambridge: Cambridge University Press, 1997), 272, 283–5.

66. Ibid., 283.
67. Wye J. Allanbrook, "Mozart's happy endings: a new look at the 'convention' of the 'lieto fine.'" *Mozart Jahrbuch*, 1984–5, 1–5.
68. Da Ponte, *Memoirs*, quoted in Bruce Alan Brown, *W. A. Mozart: Così fan tutte* (Cambridge: Cambridge University Press, 1995), 3.
69. Ibid., 10–11, and Bruce Alan Brown and John A. Rice, "Salieri's *Così*," *Cambridge Opera Journal*, 8 (1996), 17–43.
70. Alan Tyson, "Notes on the composition of Mozart's *Cosi fan tutte*," *Journal of the American Musicological Society*, 37 (1984), 356–401.
71. Friedrich Rochlitz, "Nachschrift zur Recension von Eyblers Requiem," in *Allgemeine musikalische Zeitung*, 28: 21 (24 May 1826), cols. 337–40. Quoted in Brown, *Così fan tutte*," 23.
72. Dexter Edge, "Mozart's fee for *Così fan tutte*," *Journal of the Royal Musical Association*, 116 (1991), 214–15.
73. Brown, *Così fan tutte*, 162–3.
74. Ibid. In Chapter 4 Brown proposes a primarily Ariostan origin for the work.
75. Ibid. Brown provides the most thorough introduction to Da Ponte's likely sources.
76. Richard Wagner, *Oper und Drama*. Quoted in Brown, op. cit., 172.
77. *The Musical World*, 24 January 1863, 59.
78. *The Harmonicon*, vol. VI, no. 9 (1828), 214.
79. S.M., " Mozart's Così fan tutte" *The Musical World* , 19 June 1858, 390–1. Translated from the *Niederrheinische Musik-Zeitung*.
80. John Rosselli, "Balanced on a turning point: *Così fan tutte*'s difficult history," *Times Literary Supplement* 17 June 1991, 15–16.

CHAPTER 6 – A BRIEF NOTE ON THE UNFINISHED AND MISCELLANEOUS OPERAS

1. Alfred Orel, introduction to *Apollo und Hyacinth*, Neue Mozart Ausgabe, series 2/5, vol. 1, viii–x.
2. Ibid., xii–xiii.
3. See Chapter 2 for more discussion of this kind of music.
4. Mozart to his father, 11 December 1780. *Letters*, II, 685 n.1.
5. Mozart to his father, 18 January 1781. *Letters*, II, 709, n.1.
6. Mozart to his father, 18 April 1781. *Letters*, II, 725 nn. 1, 3.
7. It was also used during the 1980s as the background music for a Master Lock advertisement, which makes sense of the text, but is an odd choice given the arcaneness of the reference.
8. Mozart to his father, 7 May 1783. *Letters*, II, 847.
9. Mozart to his father, 6 December 1783. *Letters*, II, 861.
10. Ibid.
11. Mozart to his father, 10 February 1784, *Letters*, II, 866–7.
12. The names are those used in Mozart's version, but the manuscript libretto still extant sometimes keeps the names from Cimarosa's original, thus cementing the relationship between the two libretti. See also Alessandra Campana, "Il libretto di *Lo sposo deluso*," *Mozart-Jahrbuch* (1988–9), 573–88.

CHAPTER 7 – MOZART'S THEATERS

1. See <http://www.museum.com/jb/IN/images/mgfx/37248.jpg> for a picture of the auditorium.

2. See <http://www.estatestheatre.cz/et_history.html> for some pictures and a brief history.
3. See Clive Brown, "The orchestra in Beethoven's Vienna," *Early Music*, 16 (1988), 4, for a telling photograph of this auditorium shortly before its demolition.
4. <http://www1.appstate.edu/orgs/spectacle/Pages/18thscenechange.html> is a marvelous source for computer-modeled images of eighteenth-century stage effects, including some based on Drottningholm machinery. See also Agne Beijer, *Court Theaters of Drottningholm and Gripsholm* (New York: Blom, 1972).
5. <http://www.ckrumlov.cz/uk/zamek/5nadvori/t_bd.htm> provides a variety of photographs and panoramic videos of this space.
6. Kathleen Kuzmick Hansell, "Opera and Ballet at the Regio Ducal Teatro of Milan, 1771–1776." Ph.D. dissertation, University of California at Berkeley, 1979, 135.
7. Ibid.
8. A famous contemporary picture of the theater, apparently during a ball, is available at <http://mozart.infonet.com.br/ArqF4.htm>
9. Hansell, "Opera and Ballet," 167.
10. Ibid., 124
11. That is, Ferdinand, brother of the future Joseph II, who was to be married to Beatrice D'Este, and whose wedding was celebrated in part by Mozart's *Ascanio in Alba*.
12. Charles Burney, ed. H. Edmund Poole, *Music, Men and Manners in France and Italy 1770, being the journal written by Charles Burney, Mus.D., during a tour through these countries . . .* (London: Eulenberg Books, 1974), 46.
13. Ibid., *53*.
14. Dexter Edge, "Mozart's reception in Vienna, 1787–91," *Wolfgang Amadé Mozart: Essays on his Life and his Music*, ed. Stanley Sadie (Oxford: Clarendon Press, 1996), 81.
15. Daniel Heartz, "Nicholas Jadot and the building of the Burgtheater," *Musical Quarterly*, 68 (1982), 7.
16. Edge, "Mozart's reception," 75–6, gives a detailed account.
17. Heartz, "Nicholas Jadot," 1–31.
18. Malcolm Cole, "Mozart and two theaters in Josephinian Vienna," *Opera in Context: Essays on Historical Staging from the Late Renaissance to the Time of Puccini*, ed. Mark Radice (Portland, Oregon: Amadeus, 1998), 128, gives a table comparing different scholars' estimates of the size of the stage, derived from various original floor plans. Page 135 gives the dimensions of the Burgtheater stage.
19. Heartz, "Nicholas Jadot," 10, provides a reproduction of an engraving by Bernardo Bellotto (also known as Canaletto) showing a 1759 performance of the ballet-pantomime, *Le Turc génereux*; this gives a full view of the proscenium at this time. (See ill. 2)
20. Heartz, "Nicholas Jadot," 13
21. Dexter Edge, "Mozart's Viennese Orchestras," *Early Music*, 20 (1992), 72–5, shows the lists of players for 1782/3, 1786/7 and 1788/9.
22. Bruce Alan Brown, "Vienna," §2, *Grove Music Online*, <http:www.grovemusic.com> Accessed 24 July 2006. Dorothea Link, *The National Court Theater in Mozart's Vienna: Sources and Documents, 1783–1792* (Oxford: Clarendon Press, 1998), 481.
23. Ferdinand's predecessor, Count Firmian, who actually commissioned Mozart's *Mitridate* as well as *Ascanio in Alba*, was evidently considerably less hands-on as a theatrical manager. See Hansell, "Opera and Ballet," 100.
24. The other court theater, the Kärntnertortheater, briefly continued to show ballet and French opera and plays.
25. Kurt Honolka, *Papageno: Emanuel Schikaneder, Man of the Theater in Mozart's Time*, trans. Jane Mary Wilde (Portland, Oregon: Amadeus, 1990), 77. Honolka also mentions that in 1790 the Emperor Leopold II (Joseph II's successor) granted the theater an imperial privilege, but it is not clear what financial effect this had.

26. David J. Buch, "Mozart and the Theater auf der Wieden: New Attributions and Perspectives," *Cambridge Opera Journal,* 9 (1997), 195–232.
27. Honolka, *Papageno,* 76.
28. Ibid., 75
29. Edge, "Mozart's reception," 75.
30. Honolka, *Papageno,* 76; Peter Branscombe, *W. A. Mozart: The Magic Flute* (Cambridge: Cambridge University Press, 1991), 142.
31. Cole, "Mozart and Two Theaters," 135; Honolka, *Papageno,* 75.
32. Ibid., 135; ibid., 82–4.
33. Otto Schindler, "Das Publikum in der Josephinischen Ära," *Das Burgtheater und sein Publikum* ed. Margret Dietrich (Vienna: Österreichischen Akademie der Wissenschaften, 1976), 40.
34. Ibid., 50.
35. Ibid., 46–7.
36. Edge, "Mozart's reception," 84. Dorothea Link, *The National Court Theater,* translates Zinzendorf's diary entries regarding music during this time.
37. Link, *The National Court Theater,* 487, notes that operas were usually double-cast to take account of sickness and other absences.
38. <www.baroquegestures.com> illustrates some of these basic principles, which persisted well after the baroque era, even, in part, into the twentieth century.
39. Dene Barnett, with Jeanette Massey-Westrop, *The Art of Gesture: The Practices and Principles of 18th-Century Acting* (Heidelberg: Winter, 1987) 36–67.
40. Barnett, *18th-Century Acting,* 26.
41. Metastasio, *Lettere,* no. 328. *Tutte le opere di Pietro Metastasio,* ed. Bruno Brunelli (Milan: Mondadori, 1965), vol. 3, 428–9.
42. Barnett, *18th-Century Acting,* 432–3.
43. Ibid., Chapter 28.
44. Ibid., 435–6.
45. Ibid., 387.
46. Metastasio, *Lettere,* no. 273. *Tutte le opera,* vol. 3, 337.
47. Collectively, they make exactly the gesture of surprise shown in Barnett, *18th-Century Acting,* p. 47; the right hand up and the left hand repulsing him.
48. This illustration can be seen at *Grove Music Online*/Trofonio/Images.
49. Barnett, *18th-Century Acting,* 433, mentions the larger number of stage-movement directions in comedy. Beaumarchais's *Le marriage de Figaro* seems to be particularly heavy in such directions.
50. Libretto to Anfossi, *La finta giardiniera,* reprinted in Ernest Warburton, *The Librettos of Mozart's Operas,* vol. 6 (New York,: Garland, 1992). Also in Mozart's score.
51. Barnett, *18th-Century Acting,* 426.
52. A new kind of candle, made from the oil of sperm whales.
53. D. C. Mullin, "Lighting on the eighteenth-century London stage: a reconsideration," *Theater Notebook,* 34 (1980), 77.
54. Gösta Bergman, *Lighting in the Theater* (Stockholm: Almqvist and Wiksell, 1977), 208–16.
55. Hansell, "Opera and Ballet", p.133.
56. Richard Pilbrow, "Stage lighting," in *The Cambridge Guide to Theatre,* 2nd edn, ed. Martin Banham (Cambridge: Cambridge University Press, 1995), 1025.
57. Daniel Heartz, "Nicholas Jadot," 19.
58. Bergman, *Lighting in the Theater,* 209, describes 232 wicks in the footlights at the Teatro San Carlo in Naples, for example.
59. Baker, quoted in Cole, "Mozart and Two Theaters," 135.
60. See <http://www.jan-billington.com/christofellis/en/02_age_iii.shtml> for a reproduction of an opera seria production at the Teatro Regio in Turin with such costumes.

61. See www.art.com/asp/display_artist-asp/_/crid--62211/R.Bong.htm
62. See Rudolph Angermüller, *Mozart's Operas*, preface and translation by Stewart Spencer (New York: Rizzoli, 1988), 227ff. for pictures of set designs and costumes from the couple of decades after the premiere.
63. The Montgolfier brothers' 1783 demonstration that balloon flight was possible took Europe by storm, and the balloon became a staple in scenic effects and comic riffs.
64. See <http://phonyweather.com/thunder.html> for a variety of seventeenth- and eighteenth-century ways of making thunder.
65. See <www.amadeusmozart.de/MozartOpernIdomeneo.htm>
66. Quoted in Peter Branscombe, *W. A. Mozart: Die Zauberflöte* (Cambridge: Cambridge University Press, 1991), 203.
67. See Honolka, *Papageno*, 92, for a facsimile of the premiere's playbill.
68. Cole, "Mozart and Two Theaters," 135.
69. Edge, "Mozart's Viennese Orchestras," 71, and Hansell, "Mozart's Milanese Theatrical Works," 210.
70. John Spitzer and Neal Zaslaw, *The Birth of the Orchestra: History of an Institution, 1650–1815* (Oxford: Oxford University Press, 2004), 143. See also their Appendices A and B for useful tables of sample orchestras during this period.
71. Hansell, "Mozart's Milanese Theatrical Works," 211.
72. <http://info.royaloperahouse.org/Orchestra/Index.cfm?ccs=113> Accessed 31 July 2006.
73. Edge, "Mozart's Viennese orchestras," 73.
74. Spitzer and Zaslaw, *The Birth of the Orchestra*, 149–50.

CHAPTER 8 – MOZART'S SOCIAL WORLD

1. This story is to be found as early as Boccaccio's *Decameron* (1348), but there were several eighteenth-century operas on the subject.
2. See Chapter 2, pp. 12–15, on aria types for a more detailed discussion of the musical signs of nobility.
3. Joseph Kerman, "Reading *Don Giovanni*," in Jonathan Miller, ed., *The Don Giovanni Book: Myths of Seduction and Betrayal* (New York: Schocken, 1990), 120.
4. Johann Pezzl, *Chronicle of Vienna* [1786, 1787, 1789], excerpted and translated in H. C. Robbins Landon, *Mozart and Vienna* (New York: Schirmer Books, 1991), passim.
5. This is, in fact, Figaro's life story, but although Mozart's audience certainly knew *The Barber of Seville*, the "prequel" to *The Marriage of Figaro*, in which Figaro is a free-lancing barber, there is no mention of Figaro's previous life in Mozart's opera, and for its purposes he is "simply" a servant.
6. Hester Lynch Piozzi, *Observations and Reflections Made in the Course of a Journey through France, Italy, and Germany*, ed. Herbert Barrows (Ann Arbor: University of Michigan Press, 1967). See Mary Hunter, *The Culture of Opera Buffa in Mozart's Vienna* (Princeton: Princeton University Press, 1999), 56–7.
7. Sarah Maza, *Servants and Masters in Eighteenth-Century France: The Uses of Loyalty* (Princeton: Princeton University Press, 1983), 161.
8. Ibid., 184.
9. See Bonnie G. Smith, *Changing Lives: Women in European History since 1700* (Lexington MA: D. C. Heath, 1989), 24–5.
10. Michael Bush, *Noble Privilege*, vol. 1 of *The European Nobility* (New York: Holmes & Meier, 1983), 1.
11. M. L. Bush, *Rich Noble, Poor Noble*, vol. 2 of *The European Nobility* (New York: St. Martin's Press, 1988), 3.
12. Jerzy Lukowski, *The European Nobility in the Eighteenth Century* (New York: Palgrave Macmillan, 2003), 22.

13. Norbert Elias, *The Court Society*, trans. Edmund Jephcott (New York: Pantheon Books, 1983).
14. John Shovlin, "The cultural politics of luxury in eighteenth-century France," *French Historical Studies*, 23 (2000), 577–606; Derek Offord, "Denis Fonvizin and the concept of nobility; Russian echoes of a European debate," *European History Quarterly*, 35 (2005), 9–38.
15. Heinrich Winckelmann, *Reflections on the Imitation of Greek Works in Painting and Sculpture*, trans. Elfriede Heyer and Roger C. Norton (La Salle, IL: Open Court, 1987), 33–4. Pictures of this statue can easily be found on the web: e.g. <www.artchive.com>
16. Johann Pezzl, *Chronicle of Vienna* (1786). Translated in H. C. Robbins Landon, *Mozart and Vienna*, 105.
17. See Chapter 5, pp. 154–6.
18. Bush, *Noble Privilege* p. 2.
19. Derek Beales, *Joseph II*, vol. 1, *Under the Shadow of Maria Theresia, 1741–1780* (Cambridge: Cambridge University Press, 1987), 79.

CHAPTER 9 – MOZART OPERAS IN PRODUCTION

1. Until relatively recently, what was available on DVD tended to reflect the somewhat more conservative side of Mozart opera production. But a set of DVDs (Deutsche Grammophon 00440 073 4251) released in 2007, documenting some Salzburg Festspiele productions, and some other European productions of all the operas, has somewhat redressed this imbalance, as most of the productions are innovative postmodern interpretations of these works.
2. DVD: Opus Arte LS 3006 D.
3. DVD: Archiv 440 073 026–9.
4. DVD: Decca 074 3165 8 (Hermann) and Decca 074 3087 3 DH6 (Sellars Da Ponte trilogy).
5. DVD: Arthaus Musik 100 329.
6. DVD: Opus Arte 0921 D, 2006. This production was premiered by the English National Opera in 2001.
7. Videotape: Kultur 1185.
8. Videotape: Mediascope, 1991. Reissued on DVD by Decca, 2005.
9. See my commentary on *Don Giovanni* for some historical perspective on this question.
10. The responses to Peter Sellars's productions of the Da Ponte operas are a case in point.
11. See <http://www.imdb.com/gallery/mptv/1275/Mptv/1275/5589–0020.jpg.html?hint=nm0000072>
12. Schaffer, illustrations to *The Magic Flute*, published in the *Allgemeines Europäisches Journal* between January and June 1795. Reproduced in Rudolph Angermüller, *Mozart's Operas* (New York: Rizzoli, 1988), 227.
13. This can just about be seen in the still from this production at <http://www.kent.ac.uk/sdfva/drama/DR611/Pictures/Drottningholm%20Figaro%201981.html>
14. *The Independent*, 29 June 2004.
15. DVD: Arthaus Musik 100189.
16. DVD: Kultur D1490.
17. Cf. the "making-of" segment of the Decca DVD of this work.
18. DVD: Image ID9301RADVD.
19. DVD: Opus Arte 0942D.
20. <http://upload.wikimedia.org/wikipedia/commons/2/28/Ingres,_Napoleon_on_his_Imperial_throne.jpg>
21. This is shown on the cover of the DVD.

22. See <http://upload.wikimedia.org/wikipedia/commons/6/63/Paris.louvre.winged.500 pix.jpg> for a close-up of the statue. The Louvre's "Da Vinci Code" thematic trail (<www.louvre.fr>) includes a picture of the statue's setting.

23. This refers to the hero of Goethe's novel, *The Sorrows of Young Werther*, published in 1774, but emblematic of romanticism. The hero undergoes several intense romantic experiences and eventually commits suicide.

24. Hans Neuenfels's productions – including the notorious one of *Idomeneo* featuring the severed heads of Jesus, Mohammed, the Buddha, and other religious figures – belong in this category.

25. Interview in the "making of" section of the DVD.

26. See Gundula Kreuzer, "Voices from beyond: Verdi's *Don Carlos* and the modern stage," *Cambridge Opera Journal*, 18 (2006), 151–79, for a discussion of some 1930s and '40s German productions of *Don Carlos*.

FURTHER READING

This list is for the lay reader who wants to know more about Mozart's operas or the historical context of these works. The books cited here are all in English, easily accessible in libraries or bookstores, and largely readable by people with little or no formal musical education. Readers with more specialized interests will find more resources in the endnotes.

Documentary and reference sources

Otto Erich Deutsch, *Mozart: A Documentary Biography*, trans. Eric Blom, Peter Branscombe and Jeremy Noble. London: A. & C. Black, 1965.

Emily Anderson, trans. and ed., *The Letters of Mozart and his Family,* 2nd edn, London: Macmillan, 1966.

Ernest Warburton, *The Librettos of Mozart's Operas,* 7 vols. New York: Garland, 1992.

Charles Russell, *The Don Juan Legend Before Mozart.* Ann Arbor: University of Michigan Press, 1993.

Cliff Eisen and Simon Keefe, eds, *The Cambridge Mozart Encyclopedia.* Cambridge: Cambridge University Press, 2006.

Surveys of Mozart's operas

Edward J. Dent, *Mozart's Operas*, 2nd edn. Oxford: Oxford University Press, 1960.

William Mann, *The Operas of Mozart.* New York: Oxford University Press, 1977.

Rudolph Angermüller, *Mozart's Operas*. Preface and translation by Stewart Spencer. New York: Rizzoli, 1988.

Daniel Heartz, *Mozart's Operas*. Edited, with contributing essays, by Thomas Bauman. Berkeley: University of Califormia Press, 1990.

David Cairns, *Mozart and his Operas.* Berkeley: University of California Press, 2006.

Discussions and interpretations of selected operas

Brigid Brophy, *Mozart the Dramatist.* New York: Harcourt, Brace & World, 1964.

Wye J. Allanbrook, *Rhythmic Gesture in Mozart: Le Nozze di Figaro and Don Giovanni.* Chicago: University of Chicago Press, 1983.

Andrew Steptoe, *The Mozart–Da Ponte Operas: the Cultural and Musical Background to Le nozze di Figaro, Don Giovanni and Così fan tutte.* Oxford: Clarendon Press, 1988.

Jonathan Miller, ed. *The Don Giovanni Book: Myths of Seduction and Betrayal.* New York: Schocken Books, 1990.

Nicholas Till, *Mozart and the Enlightenment: Truth, Virtue and Beauty in Mozart's Operas.* New York: Norton, 1992.
Jessica Waldoff, *Recognition in Mozart's Operas.* Oxford: Oxford University Press, 2006.

Contextual studies

Sheila Hodges, *Lorenzo Da Ponte: The Life and Times of Mozart's Librettist.* New York: Universal, 1985.
Kurt Honolka, *Papageno: Emanuel Schikaneder, Man of the Theater in Mozart's Time,* trans. Jane Mary Wilde. Portland, Oregon: Amadeus, 1990.
H. C. Robbins Landon, *Mozart and Vienna.* New York: Schirmer, 1991.
Mary Hunter and James Webster, eds, *Opera Buffa in Mozart's Vienna.* Cambridge: Cambridge University Press, 1997.
Mary Hunter, *The Culture of Opera Buffa in Mozart's Vienna.* Princeton: Princeton University Press, 1999.
Jane Glover, *Mozart's Women: His Family, His Friends, His Music.* London: Macmillan, 2005.

Cambridge Opera Guides

Julian Rushton, *W. A. Mozart: Don Giovanni.* Cambridge: Cambridge University Press, 1981.
Thomas Bauman, *W. A. Mozart: Die Entführung aus dem Serail.* Cambridge: Cambridge University Press, 1987.
Tim Carter, *W. A. Mozart: The Marriage of Figaro.* Cambridge: Cambridge University Press, 1987.
Peter Branscombe, *W. A. Mozart: Die Zauberflöte.* Cambridge: Cambridge University Press, 1991.
John Rice, *W. A. Mozart: La clemenza di Tito.* Cambridge: Cambridge University Press, 1991.
Julian Rushton, *W. A. Mozart: Idomeneo.* Cambridge: Cambridge University Press, 1993.
Bruce Alan Brown, *W. A. Mozart: Così fan tutte.* Cambridge: Cambridge University Press, 1995.

LIST OF SCREENED PRODUCTIONS CITED

This is only a list of productions cited in this book. It does not represent anything like the full (and increasing) range of screened productions available, nor does it give a representative picture of the historical record of Mozart opera films and videos. For the latter, see Ken Wlaschin, *Encyclopedia of Opera on Screen: A Guide to More Than 100 Years of Opera Films, Videos and DVDs*. New Haven: Yale University Press, 2004.

Unless otherwise noted, all productions are in DVD format.

Mitridate, re di Ponto

Director: Jean-Pierre Ponnelle. Conductor: Nikolaus Harnoncourt. Concentus Musicus Wien. Filmed in the Teatro Olimpico, Vicenza. 1987. Unitel video 071 507–3. VHS only.
Director: Graham Vick. Conductor: Paul Daniel. Royal Opera, Covent Garden. 1993. Kultur, D1490.

Die Entführung aus dem Serail

Director: François Abou Salem. Conductor: Marc Minkowski. Mozarteum Orchestra Salzburg. Vienna State Opera Choir. 1997. Image 9312RADVD.

The Marriage of Figaro

Director: Göran Järvefelt. Conductor: Arnold Östman. Chorus and Baroque Orchestra of the Drottningholm Court Theater. 1981. Image ID9301RADVD.
Director: Peter Sellars. Conductor: Craig Smith. Wiener Symphoniker. Arnold Schönberg Kammerchor. 2005. Mediascope VHS, 1991/Decca 2005: 071 4129 8 DH2.

Don Giovanni

Director: Joseph Losey. Conductor: Lorin Maazel. Orchestra and Chorus of the Paris Opera. [1978 film] 2005. Sony Pictures. VHS: Kultur 1185.
Director: Peter Sellars. Conductor: Craig Smith. Wiener Symphoniker. Arnold Schönberg Kammerchor. Mediascope VHS 1991/ Decca 2005: 0714119 9 DH2.
Director: Jürgen Flimm. Conductor: Nikolaus Harnoncourt. Chorus and Orchestra of the Opernhaus Zürich. 2001. Arthaus 100329 (NTSC) 100328 (PAL).
Director: Calixto Bieito. Conductor: Bertrand de Billy. Chorus and Orchestra of the Gran Teatro del Liceu, Barcelona. Opus Arte 0921 D.

Così fan tutte

Director: Michael Hampe. Conductor: Riccardo Muti. Chorus and Orchestra of La Scala, Milan. 1989/2004. Opus Arte LS 3006.
Director: Peter Sellars. Conductor: Craig Smith. Wiener Symphoniker. Arnold Schönberg Kammerchor. Mediascope VHS, 1991/ Decca 2005: 071 4139 7 DH2.
Director: John Eliot Gardiner. Conductor: John Eliot Gardiner. Monteverdi Choir, English Baroque Soloists. 1993/2002. Archiv 440 073 026–9.
Directors: Ursel and Karl-Ernst Herrmann. Conductor: Manfred Honeck. Chorus of the Vienna Staatsopera, Vienna Philharmonic. 2006. Decca 00440 074 3165 [Part of the Mozart M 22 complete set].

La clemenza di Tito

Director: Göran Järvefelt. Conductor: Arnold Östman. Chorus and Baroque Orchestra of the Drottningholm Court Theater. 1987. Arthaus Musik 102 009.
Directors: Ursel and Karl-Ernst Herrmann. Conductor: Sylvain Camberling. Orchestra and Chorus of the Paris Opéra. 2005. Opus Arte 0942.

The Magic Flute

(*Trollflöjten*) Director: Ingmar Bergman: Conductor: Eric Ericson. Swedish State Broadcasting Network Symphony. 1975/ 2000, Criterion 71.
Director: Axel Manthey. Conductor: Wolfgang Gönnenwein. Chorus and Orchestra of the Ludwigsburger Festspiele. 1992. Arthaus 100189.

Almost-complete set (*Der Schauspieldirektor* not included)

Mozart: M 22. Deutsche Grammophon 00440 073 4251.

A CHRONOLOGY OF MOZART'S OPERAS

Apollo et Hyacinthus. Salzburg University, 13 May 1767.
La finta semplice. Salzburg, Archbishop's palace, around 1 May 1769.
Bastien and Bastienne. Possibly Vienna, at Franz Anton Mesmer's house, 1768.
Mitridate, re di Ponto. Milan, Teatro Regio Ducal, 26 December 1770.
Ascanio in Alba. Milan, Teatro Regio Ducal, 17 October 1771.
Il sogno di Scipione. Probably Salzburg, Spring 1772.
Lucio Silla. Milan, Teatro Regio Ducal, 26 December 1772.
La finta giardiniera. Munich, Salvatortheater, 13 January 1775.
Il re pastore. Salzburg, 1775.
Zaide. Unfinished (1779/80).
Idomeneo, re di Creta. Munich, Residenztheater, 29 January 1781.
Die Entführung aus dem Serail. Vienna, Burgtheater, 16 July 1782.
L'oca del Cairo. Unfinished (1783).
Lo sposo deluso. Unfinished (1783–4).
Der Schauspieldirektor. Vienna, Schönbrunn Castle, 7 February 1786.
Le nozze di Figaro (**The Marriage of Figaro**).Vienna, Burgtheater, 1 May 1786.
Don Giovanni o sia Il dissoluto punito. Prague, Nostitz Theater, 29 October 1787: Vienna, Burgtheater, 7 May 1788.
Così fan tutte. Vienna, Burgtheater, 26 January 1790.
La clemenza di Tito. Prague, Nostitz Theater, 6 September 1791.
Die Zauberflöte (**The Magic Flute**). Vienna, Theater auf der Wieden, 30 September 1791.

INDEX

Note: Aria and ensemble titles are translated at first appearance in the text.

Freihaus complex, 231n18
French elements, 58, 62, 73, 76, 78–9, 80, 84, 181
French-language productions, 150
Frieberth, Joseph, 172
"Fuor del mar" (*Idomeneo*), 12, 14, 59

Gal, Hans, 62, 63
Galliari brothers, 40, 49, 193, 194
gambling, 30, 178, 180
De Gamerra, Giovanni, 48–50
Gardiner, John Eliot, 215
Gasparini, Quirino, 35, 36
Gassman, Florian, 178
Gayl, Joseph, 194
Gazzaniga, Giuseppe, 149
Gebler, Philipp, 79
gender, 4, 109, 125, 135, 139–44, 171, 197, 200. *See also* men; women
gender-casting, 71
generosity, 73, 88, 93, 94, 197, 200–1, 211
Generous Turk, 93, 94
genius, 18, 37, 60–1, 106, 131, 156
genres, opera, 1
George IV, 151
Gerl, Franz and Mrs., 101
German elements, 119
German-language operas, 7, 15, 76–7, 87, 96–7, 107, 181. *See also* Singspiel; *specific operas*
German-language productions, 150, 162
Germany, 77, 190. *See also specific cities*
Geroglio (*Lo sposo deluso*), 174
gestures, 22, 184, 189, 214, 222, 237n38, nn47–8
Giacinta (*La finta semplice*), 119, 124
Giardini, Felice, 52
Gilfry, Rodney, 215
Giovanni, Don (*Don Giovanni*)
  class and, 205–6
  costumes, 192–3
  ensembles, 16, 20
  interpretations, 151–4, 166–7, 215–16, 223
  in introduction, 20
  mockery of, 201, 202–3
  rank and, 198, 199
  staging, 193
  summary/synopsis, 144–7
Giulio Sabino (Sarti), 96
Giunia (*Lucio Silla*), 45–50
"Giusto ciel" (*Barber of Seville*), 136

Glasgow performances, 61
Gluck, Christoph Willibald
  Don Giovanni and, 149
  influence of, 42, 73, 76
  Mozart and, 88, 93–4, 122
  noble simplicity and, 209
  reform and, 31–2, 53
Glyndebourne productions, 61, 153, 163
"Godiam la pace" (*Idomeneo*), 65
Goethe, 102, 224, 240n23
Goldoni, Carlo
  Don Giovanni and, 149
  La finta semplice and, 121
  influence of, 119
  opera buffa and, 18, 111–16, 123
  Pamela and, 129
  at Regio Ducal, 178
Gomatz (*Zaide*), 172
Gottlieb, Anna, 101
Graham, Susan, 211, 224–5
Le Grand, 60
grand opera, 32
Greek influences, 26, 32, 154, 198, 209
Grétry, André, 107, 230n12
Grimm brothers, 106
Gripsholm theater (Sweden), 177, 182
Griselda, 200
La grotta di Trofonio (Salieri), 161–2, 164, 187
Grünbaum, Madame, 155
Gualtiero (*Griselda*), 200
Guardasoni, Domenico, 69, 70
de Guerville, Harny, 83
Guglielmi, Pietro, 50, 52
Guglielmo (*Così*), 21, 157–60, 161, 163, 165
Gustav III, 72

"Ha! wie will ich triumphieren" (*Entführung*), 92
Habsburgs, 25, 26, 39, 42, 44. *See also individual Habsburgs*
Hagenauer, Lorenz, 121, 122
hair fashions, 217, 222
Hall, Peter, 153
Hampe, Michael, 215, 221
Handel, 225–6
Hanns Wurst and Bernardon, the two heroic sons of the great knight Sacrapans, and bold liberators of Queen Leorella on the island of Lilliput, 78
Hanslick, Eduard, 62